MARTIN GOTTFRIED

HARRY N. ABRAMS, INC. · PUBLISHERS · NEW YORK

In Person

THE GREAT ENTERTAINERS

For sweet Maya, my wonderful golden

CONTENTS

ALONE AND ALIVE

The entertainer works alone. Presenting himself for approval, he steps through the curtains to dare the spotlight, and it plucks him from the darkness that might have kept him safe. Armed only with material, he hurries to satisfy the audience, or at least to survive it. He may sing, dance, or tell jokes, but whatever the routine he is a gladiator, and whether he performs in the Roman Colosseum, at a king's court, in a vaudeville theater, or on a nightclub floor, the room he is working is his arena. That is where he does his act.

"Act" and "performance" were not used to describe variety routines until the modern era of American vaudeville. It was an interesting development in word usage, for both can be applied to stage as well as personal behavior: "act" as a display of affectation and as a bit of business, a ploy (or "routine"). In theater-derived slang we "clean up our acts" or "get our acts together." An act can even be an identity. Bob Hope, for instance, is a comedy act. And we, too, are our acts. In that sense, our act is the personality we send forth as a facade, a social self to hide behind. We are known by that facade, for who can see within us? It is a self we think (or hope) will seem confident and appealing to others. The performer develops or polishes his act or facade to such an extent that his inner and outer selves become confused. Which is real? He closes the dressing-room door behind him and, exhausted by self-promotion, lays himself to rest like a shadow on a chair. If he is a top star, even that respite is denied, for, having received so much approbation, he is willing to invest his soul in the image and exploit his self for show.

Samuel Beckett based the leading characters of his great play *Waiting for Godot* on the low comics of the English music hall. These *naifs*, archetypes of mankind, clown their way through life's misfortunes and frustrations, laughing lest they weep. Like Beckett's Estragon and Vladimir, every entertainer needs a courageous naiveté in order to stand before an audience and attempt to amuse it, without company for protection. This book pays tribute to such solitary courage and celebrates every performer who ever stepped through a curtain to tumble, tap-dance, or sing his way to survival. None of them did it just for the money, but neither did anyone ever entertain simply to make an audience happy. Entertainment is a selfish act, performed because of a positive need to show off and be appreciated. The entertainers brave criticism and rejection in exchange for a spot on the bill and the ritual reward of hand claps.

Alas, they are a fading tribe. The vaudeville theaters and nightclubs are dark, abandoned, razed, converted, and gone. The casino showrooms of Las Vegas are overshadowed by newer ones in Atlantic City, where there are stages only for performers who can attract audiences that can afford to gamble high enough. Others in the shrinking circle of elite entertainers perform in cavernous concert halls where they attempt to reach audiences of four- or five-thousand people. Soon, still fewer stars will attract even larger audiences, while rock acts play arenas and

OPPOSITE:
Frank Sinatra

ABOVE:
Al Jolson

stadiums. Finally, there will be no performer-audience confrontations at all.

Television is America's major entertainment medium, but television is a demagnetizer of live performance. The presence and energy of the entertainer are lost in the electronic transmission of his image, for life disappears along the circuit boards, somewhere between the transistors and the microchips. High-fidelity recordings and equipment never can really sound like live music, being different in nature, and there is a similar eeriness in comparing the performer who prances before the camera with his electronic image on the nearby studio monitor. The image does the dance, sings the song, and smiles the smile but no energy is exchanged between performer and audience. The image on the screen is not a person. It is a composition of blips. The image has phosphors for flesh.

During television's first years, unemployed vaudevillians were willing to settle for phosphors and blips. All the jugglers, the magicians, the eccentric dancers were "between engagements," as they put it with customary bravado. In those formative years of television, network executives considered the medium a branch of theater. They scheduled many variety shows, and the entertainers were resurrected from vaudeville's grave to stock them, but it was only a midnight revel. Vaudeville might be imitated on television, but it could not be re-created because it required the spirit of live communion. Too, popular entertainment reflects the mood and style of an era, and jugglers, magicians, and eccentric

Slapstick comedy takes its name from the "slap stick," a noisy, therefore funny, stage prop used as early as the seventeenth century in the Italian commedia dell'arte. The slap stick consisted of two strips of wood tied at the handle, which when slapped against somebody would make a sharp cracking sound. In this reproduction of a print of 1689, the comic servant Columbine applies the slap stick to Harlequin. The improvisational nature of commedia dell'arte provided chances for solo turns within an ensemble.

dancers simply weren't in the 1950s fashion. But most devastating of all was television's fast-revealed and frightening ability to wear out performers and material. The phenomenon came to be called "overexposure," but the term was double-edged. For the living-room screen was watched at point-blank range. It *uncovered* the act. Even when new material was turned out, audiences quickly saw through the routine to the heart of the brave faker.

And so acts that might have been devised, tested, rewritten, polished, and then performed for years on the vaudeville circuits were done a couple of times on television and then were scrapped. The stages for the army of able, professional, working performers were almost all gone. Soon there would be nowhere "to work in one," a theatrical expression that means playing in front of the first (number one) curtain, straight out to the audience. In drama, few actors ever work there. They perform on a set that is farther back on the stage. They feign reality, and so as protection they can enjoy an imaginary fourth wall that rises between them and the audience. Only occasionally do plays require actors to come forth and address the audience. Thus, performing "in one" is generally associated with variety entertainment, with personal appearances.

Making a personal appearance, performing an act, the variety entertainer puts himself on the block. If he is a success, nobody else can share in it: all fantasies are realized, he is hailed and beloved. But if he is disapproved, given the hook, and pelted with tomatoes, then he can blame no playwright, no director. He is personally responsible for the outcome, and the absolute nature of this is reflected in show-business jargon: the entertainer who succeeds "slays them," the one who fails "dies." How strange is this ritual of exaltation and sacrifice, and how inarticulate the audience's responses: hand claps for approval, hoots for rejection. Such judgments might be expected from gorillas.

The psychological basis of this behavior must be buried deep in human psychology. Why is the comedian's role so hostile, bringing laughter but not happiness? Why does the singer seem such an innocent, so earnest and vulnerable? Why is the dancer a pet? Why is the juggler clever, the acrobat not? Why are audiences threatening, even heartless? That last question is the least perplexing. Perhaps audiences know that the urge to perform is reckless. Perhaps the power to reject encourages sadism. At the Colonial Theatre, one of New York City's first vaudeville houses, there was a ritual called the "Colonial clap." Whenever a performer was failing, the audience would begin to applaud rhythmically and the noise would build until the humiliated entertainer was forced to break off his act and flee. What primitive ritual could be more barbaric?

Except for a brief survey of origins, this book will not cover the entire history of variety entertainment (the interested reader is referred to the bibliography). It would be impossible to describe every professional act performed in America's speakeasies and cabarets, on its burlesque and vaudeville stages, in its nightclubs and concert halls. Nor could all the notable entertainers be included here, among the photographs or in the text. Apologies for the inevitable oversights are extended in advance.

Rather, this book is offered as an appreciation of the peculiarly American variety turn and of the solo entertainer, who is surely a metaphor for human individuality and bravery in facing up to life's hazards. It is presented with the rueful awareness that the end is at hand, for almost all of the stages have vanished or been rendered obsolete. And so, a hail and farewell to the array of lively acts and routines and foolish turns that past performers invented: magic tricks and contortions; bicycling; showing trained seals and bears and dogs; singing and dancing; doing impressions; telling funny stories; clowning; performing acrobatics; juggling; stripping; impersonating the opposite sex; playing musical instruments or nonmusical ones like saws, glasses, bells, and washboards; jumping on trampolines; turning somersaults; whistling. Of all God's creatures, only humans do such silly things.

Entertainers are often called children. They have traditionally been considered immoral, or merely raffish. They have lived the lives of gypsies. Wandering minstrels—vagabond variety performers—were known long before mime was introduced to Greek and Roman drama about 200 B.C. "Mime" did not then mean charades in leotards but was rather what we would now call improvisational theater: brief comedy sketches extemporized between the acts of Greek tragedies and Roman comedies.

In England during the first centuries of the Christian era, another sort of light entertainment was developed. Each Anglo-Saxon tribe had a "gleoman," who accompanied himself on the harp as he sang songs (or "lays") about local heroes and history. *Widsith*, perhaps the first poem written in English, describes the life of a fourth-century gleoman. But the most famous of their compositions is, of course, *Beowolf*. Composed by an eighth-century gleoman, it is almost the only epic of the Old English period that survives.

Mimes and gleomen had made their appearance in response to a demand for lighter entertainment, but even they proved too stuffy for some audiences. Rowdier performers were already on the way, fellows who specialized in country dances, acrobatics, and a variation on the fireside chant that came to be known as "the telling of obscene stories." The comedian had arrived.

In northern France, the wandering minstrels were called "jongleurs" and the gleomen "troubadours." The latter, like their English colleagues, sang ballads about military battles and royal romances, but the Norman troubadour enjoyed a higher status than the English gleoman. He was a fellow of respectable, even noble, birth who traveled on horseback with an entourage of jongleurs trotting behind. Arriving at a castle, he was welcomed by the lord, not as an itinerant player but as an equal. He was shown to a comfortable lodging and entertained at the host's own table. Hardly theatrical riffraff, he enjoyed the show himself. Next day, the lord's retinue of knights and ladies might gather in a meadow, beneath encircling trees festooned with ribbons and flowers. Outdoor banquet tables would already have been laden with refreshments for the local gentry. Again the jongleurs would perform. At last the troubadour himself would deign to sing. So, the star.

But it was his jongleurs, the working performers, who most closely resembled our own vaudevillians. Like the circus performers of later times, these common players made up for their lack of charisma—*star quality*— with an abundance of talent. They did cartwheels, wire-balancing acts —almost anything that might be asked for in the way of eleventh-century entertainment. In one medieval press release, a jongleur advised:

I can play the lute, the violin, the bagpipe, the syrinx, the harp, the gigue, the gittern, the symphony, the psaltery, the organistrum, the regals, the tabor and the rote. I can sing a song well and make tales and fables...I can throw knives in the air and catch them without cutting my fingers. I can do dodges with strings and balance chairs.

And for an encore he would throw a somersault and walk on his hands.

Ann-Margret

After the Norman Conquest, jongleurs swarmed across the English countryside. These foreign gleomen performed at weddings, baptisms, and knight-dubbings. Now female performers were permitted on the English stage for the first time, and these "glee maidens" accompanied the gleomen on lutes and sometimes were even permitted to join in the acrobatics and tumbling.

New variety entertainments emerged among these common jesters: puppet shows, hoop-leaping. The occasional little troupe even traveled with a lion or a camel. The trained bear proved a particularly successful addition, although Ben Jonson was perhaps overly enthusiastic when he wrote, "Good performing bears can dance at first sight and play their own tunes if need be."

Some jongleurs improved their lowly status by specializing in magic. These *tregeteurs* could make flowers and even lions seem to disappear. They would also hammer nails through their hands or snip off their own noses—an illusion accomplished with the help of "a piece of spunge with some sheep's blood in it, to be retained privately."

In 1572, because of a handful of troublemakers and ale-swillers, the merrymaking was dampened and the reputations of all itinerant players were besmirched. In a mood of moral zeal Parliament passed an Act (oh, irony of terms) decreeing "fanciers, bear-leaders, common players, minstrels and jugglers that wander abroad without license from two justices of the peace at least, should be taken, adjudged and deemed rogues, vagabonds and sturdy beggars." The unlicensed minstrel was made punishable at the stocks and the whipping post. Undaunted, the rogues, vagabonds, and sturdy beggars persisted in cartwheeling about the country, even adding comedy sketches to their increasingly popular repertoires of joke-mongering and gross obscenity.

They also found new places to work. The seeds of cabaret were sown in the courtyards of inns and taverns, where itinerant performers entertained for tossed coins. The drinking men called these entertainers "buskers," a term that would be exported to the New World with the Pilgrims. Country fairs offered an even more festive milieu for variety performance. Originating in the thirteenth century, they grew in number during the next several hundred years, providing open-air markets for goods of all kinds. A general holiday spirit prevailed, offering a natural opportunity for entertainers. The most famous was held outside London, the annual Bartholomew Fair, for which Ben Jonson's play was named, so-called because it traditionally opened on August 24, St. Bartholomew's Day. This and other great pleasure fairs offered midways where ballad-singers, conjurers, stilt-walkers, and bear-leaders could perform. The exhibition of freaks and other human oddities, while nearly as old as mankind, became institutionalized there. Other secondary attractions—"sideshows"—included the likenesses of public figures, a medieval wax museum. There were pantomimes, too—musical renditions of children's stories—and one never knew what famous actor might show up in them. For when the doldrums settled upon London Town, leading players could pick up extra pennies at one or another of these fairs. Edmund Kean himself once performed in a pantomime at Bartholomew Fair. There was no shame in it—in fact, after the theaters that the Puritans closed in 1642 had reopened, Bartholomew Fair became a prime showcase for new works. John Gay's *Beggar's Opera* was produced there in 1728.

But the two strains of entertainment, the legitimate stage and variety shows, were separating, the former appealing to the cultured, the latter to the masses. When drama moved to the indoor theaters for the winter,

the variety acts found housing in London too. Before the music halls were opened, the storytellers and clog dancers and singers of funny songs performed in the saloon theaters of such popular London pubs as the Grecian Urn and the Eagle Tavern. By 1870 there were a dozen music halls in London, with names like the Pavilion and the Eastern Music Hall. A decade later there would be opulent music halls in Drury Lane and on Westminster Bridge Road. Variety entertainment had arrived. It would fast become a fixture of British life and be exported to America.

However, comic monologues were performed in America before the turn of the century. "Girlie" and "leg" shows had for some time been popular attractions at beer halls, and in 1840 William Valentine opened the first New York variety theater. It was a modest establishment, more saloon than theater, but the idea caught on and soon similar auditoriums were popping up in storefronts across the nation. Known as "honky-tonks" or "free and easies," they combined the attractions of the saloon, the theater, and the gaming house. Then at last, in 1871, H. J. Sargent organized Sargent's Great Vaudeville Company in Louisville.

The origin of the term "vaudeville" has confounded academe. The French phrase "voix de ville" (voice of the city) would seem the likeliest source, but some scholars have speculated that the term comes from "chanson du vau," as the ballads of the early troubadour Olivier Basselin were called, or the "vive vaude" entertainments of thirteenth-century France.

It seems probable that the saloon ambience had kept variety entertainment from becoming the national rage, for there is no mass entertainment without the family trade. That would soon change. Vaudeville became America's popular entertainment. The troubadours and conjurers of the past evolved into our singers and magicians. The tellers of obscene tales, bless them, continued to tell them as comedians. The medieval jongleur who proudly advertised his multiple talents found counterparts in the vaudeville entertainers, who could do almost as much. A journeyman American vaudevillian named Sylvester Schaffer, for instance, could juggle, sharpshoot, do drawings, prestidigitate, tumble, perform with trained animals, whips, and ropes—and dance a bit. All the high-spirited vaudevillians—running breakneck, elbowing for stage space, shoving and joking and clowning—found a prance to do in the spotlight.

The spotlight is now all but snuffed out. This book was made to provide the setting, the moment, and the audience for just one more prance.

The cruel tradition of heckling originated not in variety entertainment but in the legitimate theater, and it began as actual physical punishment. Here spectators hurl potatoes at actors who dared to displease. Rotten tomatoes —less dangerous but presumably funnier—were the preferred ammunition of American vaudeville audiences.

Alone and Alive

ENTERTAINMENT STAGES

Men, women and children, who cannot live on gravity alone, need something to satisfy their gayer, lighter moods and hours, and he who ministers to this want is in a business established by the Author of our very nature.   P. T. BARNUM

In America's towns and cities during the second half of the nineteenth century, it was not uncommon for a man to unwind, after a twelve-hour work day, with a schooner of beer at his local honky-tonk. The larger places seated about three hundred of these thirsty fellows on uncomfortable folding chairs, but then comfort was not the main attraction. Beer was, and so were a rowdy male atmosphere, dance hostesses, games of chance, and continuous entertainment.

Having paid a token admission, these fellows would stop at the wine room or bar and then the gaming tables before coming in for the show. By then, some were doubtless giddy from cuddling with the bar girls, for whom they'd bought carbonated sugar-water at an exorbitant four dollars a bottle, thinking it champagne. Some of the bar girls were female impersonators, and the occasional discovery of this deception would prompt a round of rattled indignation, bluster, and ribbing. Other customers might have won or lost a few dollars at roulette, faro, poker, or spindle (an arrow-spinning game).

Once inside the makeshift theater, they would jostle and crowd their ways over the wooden chairs that were lined up in rows to face the stage. As we know from saloon scenes in countless Western movies, the drop curtain was divided into boxes containing elaborate advertisements. These six-by-two-foot rectangles, leased out at two dollars a week, touted funeral parlors, beers, liver pills, and trusses.

The raucous audience would be hushed by the bar girls as a man edged out in front of the curtain, to be greeted by good-natured whistles and catcalls. This stagehand, known as the "thespic altar boy," held a long, flaming taper with which he ignited one footlight and then the next until the skirt of the curtain glowed warmly in the orange light, reflecting it back into the eager faces in the first rows.

One of the three basic sets was in place behind the curtain. If the first sketch was to be melodramatic, the sinister "dark woods" set, with gnarled trees and twisting branches, would be there. If romance was in store, the theater would call for the "light woods" set, meaning the idyllic scene, a sunny glen painted on muslin. If the sketch was to be comic, a kitchen interior would do. Meantime, the actors would be making up with flesh-tinted greasepaint, highlighted by brilliant rouge on the cheeks and good thick black lines for wrinkles. A heavy hand on the makeup was required to make an effect in the dim gaslight.

At curtain's rise, a typical show in one of these honky-tonk theaters would begin with a chorus line of three or four buxom young women in corsets and bloomers. A song-and-dance act might follow, then a singing quartet, a contortionist, or a comedian like Jack Murphy. Murphy

OPPOSITE:
The 3 Gormans, an act with Haverly's touring minstrel show.

ABOVE:
Sophie Tucker

was representative of his trade. He had made his debut in Philadelphia, breaking in with the Log Cabin Varieties. Given his chance, he developed a solo turn, playing the banjo while telling funny stories:

"Judge, this man came home the other night, took down the front door and hit his wife with it." "No case at all," said the judge. "Any man has the right to a-door his wife."

A dramatic sketch might come next, and then another solo turn—a singer, perhaps. And as many as fifteen acts followed, stretching on until dawn. The closing number, called an "afterpiece," was a racy sketch—racy at least for the era—with a title like "After the Shower" or "The Art of Flirtation."

As these honky-tonks grew more popular, they became fancier. Some added private boxes for good customers, with sitting rooms curtained off in the rear. The business conducted back there, it has been reported, ranged from slightly advanced cuddling to outright prostitution.

The honky-tonk shows grew more elaborate. The solitary pianos of the early days were augmented by banjos and occasional clarinets. Yet professional as these places were becoming, they remained exclusively male sanctuaries. A woman contemplating a visit could anticipate not only a tarnished reputation but an evening spent fending off mashers. Ladies and children had to go elsewhere for entertainment: to a riverboat or, if no river was handy, to a Wild West or minstrel show.

The minstrel show was essentially racist, based on impersonations and caricatures of black slaves. As such, it has become a skeleton in our theatrical closet, and that is unfortunate because minstrelsy was an otherwise elegant form of musical theater. The masks and stock characters looked back to the Italian commedia dell'arte of the seventeenth and eighteenth centuries, but the shows also offered a classic and formal basis for the vaudeville bills to come. As ensemble pieces, however, they are peripheral to this appreciation of the soloists of the variety stage. When they disappeared after the Civil War, doomed by the plantation mentality on which they were based, the kind of entertainment a man could bring his family to became a very rare commodity.

Outside the cities, in the farmlands where most Americans lived, practically the only professional entertainment available was the itinerant medicine show, and that was most definitely unfit for the young and the pure. For the medicine show was only half show business. The other half was booze business. Alcohol was the only effective ingredient in the nostrums, potions, and panaceas peddled from the back of the horse-drawn wagons by teams of buffoons and straight-men—spielers. The comedy routines that they played out came quickly to the point: a sales pitch and prompt sampling.

Midway through the nineteenth century, the God-fearing in farm and city remained wary of the corruptive influence of theatricals. Show-going was considered wasteful and show folk disreputable. Why, it was practically sinful just to seek entertainment for the family.

This general attitude did not seem likely to change when one Antonio Pastor opened a new honky-tonk theater in New York City. The diminutive and ebullient Pastor was a former circus ringmaster who had moved over to the business end of show business. His Music Hall, at 199–201 Bowery, was more elegant than the usual honky-tonk, but at first its shows remained resolutely low in tone, aimed at the masculine trade. As far as Pastor was concerned, women and children could go to the museums for amusement, and that was exactly where they *did* go. For it was a "museum" that Phineas Taylor Barnum opened in 1842 to attract

them: P. T. Barnum's American Museum, on Ann Street in New York.

Now here was a bit of hokum worthy of the soon-to-be legendary showman. Barnum realized that no business could be big business until it capitalized on the family trade, which seems today as close to an eternal verity as anything in popular culture. The educational exhibits that Barnum provided to legitimize his museum were no more than a few stuffed animals in the curio section on the main floor, leftovers from the five-story museum he'd converted. However, his new exhibits were carnival sideshows and human oddities—most particularly, popularly, and sensationally, the twenty-five-inch-tall Charles S. Stratton, billed as "General Tom Thumb."

General Thumb was to sell millions of tickets, and they would be sold at a dime apiece. Outside the "dime museum," a barker—called the "Professor" but no different from his fellows on a carnival midway—would lure customers with promises of giants, midgets, bearded ladies, armless wonders, and assorted beastfolk—leopard-, bear-, snake-, and gorilla-people. Barkers would also promote such exotics as Bertha Mills, whose feet were size nineteen, and even real freaks like the original "Siamese twins," Chang and Eng.

Also on the exhibition floor of Barnum's American Museum were "platform" acts that required little space, featuring sword-swallowers, strong-men, and magicians. On the floor above was a House of Wax, filled with replicas of wife-killers, train robbers, former presidents, and, when applicable, their assassins. These kinds of exhibits had changed little since their origin at England's pleasure fairs and would remain the same in more modern days.

On the top floor of the museum was a small variety theater where brief bills of entertainment were performed hourly. Barnum's taste tended to the carnival midway. Rather than vaudeville entertainers, he favored sideshow midgets like Admiral Dot, Queen Mab, or Boston Littlefinger. To his surprise, though, audiences favored the variety shows. By the 1870s one of his bills of entertainment might have included a juggler, a clog dancer, a pair of acrobats, and a musical instrumentalist. The finale, borrowed from the honky-tonks, was an afterpiece.

Many showmen imitated Barnum's successful dime museum—opening New York's elegant Eden Musée and popular Crystal Palace; Boston's Austin and Stone's; Chicago's Epstein's; and Minneapolis's Wonderland. The museum aspects varied. Some advertised stuffed mermaids; others promoted suits of clothes made of blown glass. Soon there was tough competition for the entertainment dime and, in addition to the curio museums, by the 1880s New York also had scores of handsome honky-tonks. Besides Tony Pastor's Music Hall there were Harry Hill's in lower Manhattan, Jack Berry's Varieties in Greenwich Village and, farther uptown, in Chelsea, the Alhambra. These little theaters proliferated so quickly that performers could book themselves all the way to California and command steady salaries of as much as two hundred dollars a week.

Meantime, Pastor's new Bowery theater was a success, and he had even organized a touring company of his own. As the 1880s began, theaters were being built especially to house such shows: handsome auditoriums like the Tabor Grand in Denver, the Adelphi in Chicago, and the Howard Atheneum in Boston. Pastor built his own place, the jewel-like Fourteenth Street Theatre. Its opening date was February 8, 1881, and the featured attraction was a lengthy spoof of Gilbert and Sullivan's *Pirates of Penzance*. The Savoy operas had become the rage and, unprotected by copyright, they were shamelessly bootlegged. Rather than blatantly steal them, the more respectable producers presented

pastiches. Pastor's was called *The Pie-Rats of Pen Yan* and it featured a favorite of his, a pretty young dumpling named Lillian Russell. She would of course go on to stardom, but at this stage she was no great attraction and business was only fair.

Pastor, who had once worked for Barnum as a tumbler, clown, and ringmaster, then had an inspiration, an inspiration frankly borrowed from Barnum, whose success with the family trade was now considerable. He struck boldly, eliminating his dance hostesses and bar girls. He closed his theater's liquor, wine, and beer bars. He posted a sign back-stage warning performers against the use of such words as "slob," "sucker," "damn," "hell," and—who knows why?—"socks." Plainly he meant business, and it was to be big business. Pastor's name for it was "polite vaudeville," and the concept was revolutionary: variety entertainment for a mixed audience of men and women.

The opening date for the first show under Pastor's new policy, "entertainment clean as a hound's tooth," was October 24, 1881. The night was rainy. At the other variety theaters business was bad, but not at Tony Pastor's. The new Fourteenth Street Theatre was packed and, for the first time, with an audience that included decent women.

The little showman had of course prepared that week's bill with special care, eliminating all but the most respectable of his regular acts. Ellie Wesner opened with a couple of songs and then launched into her monologue. The Leland Sisters followed with sweet and playful duets. Pastor had slotted Dan Collyer to follow; his songs were silly ones, but

Seen here c. 1891, Lillian Russell, a Tony Pastor protégée, was in the first wave of female singers popular in the early years of American vaudeville. Pastor publicized her hourglass figure.

they had tinges of the old raciness—for instance, "Tommy, Don't Wriggle the Baby." Pastor probably sighed with relief when it got by.

Mack and Ferguson raced on stage as if to distract the audience from Collyer. They were a popular Irish dialect comedy team and their routine was well known and beloved, all the way to its climax, when Mack buried a hatchet in Ferguson's skull. Even though Ferguson wore a padded fright wig to cushion the blow, years of playing the act would leave him deaf. Lillie Western followed with her musical varieties (banjo and concertina), and then Frank McNish closed with low comedy. As a surprise finale, Pastor himself appeared in his traditional ringmaster outfit to sing a half-dozen of the thousands of songs in his repertoire.

That first night was triumphant but not revolutionary. It would not be so easy to overcome one of the major proscriptions of Western civilization and make regular theatergoers of women. The initial audience of curious women did not return, and the male customers, upon whom the day-to-day business depended, were pressing Pastor to resume traditional shows, booze, and girls. Business sagged but the showman was resolute. He compromised by designating one performance a week as Ladies' Night. At that performance, every female customer would receive a free box of chocolates. None came. He offered flowers, food (hams and bags of flour). Still they would not come.

In desperation he advertised that the first twenty-five women to buy tickets for the special ladies' show would receive free silk dresses. Silk dresses did it. Twenty-five were hardly enough. Scores of women were in line before the box office even opened. Virtually every study of American variety entertainment marks the birth of vaudeville with Pastor's silk-dress promotion.

Tony Pastor's clean-up campaign was doubtless necessary to overcome the historically sleazy reputation of variety entertainment, but his eagerness to avoid even a hint of the risqué would ultimately lead to excessive prudishness. A practically priggish conservatism developed in vaudeville that detracted from the ribald spirit that had always provided a certain dash. Vaudeville paid the price for acceptance by upholding a level of decency not merely fit for women and children but sufficient to satisfy the demands of an inquisitor. As a result of this self-censorship, a curious blend of low urges and high morality would for decades characterize *all* American entertainment—theater, the movies, television. Stage invective would be limited to juvenile epithets; in the movies, not even married couples would sleep in the same bed, and life would go on without bodily functions; television entertainment would be sanitized as if for an audience of children exclusively.

Perhaps the show makers of Pastor's time as well as our own endured these limitations because they were seeking not only family business but professional and personal acceptance. It was not many years, after all, since they had been barred from polite society; certain hotels and communities still excluded them. Perhaps for all these reasons, vaudeville was to become puritanical beyond the dictates of plain sense. There seemed to prevail a basic fear that one blue joke or sexual innuendo, one off-color sketch or frank expletive would not merely alienate the family trade but destroy the hard-won offstage respectability. It would be back to the honky-tonks and the fleabag hotels for the rogues, vagabonds, and sturdy beggars. This, then, was the bargain: the hypocritical acceptance of a moral code to which neither performers nor audiences actually adhered.

Pastor's Fourteenth Street Theatre became the most famous vaudeville house in America. Its roster of performers was brilliant, for only the best could play polite vaudeville, only the best could be thoroughly entertaining without smuttiness—and only the best played Pastor's: Harrigan and Hart, Weber and Fields, the Four Cohans, Buster Keaton, Nat Goodwin, and of course Lillian Russell. Audiences flocked to see these ascendant stars and doubtless to see Pastor himself as well. He appeared in the lobby at almost every performance in his tails, high-heeled boots and collapsible top hat. On a lucky night an audience might even find him strolling on stage to sing his theme song:

> Are you going to the ball this evening?
> No, not this evening! Some other evening!
> Good evening!

They loved him, they loved his high spirits and good humor, and so did the performers who worked for him. Pastor was said never to have "closed" —that is, fired—an act. His attitude toward performers was so sentimental that when reminded of his house band's ineptitude he once remarked, "I know they're terrible but they're my old boys and they can die here." And he could well afford to be magnanimous. He had vaudeville all to himself. The competition was still in Boston.

Benjamin Franklin Keith had cut his teeth in show business as a "candy butcher," hawking chocolates and racy gazettes during intermissions at primitive Boston variety houses. He had a real talent for discovering (or inventing) freaks, and when he left burlesque to open a curio museum he revealed another gift, a knack for naming them: the Dog-Faced Boy (a youth with a badly splotched complexion); Baby Alice, the Midget Wonder (a premature baby); and the Three-Headed Songstress (an optical illusion).

Keith found an ambitious and energetic young partner in Edward F. Albee—whose grandson is the well-known playwright—and expanded operations, acquiring a second museum and putting up a variety theater in Philadelphia. Soon he replaced his freak shows with popular acts and low comics. In 1893 Keith and Albee opened a theater just blocks from Pastor's and took advantage of what Keith perceived as Pastor's weaknesses. Their Union Square Theatre was bigger than the Fourteenth Street Theatre and they offered higher salaries to lure the best performers, leaving the sentimental Pastor with every worn-out and needy entertainer who begged him for a booking. Pastor had also cut back to two shows a day, and Keith and Albee began running continuous shows.

Still Pastor lorded it over the competition. Did not songwriters still clamor to have their latest numbers aired at his place? Introducing a song at Tony Pastor's, it was believed, could guarantee it national popularity. Influential as Pastor was in popularizing songs like the smash hit "Wait Till the Sun Shines, Nellie," the little impresario considered comedy acts the key to variety success. Though he avoided the cruder ethnic sketches that were attracting the crowds to Keith's theater—"The Sport and the Jew," "Irish by Name but Coon by Birth," and "The Merry Wop"—by today's standards his comedy acts were, as Joe Laurie, Jr., dryly remarked in *Vaudeville*, rather less than witty:

In those days the corn was very green. Actors laid them in the aisles with such sparkling chestnuts as, "I sent my wife to the Thousand Islands for a vacation—a week on each island." Or, "Are oysters healthy?" "I never heard them complain." Or, "You can drive a horse to drink but a pencil must be lead."

And any gag employing false teeth or hair, a wooden leg or a mother-in-law panicked the house.

For thirty years, Eddie Foy starred in both vaudeville and legitimate theater. In 1913, at the age of fifty-nine, he came out of retirement to form the most famous of all family acts, "Eddie Foy and the Seven Little Foys." Here he does his youthful vaudeville turn, "Why Do They Call Me a Gibson Girl?" in the Broadway show The Orchid.

Plainly and regrettably, the line between popular entertainment and the higher theatrical arts was one no self-respecting writer would cross.

Albee hounded Pastor as if the entire vaudeville business depended on the New York market. Although he was supposedly Keith's executive assistant, it was he who wielded the power. He raised star salaries higher and cut the admission price to fifty cents. In response, Pastor dropped

his own admission to thirty cents and remained confident enough to take a full-page advertisement in the Christmas edition of the *Dramatic Mirror*, boasting that his Fourteenth Street Theatre was "the first specialty and vaudeville theater in America catering to polite tastes," and that its clientele included "the best families of the metropolis."

Albee pressed Keith to build more and bigger theaters: the Keith Colonial in Boston, the Palace in Cleveland, a second house in Boston, and another in New York. Relegating his chief to the background, and ever more aggressive, ruthless, and now widely despised and feared, Albee was fast becoming czar of vaudeville and the Keith houses the most important "wheel" (booking circuit) in the country. Only the top acts played it. This, now, was the big time.

The expression, "big time," like "small time," is an outgrowth of the vaudevillians' use of the word "time." An act would sign a contract for a certain number of work weeks on one of the vaudeville wheels. Such a stint was known as "Keith time" or "Orpheum time," and, then, as "playing the Keith time." Because these were major wheels that offered the most comfortable theaters, the biggest and most polite audiences, the highest pay, and the best working conditions, playing them was known as playing the "big time." The "medium" and "small" times referred to lesser circuits with smaller salaries and meaner conditions.

Moving from one circuit to the next, as if on meshing gears, an act could be booked as far as two years in advance without scheduling the

The tiny Anna Held, another reigning queen among vaudeville's lady singers, was married to the great Flo Ziegfeld, who boasted to the press that she took daily baths in fresh milk.

same theater twice. Thus a comedy sketch, dance routine, or set of songs could remain unchanged and provide a performer's livelihood for years. No wonder, then, the addition of even one joke to a routine was considered a major revision. Vaudevillians would wait for remote engagements to test new material so that no harm would be done to the dear-as-life act, should the new material fail. In this way, routines were protected as they were polished—as well they might be, for an act was all a performer had. It was his living. Naturally, anyone who stole material, even so much as a joke, was considered vile. Vaudevillians even established a central office where, after being written out and sealed, acts could be registered so as to establish their true and original authorship.

The Keith wheel was considered the biggest time of all because it paid the highest salaries and offered the best working conditions in the largest, most luxurious, and greatest number of theaters. Its performers played only two shows a day—Albee having reimposed that on Keith, though hardly out of sympathy for performers. Albee simply believed it to be efficient scheduling as well as an argument for lower pay: once he had performers dependent upon him he slashed their salaries.

On the medium time, the grind might be four performances a day, and on the small time an act could work for six or even eight performances a day, with the pay as little as twenty-five dollars a week. This was known as the "death trail," or "the aching heart" to those unfortunate enough to be playing storefronts, virtually honky-tonks, in one-night stands in the boondocks.

Depressed by Albee's competitive tactics, Tony Pastor retired in 1908, but by then Keith had other Eastern competitors: F. F. Proctor, Marcus Loew, Klaw and Erlanger, and William Morris. As for the rest of the country, Martin Beck's Orpheum circuit shared the Midwest with the Kohl and Castle wheel, while Considine-Sullivan and Alexander Pantages controlled the West Coast.

This, then, was the start of vaudeville's brilliant era. A host of motley jesters was to blanket the country, confidently booking themselves hundreds of performances in advance, the top stars earning as much as several thousand dollars a week. The center stage was in New York City, now the country's entertainment capital. There, splendid theaters boasted a peak-caliber eight-act variety bill, which had developed a ritualistic quality.

As Bill Smith explained in *The Vaudevillians*, an eight-act show began with a "dumb" (silent) act—an acrobat, or a bicyclist, or perhaps an animal-trainer. The second place—traditionally the worst spot on the bill because it was the first talking act, performed while the audience was usually still arriving—was filled by a newcomer, a minor comedian, or a female singer. There followed a "tab" show (a tabloid, or abbreviated, version of a recent Broadway success) or a "flash" act, meaning an act with a large company, elaborate costumes, and its own scenery.

The fourth and fifth spots on this typical agenda were usually filled by a solid performer, perhaps an established comedy team, or by a rowdy act like "School Days," one of Gus Edwards's kiddie groups, or perhaps the Marx Brothers' "Fun in Hi Skule." Sixth on the bill was approaching the cream of the show, and this niche called for a class act, perhaps a dance team. Then came the headliner, *always* seventh and next to last. The closing spot, considered a throwaway since many customers left after the star turn, was usually another dumb act.

If the program was ritualized, the acts were not. Their variety was limited only by the performers' imaginations, and there were no limitations on originality, brilliance, or chutzpah. Entertainers trotted on stage

seeking no less than to overwhelm the audience, and whether the reaction was enthusiasm or contempt, nothing they did was ever ludicrous enough to be truly surprising, for the ludicrous was merely everyday and some acts were magnificently preposterous. The Cherry Sisters, for instance, were billed as "The World's Worst Act." They once sued a newspaper for libel on the basis of an insulting review, and after watching the act the judge ruled against them. A net was stretched across the stage whenever Effie and Addie Cherry played Hammerstein's Victoria Theatre in New York, to protect them from tossed eggs and tomatoes. Beginning as five farm girls and ending as two, the Cherry Sisters insisted that they were supposed to be *good*. They enjoyed a thirty-year vaudeville career on the premise of being awful and not knowing it.

Other curious acts might show up on a bill, such as "Francis White, the World's Smallest Dancer," or "Willard, the Man Who Grows." Willard would chat with audience volunteers while the backdrop behind him inched downward. The strong horizontal line that was behind him at waist level when he began would end up around his hips—hence, growth. McNaughton, the Human Tank, swallowed frogs, and Charlie Chase ate lightbulbs. Swain's Cats and Rats raced around a track, the cats astride the rats, and The Lunatic Bakers jumped in and out of ovens. Cantor Joseph Rosenblatt sang "Molly Machree" and the armless Lutz Brothers assembled an engine with their feet. The team of Marguerite Webb and Jack Connelly played the piano with fruit. Annie May Abbott, the Georgia Magnet, defied anyone in the audience to lift her.

ABOVE:
The professionally awful Cherry Sisters, Effie and Addie, shown here c. 1900

OPPOSITE:
Nora Bayes was an emotional woman who didn't hesitate to open her heart and speak her mind in public. Passionately jealous, whether of lovers or competitors, Bayes was blackballed by the Palace management after she complained about Sophie Tucker's billing, and she spent the last weeks of her life begging to be reinstated at any salary. She died on the day her return was announced.

Tops among the odd acts, believe it or not, was Helen Keller, assisted by Annie Sullivan. They were more sober personages in later years but in those cheerful and halcyon days they headlined in vaudeville, Keller using her fingers to read the lips of audience volunteers. Nobody considered this disrespectful or insensitive. Show business was a leveler. And in such sweet times, beyond chastisement, playing the Keith circuit became a fair mark of success.

Yet, several successful theaters in New York notwithstanding, the frustrated Albee could not establish a flagship house there. First Tony Pastor had taken center stage, and then Oscar Hammerstein grabbed the spotlight. A multimillionaire inventor of cigar-making machines, Hammerstein was a fellow with a history of failed theaters. He had indulged his enthusiasm for show business by building auditoriums: first, in 1880, the Harlem Opera House; then, in 1895, the Columbia, uptown on East One Hundred Twenty-fifth Street; and after that, the plush Olympia Music Hall, on Broadway at Forty-fifth Street; and finally, in 1906, the Manhattan Opera House, on Thirty-fourth Street. These various white elephants were done in by architectural errors, cost overruns, and disastrous programing. Hammerstein's love of lavish entertainment, grand opera in particular, was not supported by business sense or even a reliable showmanship (only by his cigar-making machines). One of his grandiose notions, for instance, was a vaudeville version of a three-ring circus, with three acts performed simultaneously. In 1893 he accepted a bet with conductor Gustav Kerber and in forty-eight hours composed a grand opera, *The Koh-i-Noor Diamond*. Kerber refused to pay on the grounds that Hammerstein's opera was terrible, but the ingenuous impresario produced it anyhow, on the stage of his Harlem Opera House. *The Koh-i-Noor Diamond* attracted a pathetic four hundred dollars in ticket sales at its single performance.

When in 1898 Hammerstein's $350-thousand Olympia was sold out from under him, he was left destitute. Friends organized benefits at the various music halls he'd built and lost. The undauntable Hammerstein took the money and, a hopeless case, put up yet another theater, the 1,250-seat Victoria at Seventh Avenue and Forty-second Street, and for once his gamble paid off. The Victoria became America's premier vaudeville showcase, known to entertainers simply as "the corner." It would ultimately earn Hammerstein five million dollars and during the next seventeen years provide a stage for the country's greatest performers.

Of course, it was not Hammerstein who was responsible for the Victoria's success. It was his son Willie, a fellow as reserved as his father was flamboyant. Behind Willie's dour facade, however, were the gaudy colors of an inherited showmanship, and the colors showed where they mattered most: in the operation of the theater. For instance, Willie had no qualms about advertising the farewell appearance of the fabled cooch dancer Carmencita, six years after her death. Audiences accepted the impersonator as if deception were a normal part of show business, which of course it was. Over the big auditorium, Hammerstein built another called the Paradise Roof. There he promoted "Hy-Tone Vaudeville," with acts more refined than those in the music hall below. The afterpieces, however, were usually played by performers who had just finished the show downstairs.

Willie Hammerstein served refreshments in the glass-walled Paradise Roof. He installed as hostess a young black woman, whose expression was even grimmer than his own. Known as Silent Sue, she glared at the customers and they were dared to make her smile. Silent Sue could not smile supposedly because her facial muscles were paralyzed. Spreading such a rumor was typical of Hammerstein's showmanly style.

Another example of it was hiring Evelyn Nesbit to appear at the Victoria. Miss Nesbit was the beautiful wife of Harry K. Thaw, who in a jealous rage murdered her lover, the prominent architect Stanford White. Thaw had been committed to a state hospital for the criminally insane. Evelyn capitalized on the tragedy by performing in vaudeville. Such appearances by notorious public figures were known as "freak acts" and Willie Hammerstein was given credit (or blame) for originating the genre. He booked prizefighters and explorers at the Victoria too, but along with his audience he seemed to prefer swindlers like Barney Bertsche, forgers like George Schroeder, bank robbers like Ed Morrell, and just about anyone involved with murder.

As 1913 began, Hammerstein was scheduling these and otherwise accomplished performers far in advance as he prepared to deal with the mighty competition of the Palace Theatre, rising some five blocks to the north. When that plush 1,700-seat auditorium was originally announced, he had been less concerned, probably feeling confident on his home ground. The builder was Martin Beck, the Midwest vaudeville entrepreneur, who was hoping to crash the New York market. Neither Beck nor Hammerstein, however, had reckoned with Edward Albee, who was half crazy on the subject of the Keith circuit's being without a flagship theater in New York. The Palace apparently snapped his tolerance. Albee just would not countenance an outlander's strolling in with a "palace" and gaining squatter's rights to the territory in the bargain. So he simply saw to it that no performers were available to Beck. This wasn't hard to do, as his United Booking Office controlled every major act in the country. And when that happened, Beck's financial backing van-

Swain's Birds, an early vaudeville act

ished and Albee took control of the big theater, the most beautiful vaudeville house in the nation.

When the Palace finally opened later in 1913, its marquee bore the Keith nameplate, and Albee had his flagship theater. It was to become a legend. No name is so closely identified with top-flight vaudeville as the

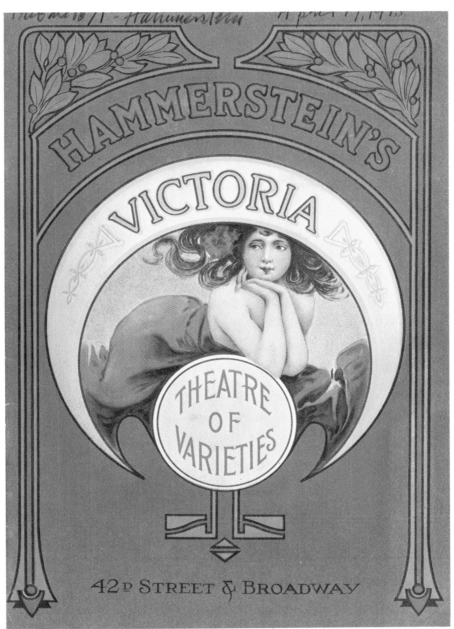

The last of Oscar Hammerstein's huge theaters was the Victoria, at the corner of Seventh Avenue and Forty-second Street. Thanks to the showmanship of his son Willie, it was the first of the old man's elephants that was not white. Because of the popularity of Willie's "freak acts," the Victoria became known as the "nut house."

Palace Theatre, and to this day, "playing the Palace" means being at the very top as an entertainer.

But for a while Hammerstein's Victoria remained New York City's premier vaudeville house. Just to be near it, performers liked to hang out on the street in front and talk show business. The Palace's managing director and booking agent, Eddie Valentine Dowling, floundered for an entertainment policy to distinguish it from the crowd and from the Victoria particularly, and nothing seemed to work. It was as if Hammerstein had cornered the showmanship market. Eventually, Dowling was inspired to import Sarah Bernhardt from France to star in a one-act play (playlets were not uncommon in vaudeville). The Divine Sarah insisted on being paid in gold coin immediately after every performance, but she was worth every karat. For with her engagement, the Palace would become identified with vaudeville that was prestigious enough to rank with the legitimate theater.

Now, the difference between vaudeville and the Broadway legitimate theater was simple: vaudeville was a program of variety acts that was performed two (or more) times a day and changed every week. Legitimate theater was a musical or dramatic show that played only eight performances a week, running unaltered as long as audiences supported it. Broadway's musical revues might resemble vaudeville in offering a

After vaudeville audiences had lost interest in the scandal that rocketed Evelyn Nesbit to notoriety, she was faced with either oblivion or the development of an act based on some talent she had not yet displayed. The beautiful former chorus girl found a dance partner in a boxer named Jack Clifford, with whom she performed at B. F. Keith's Alhambra Theatre.

series of entertainers and sketches, but they aimed to please a more sophisticated taste; they offered new songs; the program never changed; and there was not the variety—the jugglers, magicians, acrobats, and comedy acts—that gave vaudeville its tempo.

For performers, however, there was a much more significant difference between vaudeville and the legitimate theater: prestige. The legitimate theater was the *legitimate* theater. The Palace would change that, but while the Victoria reigned, deluxe it may have been but vaudeville it still was.

At the new Palace, the rules of propriety were as strict as they had been when Tony Pastor first introduced polite vaudeville. "Remember," a sign backstage read, "this theater caters to ladies and gentlemen and children. Vulgarity will not be tolerated. Check with manager before using any material you have any doubt about. Don't use the words hell, damn, devil, cockroach, spit, etc."

After Eddie Dowling announced Sarah Bernhardt's imminent appearance at the Palace, Willie Hammerstein countered by signing his favorite freak act, Evelyn Nesbit, for a return engagement at a considerable three thousand dollars a week. It seemed, initially, as if for once Willie had miscalculated. This woman who had inspired murderous jealousy no longer seemed able to inspire audiences. Business at the Victoria was slow until, by a coincidence still difficult to believe, her ex-husband, Harry Thaw, escaped from Matawan State Hospital.

When Thaw was found in Canada, Willie had a friend up there send a wire signed "H.K.T." which contained a threat to kill Evelyn plus a threat to sue the theater if the name of Thaw was not instantly removed from the billing. Thaw did not come back to New York but largely due to the way Willie Hammerstein ballyhooed the news of his escape, Evelyn remained the box office draw at his theatre for eight weeks, attracting $175,000 during that run. (Charles and Louise Samuels, *Once Upon a Stage*)

The stunt was to be Willie's last, for he died the next year, and without his wonderfully sobersided flamboyance the Victoria faded and was sold and razed. The Palace, now without any real competition, rose to glory and its weekly show became an event. Afficionados would attend the Monday matinee just to be first to see the new bill. They would catch the classic sketches repeatedly, searching for refinements. Tickets weren't cheap (a dollar and a half for an orchestra seat), but there in the plushest showcase for the country's favorite entertainment medium the top entertainers in the country played before the toughest audiences. The Palace was the ranking stage in a field of thousands from tents in the farmlands to other Palaces that had sprung up in emulation of the first, in cities from coast to coast.

The one and only original Palace Theatre featured only the best. The great women singers who had dominated show business since the turn of the century—Eva Tanguay, Nora Bayes, Elsie Janis, Sophie Tucker, and other troupers in feathers and hats—were the backbone of its original roster. The wonderful funnymen played there, such teams as Smith and Dale; Burns and Allen; Clayton, Jackson, and Durante. True, Ed Wynn, Bert Lahr, and the other great clowns favored the legitimate theater, but clowning was a European tradition as was the theater. America's great innovation was the monologist, and these fearless talkers grew up on the Palace's stage—Julius Tannen, Lou Holtz, Milton Berle, Joe Frisco, Fred Allen, Frank Tinney, and the greatest of all, Jack Benny and Frank Fay. (Bob Hope played the Palace too, early in his career. He was so discouraged that he had to be talked out of quitting show business.)

B.F. Keith's

Palace Theatre

Broadway at 47th Street

OPPOSITE, ABOVE LEFT:
Evelyn Nesbit was one of Willie Hammerstein's "freak acts," offering not talent but notoriety. What Evelyn was notorious for was sex appeal.

OPPOSITE, ABOVE RIGHT:
If Eva Tanguay had been tempestuous but untalented, Elsie Janis was just the reverse—meek but perhaps the most gifted of all the vaudeville actresses. A headliner in her teens, she could sing, dance, perform acrobatics, and do impressions, but she achieved her most glorious successes in troop shows, entertaining American doughboys overseas. It was there that she discovered and sponsored (and, some say, fell in love with) Maurice Chevalier.

OPPOSITE, BELOW LEFT:
Imposing in her brimmed hats and endless boas, Nora Bayes was nevertheless victimized by her own romantic and emotional soul. She talked too much about her private life onstage and backstage and complained so much about her competitors that Eddie Dowling, the Palace's managing director, once pushed her out the stage door and didn't let her back in for the show.

OPPOSITE, BELOW RIGHT:
Although she was born in Warsaw, Anna Held's specialty was playing the French coquette and singing (into a hand-held mirror) such songs as "I Just Can't Make My Eyes Behave." Married to Flo Ziegfeld, this great singing lady never appeared in his Follies.

OVERLEAF, LEFT:
Irene Foote was a New York debutante when she met and married a little-known English song-and-dance man named Vernon Castle. As a team, personifying elegance and romance, Vernon and Irene Castle became idols of the American stage. They built a beautiful nightclub and called it "Castles in the Air." Irene's hair and dress styles set the fashion for a generation of women. As romance would have it, Vernon became a World War I pilot and died in a flaming crash.

OVERLEAF, RIGHT:
The dance team of Fred and Adele Astaire, one year after turning professional. It was 1905, he was five, she six, and they were already touring on the medium time.

There were other big-time vaudeville houses in New York City—the Riverside and the Riviera on upper Broadway, and Proctor's Fifth Avenue downtown, and the Orpheum in Brooklyn—but for a first-class evening of first-class entertainment in a first-class setting, as lavish and special an evening as any Broadway theater might offer, the Palace was guaranteed gala, and tickets were scalped outside almost every night.

The beginning of the end came with the Wall Street Crash. Suddenly, there was little money available for frivolity. The radio networks were already established, and a depressed population preferred to stay at home and hear the best entertainers for nothing rather than go out and pay for second best at a local vaudeville theater. Many city-dwellers who still wanted to go out for an evening preferred the activity of dancing along with the new orchestras to the passivity of theatrical spectatorship. Too, hard times inspire a certain physical recklessness that can serve as a vent for frustration, nervousness, and rage. Dancing is a readily available and acceptable outlet. It thrived in the Crash years as it would in wartimes.

The Palace's downfall began in 1929, when a three-on-Sundays policy was instituted. Then Albee was forced to lift his ban on radio performers, bringing in Eddie Cantor and George Jessel for eight weeks each in

Miss NORA BAYES   The Theatre Magazine Co.,

1930. By 1932 the operation was fraying at the edges. The great theater stooped to four shows a day, alternating with movies. Within months, the shows were dropped. The golden age was over.

Personal entertainment is a performing art without strict form. Each entertainer creates his own form; he is the art as well as the artist. His creation, his show, his act cannot be read or hung on a wall, or be re-created by anyone else. It must be performed on a stage in front of

The greatest star and the hottest attraction in all of vaudeville was Eva Tanguay, the "I Don't Care Girl," who by her own admission could neither sing nor dance. Early in her career, Tanguay socked another chorus girl who was upstaging her and discovered the value of publicity. Her sexual adventures, fiery temper, and unpredictable stage behavior kept her in headlines and business.

ABOVE:

Though in her day vaudeville was striving to shed its risqué reputation, Sophie Tucker was insistently, exuberantly, and triumphantly bawdy. She started out, at the turn of the century, singing in blackface, a "coonshouter" in a New York beer hall (some consider this the first cabaret entertainment in America). Tucker found regular work as a rollicking and lusty act. Pictured here in 1914, she had progressed in vaudeville to the big time of Oscar Hammerstein's Victoria and B. F. Keith's Palace. Always unique, "The Soph" survived after the other singing ladies of early vaudeville went out of style.

BELOW:

By professional consensus, at the very top of the vaudeville class were Jack Benny and Frank Fay. Fay's ego, awesome in good times, was just as inflated when its owner was under siege. Late in his career, when things were going badly, Fay returned to the Palace to share emcee duties with his wife, the glamorous movie star Barbara Stanwyck. After two weeks of a three-week engagement that everyone in show business knew was thanks to Stanwyck, Fay skipped out, leaving her to finish alone (Gus Van stepped in as his replacement).

an audience. Without that stage and audience, he and the act do not exist.

As America's thousands of vaudeville theaters were shutting down, entertainers were pushed to huddle in the few remaining spotlights; on the last stages. But in the youthful time of vaudeville, as in all youthful times, decay and change and death itself lay ahead, in a future not only unforeseeable but unimaginable. America's great entertainers still had time, while there still was time, to caper across the great vaudeville stages.

AL JOLSON
The Greatest Entertainer in the World

If anyone epitomizes the singular excitement of live performance and its ephemeral, unrecordable nature, that figure is Al Jolson. Billed as "The World's Greatest Entertainer," he probably was just that. By almost every available account, his performances were electrifying and his appeal crossed all boundaries of taste and intelligence.

To say that he was a singer is to call Fred Astaire a dancer, Jack Benny a comedian, or Liberace a piano player. He invented a new kind of singing and a new kind of song—big numbers done in big, over-whelming ways. Jolson would move up stage and down, from one wing to the other, dancing, skipping, getting down on one knee and wringing his hands, then rising to spread his arms in exaltation. Song singing, a passive and nearly inane activity, had been made into performance.

He had a voice of size, a rich baritone that landed on each note with bell-like purity; his rhythmic impulse was metronomic; and his musician-ship was influenced by the improvisations and slides of Dixieland jazz. But the songs themselves were an utterly new sort. Soaring numbers conceived for theatrical effect, they were designed especially for the Jolson style; high-stepping, expansive, and totally American songs: "Swanee," "My Mammy," "Rockabye Your Baby with a Dixie Melody," "Toot, Toot, Tootsie," "There's a Rainbow 'round My Shoulder," "I'm Sittin' on Top of the World." Nobody had ever sung such extroverted numbers before, at least not with the dominating verve that Jolson flashed. Theater music had been light and cheerful until then, or else downright florid. And nobody had attempted the flat-out bravura that Jolson demon-strated as he ran on stage (he would never just walk) to grab the spotlight as if with his hand and not let go of it, rocking and socking. Future star singers and theatrical belters who had never seen Al Jolson would owe their careers to him, for he invented big singing.

Al Jolson's movies and records provide few clues to the effect he created onstage, the effect of a man possessed, according to the critic Gilbert Millstein. But there are enough descriptions available to piece together an impression of what it must have been like to be in this performer's shock range.

Jolson had, in 1909, left a trio (which included his brother Harry) to go out as a single. After a year in vaudeville's medium time, he felt cocky enough to take full-page advertisements in the theatrical newspa-pers announcing, "You never heard of me but you will!" He left vaudeville for the prestigious Dockstader's Minstrels, and there he developed the black musical and verbal intonations to go with his blackface makeup. The Minstrels led to a small part in *La Belle Paree!*, a musical comedy that was opening the palatial Winter Garden Theatre on Broadway. The overlong show received dismal reviews, none of which singled out the twenty-five-year-old blackface singer. At the third performance, the au-dience had been decimated by walk-outs when he made his usual entrance. Pearl Sieben, Jolson's biographer, describes the occasion:

He walked to the center of the stage. The single spotlight hit him. He shaded his eyes with one hand and gazed out to the audience.

"Lots of brave folks out there," he said. "Either that or you can't read." There was a spattering of uneasy laughter. "Come to think of it," he went on, "after the reviews we got, there's a lot of brave folks up here on the stage." The laughter increased. It was infectious. Al pointed to the audience. "Hey," he said, "I know you. You was in the audience the last time I played Brighton

Beach. You used to like my act. What's the matter, you come into this classy joint you think you shouldn't have a good time? C'mon, this place ain't so much. I remember when it was the Horse Exchange." A wave of laughter spread through the audience. "That's better. Now I got a few songs to sing—if you'll listen."

The next day's papers told of a new star who had captured the sophisticated Winter Garden audience.

Talent, if not the least of it, is only one key to a performer's success. The way that the talent is used, how it is communicated, how it is packaged counts just as much, and Jolson had already developed idiosyncracies enough to distinguish him from all the other blackface singers. It was certainly brash to break character in a musical comedy and chat with the audience; and it was risking annoyance to be arrogant about it. But he was "Joley" to everyone now and everyone was a "mug" or a "kid" to him, and his casual style was disarming. Audiences always sense an entertainer's pleasure or ease onstage, and they share in it.

Although *La Belle Paree!* had a Jerome Kern score, it was common in the musical theater of the time to interpolate additional songs, and Jolson added a Stephen Foster medley that included "Oh, Susanna," "Camptown Races," and "I Dream of Jeannie." He would ever after be expected to interrupt his shows and announce that he was going to treat the audience to some singing, and the hell with the plot. They came to count on it (as the actors in the cast came to resent it), awaiting Jolson's tag line, "You ain't heard nothin' yet."

He wore a nappy wig over the blackface makeup, a dark blue suit that was short at the cuffs, a floppy bow tie, and white gloves. Those gloves would develop a life of their own as he introduced an entire vocabulary of hand language—palms up or down or out, fingers jabbing, fists punching—to go along with the poses and gestures that added choreographic flair and drama to the mere act of singing. Jolson was becoming an entire act. He would skip, shuffle, leap down into the audience and dash up one aisle and down the other, stopping to serenade a pretty girl, an old woman, a child. Corniness works—don't forget it. Then he was back onstage, turning away from the audience but never letting it out of eye contact. Now his eyes were rolled into the corners of the sockets, staring, winking. He would freeze in that pose and then pop into a fast soft-shoe or a buck-and-wing, until the suspenseful beat began. Then he would segue into a melodramatic, incantatory recitation.

> *Mammy, I'm-a-comin'*
> *Sor-sorry that I made you wait,*
> *Oh mammy, mammy, I'm comin'*
> *Oh God I hope—I hope I'm not too late!*

It wasn't over yet. He would clap his hands and jab a finger, and then he would tilt his head back, arch his spine, roll his eyeballs heavenward, and spread-eagle his arms to climax.

> *Mammy, don't you know me?*
> *It's your little baby!*

And finally, punching and peaking,

> *I'd walk a million miles*
> *For one of your smiles,*
> *My ma-aaa-my!*

ABOVE:

Al Jolson sheet music cover

BELOW:

Al Jolson's career was resurrected by the hugely successful 1947 film The Jolson Story. *Here he rehearses for a comeback appearance at a New York movie-presentation house.*

GEORGE JESSEL

The California branch of vaudeville's top comedians—the group that
had succeeded in radio—was an arrogant lot. George Burns, Jack
Benny, Groucho Marx, Milton Berle. They were competitive and
argumentative, but there was one thing they agreed on: the funniest man
of all was George Jessel. The problem with Jessel, the consensus seemed
to be, was that he spread himself too thin. He was an actor and a singer
as well as a monologist. He could come through onstage (there were
comedians' comedians who couldn't) but he never was as funny in performance as he was among fellow funnymen. For instance, Burns couldn't
get over Jessel's impromptu cold-war crack, "You guys think the Russians can't invent an atom bomb just because they dance sitting down."
And Eddie Cantor loved Jessel's ad-lib at a White House luncheon,
"Never before has so little chicken served so many."

Jessel had starred on Broadway in *The Jazz Singer* and had worked
regularly as a monologist in vaudeville. His opening line was among the
most famous: "Hello, mom? This is your son Georgie. You know. From
the checks." But between a love of fun and perhaps too easy a flow of
natural talent, he let his career go to flab and, while he never wanted for
work, neither did he ever win from the public an acclaim commensurate
with that of his colleagues. Instead, he became a caricature of himself,
ultimately to be better known as a subject of impressions than for his
own great gifts.

As the Palace began to show the first
signs of decline, vaudeville mogul
Edward Albee was forced to lift his
ban on radio performers, hiring George
Jessell (left) and Eddie Cantor for an
extended engagement as co-emcees.

George Jessel at the Palace, doing
his impression of Eddie Cantor

CLOWNING AROUND

A performer watched an opening act. A comic barrelled onstage with a red nose a blue wig, green makeup, teeth blacked out, baggy pants, funny hat, a loud vest, slap shoes, an outsized checkered coat and a big heavy watch chain. "By the looks of that guy," the performer said to the stage manager, "he must be a very funny comedian." The stage manager replied, "That's the straight man."
JOE LAURIE, JR., *Vaudeville*

The wild and raucous comedians who had been doted upon by the honky-tonk audiences were perhaps pioneers but they were also the cavemen of comedy. Their senses of humor were too broad and (though it's hard to imagine) sometimes even too ethnic for the more refined audiences of "polite vaudeville." The early crowds at Tony Pastor's had enough of the honky-tonk in their blood to be amused by the mayhem of Mack and Ferguson, but not for long. Soon they were asking for more sophistication than a hatchet in the skull. Dialect provided it. Almost any accent was considered funny: Italian, Jewish, Russian, Irish. And Dutch:

A: I am delightfulness to meet you.
B: The disgust is all mine.

This inspired exchange was dreamed up by Joe Weber and Lew Fields, a star dialect-comedy team that did make the successful transition from honky-tonk to vaudeville. They too had started out as a knockabout act, "The Skull Crackers," but the two twelve-year-olds worked out the characters of Mike (Weber) and Myer (Fields) and soon discarded the bludgeon of slapstick for false whiskers, checkered suits, flat derbies, and the drier pleasures of verbal riposte.

Mike: I receivedidid a letter from moin goil but I don't know how to writteninin her back.
Myer: Writteninin her back! Such an edumuncation you got it? Writteninin her back! You mean rotteninin her back! How can you answer her ven you don't know how to write?
Mike: Dot makes no nefer mind. She don't know how to read.

It is difficult but not impossible to envision the circumstances that made such dialect jokes hilarious, but we can certainly understand why audiences were amused by this classic exchange:

Myer: Who was that lady I saw you with?
Mike: That was no lady. That was my wife.

OPPOSITE:
The Marx Brothers' stage identities were established early. They lavished a wealth of career time developing, mining, and finally becoming these characters.

ABOVE:
Jimmy Durante

Fat and skinny was the formula for teams. The straight man was skinny because fat presumably looked funny. About the same height and build, Weber and Fields used padding and elevator shoes to create the impression of fat and skinny, and by the turn of the century they were earning two thousand dollars a week apiece with such material as:

Myer: Tell it, vot is you playing?
Mike: Pool, ain't it?
Myer: You got to name vot ball you shoot.
Mike: Good! I name it Rudolph.

Such routines could be used for years as an act looped one circuit before hooking onto the next. Probably no routine was ever plied more continuously than Joe Smith and Charles Dale's classic "Doctor Kronkite." This was essentially a prototype burlesque sketch, calling for a comic, a straight man, and a dumb blonde. Smith and Dale squeezed a buxom actress into a nurse's uniform and took the doctor's office sketch to the top of vaudeville.

Smith (the patient): I've got a rheumatism.
Dale (Dr. Kronkite): Where do you have this rheumatism?
Smith: On the back of my neck.
Dale: That's a good place for it. Where would you *like* a rheumatism?
Smith: On the back of *your* neck.

Although Joe Weber (left) and Lou Fields broke up their act while young, they periodically reunited and at one point even bought their own Broadway theater.

Smith and Dale were so popular they were able to play repeat engagements without changing the act, for knowing every line and bit of business seemed only to heighten the fun. It was no longer the humor of the exchanges that delighted afficionados. Rather, they savored the ritual of the Smith and Dale routine and the refinements of its presentation.

Dale (singing): Take off the coat, my boy
Take off the coat, my boy
Take off the coat, my boy
Smith and Dale (together): The coat is off.

What's *that*? Such strange humor is a uniquely American eccentricity. By and large, our professional monologue comedy is a comparatively straightforward affair, with codified joke patterns, logical sequences, and punch lines that are based on conventional elements of surprise and truth, but an earlier strain of offbeat and even anarchic humor, dark with the bizarre, lends our low team-comedy rich glimmerings of madness. For those who look, it can be found in the modern era too: for example, in Laurel and Hardy, Martin and Lewis, Dan Ackroyd, and the late John Belushi.

Anarchy but not madness lay at the heart of the Marx Brothers' vaudeville act. Their earliest routine, "Fun in Hi Skule," was one of countless schoolroom sketches that kept stagestruck youngsters from tap-dancing in the streets. According to Joe Adamson's *Groucho, Harpo, Chico and Sometimes Zeppo*, "It was a wild, bounding, violent, disordered, post-adolescent act that the Marx Brothers hit vaudeville with, week after week, town after town, for fifteen years . . . witnesses swear that they

(Joe) Smith and (Charles) Dale in their classic "Dr. Kronkite" sketch

destroyed props, backdrops, costumes and sometimes promoted physical damage to the theater." Yet the Marx Brothers' humor, for all its rambunctiousness, was essentially *verbal*, based on intelligence and the lucidity of literal-mindedness:

Groucho: What are the principal parts of a cat?
Gummo: Eyes, ears, neck, tail, feet.
Groucho: You've forgotten the most important part. What does a cat have that you don't have?
Gummo: Kittens.

It was unusual for Gummo to have a punch line since he was the straight man in what was otherwise a barrelhousing act.

The premise of "Fun in Hi Skule" was no more than to set the Marxes running amok. When these inspired zanies outgrew that setting, they created a new act that involved a policeman searching for stolen silverware. Having won the cop's approval, Harpo would unwisely offer to shake hands. Promptly, a dozen knives would come clattering out of his voluminous coat sleeve. This got such a laugh that Harpo gradually increased the number of knives to about two dozen, producing a grand jangling crash. He even added a coffeepot as a final salvo. The bit was so funny

The Marx Brothers in their moppet act,
"The Four Nightingales"

that, years later, he repeated it in the film *A Night at the Opera*.

The explosion that was the Marx Brothers, then, was one of ordered chaos rather than outright anarchy. Effective comedy must have energy, but it also requires structure, editing, shape, and timing. There is a difference, after all, between inspired creativity and formless abandon. The Marx Brothers seemed instinctively to sense that difference. They also worked with a purpose: their unique mixture of high verbal comedy and low pratfalls was aimed at puncturing pomposity. It was this sense at the core of nonsense that invigorated their work. When in 1924 they moved from vaudeville to Broadway, they were suddenly discovered as artistes by the intelligentsia. That show, a revue called *I'll Say She Is*, merely incorporated the routines they had developed on the variety stage. (Artistic status did not go to their heads, though Broadway did give them the respectability their mother, Minnie, so dearly desired. Already headed for Hollywood, the Marx Brothers performed in several more Broadway shows, but their days of in-person performance were all but ended.)

It is probable that no act in all of American variety entertainment surpassed the Marx Brothers' high-spirited and inspired lunacy. While their work in such movie classics as *Horse Feathers*, *A Day at the Races*, and *The Coconuts* is preserved and can continue to regale new audiences, it is not an equal exchange for their personal appearances. If value is the cost of replacement, the very dearness of the live entertainer lies in his ephemeral quality. What makes the entertainer precious is his mortality and the uniqueness of each performance.

For that reason, the team of Bert Williams and George Walker was worth a fortune to see. They did not work together for long, and there are no recordings of their act, which was one of the biggest in vaudeville. They were black men in an era of primitive racism, when discrimination was an everyday part of life (Walker himself was badly mugged during New York's 1900 race riots).

Walker was the straight man. He played the part of a hustling smoothie. Williams was the slow-witted clown, whose clear logic proved funny.

Williams: And what am I to do with this satchel?
Walker: All you got to do is bring it to me at a place where I tell you.
Williams: When they come to count up the cash and find it short, then what?
Walker: By that time we'll be far, far away—where the birds are singing sweetly and the flowers are in bloom.
Williams: And if they catch us they'll put us so far, far away we never will hear no birds singin'. And everybody knows you can't smell no flowers through a stone wall.

While Walker and Williams were definitely a "colored act" and even had to wear blackface makeup to look like stage darkies, they didn't play in exaggerated minstrel style. An articulate man, George Walker spoke his mind. "The one hope of the colored performer," he said, "must be in making a radical departure from the old, 'darky' style of singing and dancing . . . there is an artistic side of the black race and if it could be properly developed on stage I believe the theatergoing public would profit much by it." This was courageous and perceptive for 1910 but Walker did not live to see his dream realized. He died in 1911, a victim of extravagant living as much as of disease. The team was at its peak and he but thirty-nine. Bert Williams went on to become one of the *Ziegfeld Follies'* greatest stars.

Another major ethnic comedy team in big-time vaudeville was Willie and Eugene Howard, a Jewish (or "Hebe") act. Although the Howard Brothers' dialect and visual clowning betrayed their origins on the honky-

tonk stage, their comedy was not quite as simple-minded as that of Weber and Fields, and, unlike Smith and Dale or Weber and Fields, the Howards did not do the same act repeatedly. As a matter of fact, for some afficionados of vaudeville, the Howards represented the ultimate in team comedy. On tour they might perform a sketch about Arctic explorers surviving on matzo-ball soup, or recruit a couple of chorus girls to join them in an operatic quartet where the men were less interested in the aria than in the sopranos' cleavage.

The best of the routines was "Tomorrow Comes the Revolution." In this, a pathetic looking Willie, with his tiny frame, old clothes, and burning eyes, was perfect as a Communist agitator lecturing a crowd from a soapbox. He promises them relief from those bloodsuckers who have always exploited the poor, the greedy capitalists. "Tomorrow, like them, you will eat strawberries and cream." Whereupon one of his listeners pipes up, "But I don't like strawberries and cream." Willie scowls, scarcely believing his ears. Then he thunders, "Tomorrow comes the revolution, you nothing. Tomorrow you will eat strawberries and you'll like it." (Charles and Louise Samuels, *Once Upon a Stage*)

Such material may not seem particularly amusing today, but comedy is the product of material and delivery and the tone of the times. Since such tones change with fashion, most comedy dates quickly and badly. If so many people admired Willie and Eugene Howard, we can only accept the praise as deserved. Yet, explain this: some of the earliest of the George Burns and Gracie Allen routines remain funny. Even on paper.

Originally, Burns had been the comic, with baggy pants and a turned-up hat, and Gracie the straight, or "feeder." The act failed, but "even Gracie's straight lines got laughs," Burns remembered. "She had a funny delivery, very sharp and quick and cute." The success or failure of a team could ride on a decision as simple as switching roles, and once Burns and Allen had switched theirs, he concentrated on tailoring the material to her silly sanity. Vaudeville surely produced few writers of comedy superior to George Burns.

Bert Wheeler (right) never found a steady partner. Here he works with Bob Woolsey. Wheeler had his start in one of Gus Edwards's kiddie troupes, as did performers as diverse as Eddie Cantor, Sally Rand, and Groucho Marx.

ABOVE:
Bert Williams (left) and George Walker

BELOW:
The blackface comedy team of (Jim) McIntyre and (Tom) Heath topped variety bills for fifty years, starting out in the honky-tonks and winding up at the Palace.

George: I've got an idea. I'm going to ask you something, then you ask me the same thing. In other words, I am going to be the comedian.

Gracie: I know what you mean. You're going to be the funny fellow.

George: That's the idea.

Gracie: Well, go ahead. Be funny.

George: Well, I might have a little trouble, but this is what I mean. If I should say to you, "Why are apples green?" all you have to do is repeat the same thing. You say, "I don't know. Why are apples green?" Whatever I say, you say.

Gracie: I get the idea. I repeat what you say and then you tell the answer.

George: That's it. Well, here we go. What fellow in the army wears the biggest hat?

Gracie: I don't know. Why are apples green?

George: Now don't be silly. When I say, "What fellow in the army wears the biggest hat?" you must say: "I don't know. What fellow in the army wears the biggest hat?"

Gracie: Oh, I got it. Yeah, you're the comedian.

George: All right now. What fellow in the army wears the biggest hat?

Gracie: The fellow with the biggest head.

George: I certainly am the comedian.

Gracie: I think so. Try another one.

George: All right, here's another one. What is it that sings and has four legs?

Gracie: Two canaries.

George: I picked out a good game.

George Burns succinctly describes this sketch as a "streetcorner act"—a comic and a straight simply standing there, exchanging setups and punch lines. The writing is his and it is flawless. There is no waste. The straight

George Burns and Gracie Allen combined the high comedy of the monologist with the low comedy of the vaudeville team and came up classics.

Eddie Jackson (left), Jimmy Durante (center), and Lou Clayton lived out the movie cliche of facing a break-up because only one of them (Durante) was offered a chance in Hollywood. Durante took his partners west with him, making them his managers. The trio continued to revive their act at benefits and private parties.

lines, patiently repeated, set up not just the jokes but, more important, the audience. Even throwaway lines aren't throwaways—"That's the idea" and "I get the idea" provide flow, while "You're going to be the funny fellow" and "You're the comedian" are double-edged. The lines also point out to us that we are being given a lecture-demonstration on comedy technique, all the way to the wry final line, "I picked out a good game." It is difficult to imagine a comedy routine more perfectly written than this example. George Burns has always seemed modest and a gentleman, crediting Gracie Allen with doing all of the work. The truth is, the act would not have succeeded without her character and it would not have succeeded without his material. It took them far from the ethnic clowning of Weber and Fields, the burlesque of Smith and Dale, the lampoons of Willie and Eugene Howard. Most of the top vaudeville teams would be left behind after the dawn of the radio era—Bobby Clark and Paul McCullough, Ed Gallagher and Al Shean, even the popular blackface team of Jim McIntyre and Tom Heath. Radio was a medium of talk, and not only were Burns and Allen a talking team but their talk was deadpan. They were a two-part monologist. There would continue to be teams in older styles, such as the burlesquers Bud Abbott and Lou Costello and, a good many years later, Dean Martin and Jerry Lewis. But the future was unmistakable: low-comedy teams were destined for oblivion, among the first wave of entertainers to slip out to sea with vaudeville.

Clowning Around

THE FIRST FUNNY TALKERS

Of all the entertainers, none is braver than the monologist because the audience lies in wait for him and he knows it. For him the house saves the most devastating rejection: a stony silence in the face of ever more desperate efforts to amuse. The person who tries to make us laugh is at the tough end of a dare. Perhaps this hostile relationship can be explained by the abstractness of humor and the involuntary nature of laughter. The person who tries to make us laugh is someone to fear because he can literally disarm us—lower our rational defenses and, at that, merely with words. The laugh he "gets" is one he forces from us; it is a laugh of reflexive comprehension, won despite our resistance, leaving us momentarily out of control of ourselves mentally and physically. For "helpless with laughter" is not just an expression. There isn't much else that you can do when you are laughing.

No question, the laugh the monologist is after has nothing to do with happiness. The laugh of happiness comes from the heart, and even the laugh a clown gets is cheerful, but there is no joy in a monologist's laughs. They come from the head. And these are probably all reasons why there is tension, armor, and hostility in his vicinity.

When he wins, when he does get the laugh, the victory is only a temporary one. He must repeat the trick if his act is to succeed, and repeat it to the end. If the audience wins, if it finds him unamusing, its victory is sour. It glares in grim superiority while he sweats, squirms, and even strikes back:

These are the jokes, folks.
What is this, a cemetery?

The clown has it easier. A descendant of the court jester, he cuts an endearing figure. His appearance, his behavior, his facial expressions, his clothes are all funny-looking. He is either a fool or a child and is free of blame should he fail to get a laugh, because he is an innocent. Even when he succeeds, when he makes us laugh, we are pleased. The audience has no sense of being outwitted by an Ed Wynn, a Bert Lahr, a Sid Caesar; there is no sense of domination, and so people love the clown and would trust their children with him. But who would trust a child with a monologist or, still worse, his angry successor, the stand-up comedian?

Although monologists can be traced to the medieval tellers of obscene stories, the ones at the turn-of-the-century honky-tonks were considered lesser performers than the clowns, the team zanies, and the buffoons. The honky-tonk monologist was, in fact, employed only before the show, to settle the rowdy audience. He might be permitted a few of the clown's devices, such as blackface or dialect, but once the show began only the guileless funny man and his pratfalls were considered funny.

If the monologist is defined as a man who attempts to amuse an audience simply by saying funny things, then one of the first to perform on a main bill at a honky-tonk was Walter C. Kelly. A transitional figure, Kelly is unfortunately remembered as the racist who in 1909 refused to work on the same bill as Bert Williams. But Kelly's act was a major and popular one. It was called "The Virginia Judge." He would stride on stage in judicial robes, sit down at a desk, and slam the gavel. He would then play the roles of various attorneys and defendants, using Italian, Dutch, Jewish, or Irish dialects. Here was the start of the modern comedian's confrontation with the audience. It would ultimately lead to the vaudeville monologist who faced up to the public with only words and ideas in his defense. The challenge was clear: make them laugh—or die in the attempt.

Sensing the awful risk in this, the great clown Ed Wynn created a routine on the subject, introducing it on March 24, 1913, on the opening-night bill at the brand-new Palace Theatre, where—ironically enough—the uniquely American monologist would be bred and developed. Wynn's act, called "The King's Jester," was about a grouchy king who was doomed to die unless someone made him laugh. All the jesters in the realm were summoned to try and save his life. Those who failed were put to death—a neat metaphor for comedy's life-giving energy and the comedian's death-defying task. (Wynn's perceptive sketch deserved a better ending: the jester finally gets a laugh out of the king by whispering a joke in his ear and adding, "I didn't know you wanted to hear *that* kind of joke.")

The Yiddish dialectician Joe Welch came even closer than Walter C. Kelly to direct storytelling. Welch would shuffle miserably on stage in shabby clothes, as forlorn as a beggar. Standing stooped, his shoulders hunched, he would stare balefully at the audience, blink back tears, agonized and despairing. Only then would he utter his opening line: "Maybe you t'ink I'm heppy?"

As sight gags, dialect, and outlandish costumes were displaced by verbal humor, monologists grew conservative in dress and sober in manner, a style borrowed from the straight men of burlesque. They would eventually wear business suits and speak carefully, as if taking the part of sanity, logic, and the audience. Good diction was originally used to contrast with the clown's dialect and foolishness. It was now essential, for the laughs depended on the words alone and this resulted in the ornate manner of speech that would characterize monologists for many years. A detailed, almost Dickensian kind of storytelling went along with it. An early example by the popular vaudevillian George Fuller Golden was reconstructed by Joe Laurie, Jr., in *Vaudeville*:

One day I was riding on top of a bus in London with my friend Casey. I was nearly worn out with several hours of sightseeing, and the bustle and excitement of the London streets, the hoi polloi, the Billingsgate and the rattle were becoming unbearable when we came in sight of Westminster Abbey. Just as we did so, the chimes burst forth with joyous melody and I said to Casey, "Isn't that sublime? Isn't it glorious to hear those chimes pealing and doesn't it inspire one with renewed vigor?" Casey leaned over with one hand to his ear and said, "You'll have to speak a little louder, George. I can't hear you." I said,

"Those magnificent chimes. Do you not hear them pealing? Do they not imbue you with a feeling of reverence? Do they not awaken tender memories of the past?" Casey again leaned forward and said, "I can't hear you. You'll have to talk louder." I got as close to him as possible and said, "Do you not hear the melodious pealing of the chimes? Do they not recall the salutation of Old Trinity on the Sabbath morning? Do they not take you back to the dim vistas of the past when the world was young and touch your heart with a feeling of pathos?" Casey put his mouth close to my ear and said, "Those damn bells are making such a hell of a racket, George, I can't hear you!"

Monologists were to prove especially welcome in vaudeville because they could double as masters of ceremony. They were the only "civilians" on the bill, working in street clothes and speaking like normal people. Of course the suit and tie were the monologists' equivalent of baggy pants; careful diction their version of dialect. But, taken straight, the act would do for a master of ceremonies.

Among the first generation of vaudeville monologists, Roger Imhoff and Julius Tannen are credited with originating the basic style of appearance and performance. Sober in mien and conservative in dress, Tannen was positively mortician-like. "Pardon me for being late," he'd begin grimly, "but I squeezed out too much toothpaste and couldn't get it back in." Most monologists imitated this subdued and understated style. "Senator" Ed Ford would introduce himself by saying, "Although my name is Ford and I was assembled in Michigan, I am in no way related to

Only the most sophisticated clowns could survive vaudeville and follow radio and America into the era of monologists. The great Bert Lahr was one of the survivors. He created his classic routines for Broadway revues.

A Palace headliner, Frank Tinney was thrown and eventually destroyed by radio.

Ed Wynn "The Perfect Fool."

that obscure Middle Western manufacturer who put a radiator on a roller skate and called it an auto."

Although every monologist considered his act topical, most concentrated on the general. The idea was to develop humorous possibilities by threading a line of reason through the loopholes of improbability. Calmness and a straight face were considered powerful attributes, the smile a tool to be used only at the punch line, to cue the audience and give it a laughing start. Smooth continuity was the basis of the craft, linking the anecdotes with logical connections rather than rattling them off in arbitrary order. Frank Tinney was an exemplar of the style. He would amble onstage and, with mock innocence, tell an intentionally bad joke such as, "I asked an acquaintance, 'Lend me a dollar for a week, old man,' and the fellow replied, 'Who is the weak old man?'" The audience would groan at the awful pun, and Tinney would give them plenty of time to do so, lighting a cigar and puffing at it a couple of times. Then he would plead the merits of the joke with the conductor in the orchestra pit, suggesting that the only thing needed to make it funny was the appropriate musical accompaniment.

Joe Cook was another sedate headliner.

I will give an imitation of four Hawaiians. This is one. [He whistles] This is another. [He strums a mandolin] And this is a third. [He taps a toe] I could imitate four Hawaiians just as easily but I will give you the reason I don't. You see, I bought a horse for $50 and it turned out to be a running horse. I was offered $15,000 for him and I took it. I built a house with the $15,000 and when it was finished a neighbor offered me $100,000 for it. He said my house stood right where he wanted to dig a well. So I took the $100,000 to accommodate him. I invested the $100,000 in peanuts and that year there was a peanut famine, so I sold the peanuts for $350,000. Now why should a man with $350,000 bother to imitate four Hawaiians? [Exit]

Other front-rank monologists were George Jessel, Jack Benny, Lou Holtz, Milton Berle, Frank Fay, and the unique Joe Frisco. Frisco had begun as an eccentric dancer, with a peculiar number he called the "Frisco Shuffle." Eccentric dancing is a good example of the abstract humor that runs through American comedy. Funny because perverse, it was the antithesis of the graceful movements that traditional dancers aspire to. Frisco's jerky dance steps, angular but engagingly awkward,

ABOVE LEFT:
Walter C. Kelly is generally credited with having launched the all-talking comedian of American vaudeville with his act, "The Virginia Judge."

ABOVE RIGHT:
Julius Tannen was the first comedian to discard the funny clothes and makeup, and run the risk for laughs on wits alone.

In Person:
The Great Entertainers

were a choreographic version of his own deadpan comedy. Like his hat tricks and fancy cigar-smoking, eccentric dancing was a way of doing monologues without speaking. In fact, Frisco did everything but talk, for when he finally did speak it was clear what he had to be silent about: Joe Frisco was a stutterer. Speaking proved to be like doing his eccentric dance—it was an affirmation of his own style as acceptable and appealing, even though it was different from everyone else's. Only then was he able to use it freely and without embarrassment. In time, Joe Frisco gained such confidence that he was recognized as one of the fastest and most original comic minds on the vaudeville stage. As for the stutter, it came to be his trademark.

Even in company as brilliant as Frisco's, one stand-up comedian stood apart: Frank Fay. George Burns said, "He was the greatest single monologist I've ever seen." Fay was the first monologist to abandon all exaggeration of appearance and speech. The garrulous Lou Holtz and George Jessel had a hint of the Yiddish in their styles; Milton Berle couldn't resist clowning and making faces; Jack Benny played the violin; and Fred Allen and W. C. Fields still juggled.

Tall, lithe, Frank Fay would stroll on stage, the essence of debonair. He was stylishly dressed, he moved like a dancer, and his wavy red hair was a show in itself. Audiences were mad for him. His voice was resonant, his diction crystal clear, and his hands did figure eights as he wove arch and sophisticated patterns of finely drawn anecdote and fantasy. He was the consummate professional, as his colleagues readily agreed. But he was not their favorite human being. For one thing, he had a reputation for anti-Semitism, which did not endear him to the many Jews in vaudeville. For another, he was an overbearing egoist, a trait possibly acceptable in a field that fundamentally involved ego, except that Fay's conceit was untempered by humor and his cruelty to other performers was a byword. It was not unusual for Fay to sadistically whisper an insult to an entertainer waiting in the wings to go on.

He could do wonderful and novel routines—an imitation of John Barrymore doing the Charleston, or of Enrico Caruso singing "Darktown Strutters Ball." According to George Burns, "He was a master performer. Fabulous. Everybody copied him. Jack Benny came from Fay's school."

A youthful Milton Berle, wisecracking with the conductor at the Palace Theatre about 1937. Berle must be ranked with Bob Hope and Jack Benny among the most enduring of America's monologists. His career spanned half a century and he was perhaps the most versatile of all, a stand-up, a sketch comedian, and a clown. His willingness to do anything for a laugh and his obliviousness to all else around him in a single-minded devotion to the audience made this man an almost expressionistic figure.

But he became the biggest vaudeville name to be destroyed by radio (except for a brief comeback as the star of the Broadway play *Harvey*). Although nightclubs might have kept him busy for years, Fay's ego was crushed, and a performer without an ego is like (or perhaps exactly the same as) a pilot who is afraid of heights.

Some years after Fay had retired to obscurity, abandoned by his wife, Barbara Stanwyck, to his arrogance and anger, Burns recalled:

He was asked to be master of ceremonies at the May Fair in Hollywood. The May Fair was a big thing where everybody went. We all wore tails, Jack Benny in tails, myself in tails. And they asked Fay to be master of ceremonies, and nobody greater. And Fay got up there that night and he looked around and everybody was working but him. That's when he was at his greatest. With sarcasm.

As he said something, somebody heckled him. And he stopped and he said, "Who said that?" And at the table they said, "Groucho Marx." He said, "Oh?" And he said, "Groucho, come up here. We'll talk, you and I." And Groucho wouldn't get up. And Fay looked over to him, very charmingly, and he said to him, "You do need Zeppo, don't you?" That's how great he was. "You do need Zeppo." That's Fay at his best. Or anybody at their best.

Frank Fay's debonair appearance and his vanity about it had set him off from the other monologists in vaudeville. Trademarks were eagerly, even desperately, sought out by these fast talkers: anything to separate them from the crowd. W. C. Fields's style was boozing and misanthropy. George Jessel was remembered as the fellow who was always making telephone calls to his mother. Fred Allen juggled. Jack Benny began as a musical act, and even after concentrating on comedy he leaned on the violin for recognition.

Benny had originally called himself "Ben K. Benny" (his real name was Benny Kubelsky). He did a double with a pianist named Lyman Woods, and in 1917 they'd even played the Palace. It was the second slot, worst on the bill, but it was still the Palace. The act was essentially musical and Benny's comedy was limited to mugging while he was fiddling, or holding the violin in funny ways.

When he decided to go it alone, he billed himself as "Ben K. Benny —Fiddle Funology" until the bandleader-comedian Ben Bernie complained about the similarity of names. The central office that had jurisdiction over such disputes judged Kubelsky the imitator. His act became "Jack Benny: Fun with a Fiddle," then "A Few Minutes with Jack Benny," and finally "Jack Benny: Aristocrat of Humor."

Aristocratic his humor was, and early on, too. When he began developing comedy about stinginess, he did not depend on mere jokes. Tone of voice or a mild hint might be trigger enough for a humorous connection. For example, telling about a dinner date he'd had, Benny would say, "She got so excited she dropped her *tray*." Pauses and timing were devices that Benny used early in his career. He would recount an evening of fun at the greyhound races. He had bet two dollars, pause. On the rabbit, pause. To show.

By 1924 Jack Benny was headlining at the Palace. Two years later he turned to the legitimate theater, appearing in the revue *Great Temptations*, and for the next several years he worked only in big-time vaudeville. Whether it was he who had influenced Frank Fay or the other way around, the pair were to represent the most highly developed form of monology known to vaudeville.

As for the low comedians, most were fading into burlesque and then oblivion. The survivors—Ed Wynn, Bobby Clark, Bert Lahr, Bea Lillie

Jack Benny at fifteen. His first solo act contained more fiddling than "funology."

—performed in the legitimate theater, but it was only by sheer dint of greatness that they endured, genius transcending fashion. The clown, low comedian, and cut-up, no matter how inspired, was too broad a performer for increasingly sophisticated tastes, and blind radio hastened his demise. The comedian's world, like the movies, was entering an era of all-talkies.

HARRY LAUDER
The Original Scotsman

Harry Lauder is the only evidence needed to prove the unpredictability of show business. In 1907 this little fellow arrived from Scotland to make his first American appearance. He was already thirty-seven, ancient for a debut. To the drone of bagpipes, he strolled on stage wearing a plaid kilt and high stockings. He leaned on his crooked walking stick and smiled warmly at the audience, and what in the world were these tough New Yorkers to make of him? His knobby knees were exposed. A tam-o'-shanter was perched on his head. A stock Scotsman? This was the original.

For 24 minutes, Mr. Lauder stood before the footlights as a woebegone youngster, looking over the mutilated toys removed from several pockets . . . he recited a meeting with an old man and instantly would become the old man. . . . While as a boy, Mr. Lauder sang "The Softest of the Family." . . . For the opening the Scotchman did a party (where different persons were called upon) concluding with "Stop Your Tickling, Jack!" and "My Scotch Blue Bell." . . . For the finale, a pretty blonde girl came stealing upon the stage and was introduced as "That's her," his Scotch blue bell. The audience believed just what Mr. Lauder said. He is never "on the stage" during the act. . . . After a speech and tumultuous applause, Mr. Lauder sang "We Parted on the Shore" dressed as a sailor who had never been to sea. . . . Booked to remain in New York for five weeks, he could remain for six months.

An ovation never equalled on the variety stage was his reception. (Sime Silverman, *Variety*, November 9, 1907)

Harry Lauder would make twenty-two cross-country appearances in America, the last half-dozen billed as "farewell tours." No matter how long he was onstage, and sometimes it was as much as an hour and a half, audiences never wearied of him. His bag of stage tricks—singing, telling anecdotes, confiding personal feelings, reenacting incidents from his past—simply *worked* on them. (Skeptics beware! Contrivance is no sin on the stage. All show business is hokum.)

Harry Lauder only played in his own show, never in the *Ziegfeld Follies*, and never on any vaudeville bill—except for the greatest show he ever was a part of. It was the opening night of his 1911 national tour, and the black-tie audience was already assembling in the huge Manhattan Opera House, but Lauder's ocean liner had been delayed by stormy Atlantic weather. His agent, William Morris, began to telephone performers all around New York, with the idea that they would entertain in an emergency all-star vaudeville show until the ship tied up and Lauder could get to the theater.

Some twenty volunteer acts showed up, including Blossom Seeley, Leon Errol, and the Dolly Sisters. Between numbers, the audience was kept apprised of Lauder's progress—how far out at sea the liner was, when it was being met by the tugboats.

The parade of acts continued. Carter de Haven was the master of ceremonies. The great monologist Frank Tinney arrived toward midnight, still in blackface, having finished his evening's performance at the *Ziegfeld Follies*. Irving Berlin sang, accompanying himself on the piano.

When de Haven announced that Lauder had arrived at the Battery, had been met by a limousine, and was on his way uptown, a great roar arose in the theater. Was not this evening laced with the excitement of the once-in-a-lifetime?

At one o'clock in the morning, still in street clothes, Lauder strolled

on stage to a tremendous ovation. He was carrying a sheaf of music, the orchestra parts for his act, all he'd been allowed to take from the ship's hold. He walked to center stage. The applause and cheers were unrelenting. He smiled and waved to the audience and then held his arms up high, gesturing for silence. The excitement, though, was too invigorating to be easily relinquished. Finally hushing the exhilarated crowd, Lauder said in his familiar and beloved burr, "Aye, aye, I'm tellin' you, it's been a verra frantic rush. But now, if you will bear with me, I will go through the program of songs I did at the ship's concert out in the Atlantic last Saturday night."

He sang and chatted, told stories, murmured confidences, and even did a Highland reel. As a special treat, he included two new songs, "Every Laddie Loves a Lassie" and a number destined to be an enormous hit, "Roamin' in the Gloamin'." Evidently, he had no trouble meeting the challenge of following twenty major acts and a three-hour introduction.

How to account for Lauder's success? The explanation lies in the chemistry between performer and spectator. Harry Lauder could have happened at any time. An audience is always capable of unleashing its enthusiasm, ever waiting for a Pied Piper.

Harry Lauder was the prototype Scotsman.

HARRY LANGDON

Harry Langdon is best known for work in Mack Sennett's movies, but he first established himself on the stage. A graduate of medicine shows and dime circuses, he dropped blackface makeup to develop a vaudeville act that played, almost unchanged, from 1906 until 1923. Langdon would drive on stage in a car that promptly broke down. He would then work at fixing it, and the comedy lay in his tempo—which grew slower through the years—as well as in his physical responses to the situation. He would caress the stalled car, kiss it, warn it with a wagging finger, and all the time look back and forth from auto to audience. In this increasingly stylized act, whiteface makeup would make Langdon's baby face seem rounder, his eyes ever wider. He was a pantomimist as much as comedian. Though his Hollywood success was great, film could never capture the precisely timed and controlled exchange between the innocent onstage and his charmed audience.

OPPOSITE:
Harry Langdon as mime

ABOVE:
Harry Langdon doing his impression of Harry Lauder.

ZIEGFELD
MOULIN ROUGE

(Formerly NEW YORK THEATRE)

KLAW and ERLANGER - Lessees -

Management F. ZIEGFELD Jr.

THE ZIEGFELD FOLLIES

Although entertainers historically suffered from social snubs and second-class citizenship, they also created their own rankings of prestige. In vaudeville, for instance, there were strict classes of billing that applied both to a show's running order and to the size of a name on the poster. (The term "billing" originated with the bill of acts that was posted in front of a variety theater, but it came to refer to any mention of a performer's name.) Honky-tonks were considered above dime museums but two steps beneath vaudeville; burlesque was one step down, the legitimate theater of Broadway one step up. There was always some gauge to determine greater or lesser prestige, and if there wasn't, then one would be created. Part of this was theatrical snobbery and egotism but the larger part was defensiveness, for the distinction between performance and ego is a blurry one. You are your act—protect your act—protect yourself.

One issue was never resolved: whether the acme of stardom was playing the Palace or the *Ziegfeld Follies*. The Palace, of course, was the pinnacle of international vaudeville, but vaudeville it remained, while the *Follies* was the legitimate theater. Some of the entertainment royalty, such as Al Jolson, Bea Lillie, and Bert Lahr, felt they'd finessed the Palace versus the *Follies* issue by performing only in Broadway musical comedies and sharing the stage with no other acts. Harry Lauder, too, toured only with his own show. The niceties notwithstanding, one thing was certain: star billing in the *Ziegfeld Follies* was a measure of great accomplishment, and those who earned it were an elite among American entertainers.

Producer Florenz ("Flo," or "Ziggy") Ziegfeld presented the first of his shows in 1907. It was a "revue"—the French spelling of "review" was considered fancy; the French spelling of *anything* was considered fancy. A revue was a series of acts not unlike a vaudeville show except that instead of being changed weekly, the bill would remain the same as long as the public continued to buy tickets. Songs would be written for it, and original comedy sketches—not low comedy but humor aspiring to some sophistication. To all of this, Ziegfeld added resplendent production numbers featuring beautiful young women. Indeed, they were the theme of the *Follies*, which was subtitled *Glorifying the American Girl*. Beautiful girls distinguished the *Follies* from all other Broadway revues.

Twenty-one of these flamboyant and elaborate shows were presented under Flo Ziegfeld's aegis between 1907 and 1932, and while another four were done after his death it is a striking coincidence, I think, that the last of the *Follies* personally produced by Ziegfeld opened in the same year that the Palace concluded its top-flight vaudeville policy. Our most prolific era of personal performance had come to a conclusive end.

Most of the *Ziegfeld Follies* were presented in the beautiful New Amsterdam Theatre on Forty-second Street. Among the stars were such singers as Ruth Etting, Nora Bayes and Jack Norworth, Eva Tanguay,

OPPOSITE:
Ziegfeld Follies *poster*

ABOVE:
Marilyn Miller

Sophie Tucker, the Dolly Sisters, and Marilyn Miller. But the era be-
longed to the comedians, and they were the biggest *Follies* stars: Will
Rogers, W. C. Fields, Fanny Brice, Ed Wynn, Eddie Cantor, and, perhaps the greatest of all, Bert Williams.

When Williams's long-time partner, George Walker, suffered a mortal
illness, the Nassau-born comedian became a single and was booked to
star in the 1910 *Ziegfeld Follies*. It was an awesome measure of his
success because, although there had been black performers in white
vaudeville (Charlie Case, notably), they were not common and certainly
not headliners on the big time. However, Flo Ziegfeld was no Branch
Rickey and he backed out of an original plan to include Williams with
white performers in a comedy sketch. Williams was only allowed to do
his solo spot. He brought down the house. Even racist audiences forget
their bigotry in the presence of the live entertainer.

Bert Williams worked as a tramp clown in seedy formal clothes. He
wore a battered top hat and shabby tails. He had his trousers too short
and his shoes too big, with blackface makeup over his own tan skin,
just as it had been when he'd worked with Walker. He opened his act
leaning against one side of the proscenium arch, a baby spotlight on
his outstretched white gloves. Then he brought the audience along
with monologues, songs, and mime. He might play all the parts in
a silent poker game—dealing, betting, glancing up and down or at
the other fellow's cards. Or, if he spoke, his manner would be confidential, his voice friendly and subdued, the shuffling style and Southern
intonations mocking.

Where I'm living now is a nice place, but you have to go along a road between

ABOVE:
*Joseph Urban's rendering of his
proposed Ziegfeld Theatre. The
celebrated Viennese architect also
designed the interiors for this
Manhattan showplace. It was razed in
1967 and replaced by an office
building.*

OPPOSITE, ABOVE:
*Florenz "Flo" Ziegfeld with his chorus
girls*

OPPOSITE, BELOW:
*Nora Bayes (Leonora Goldberg) was
already a headliner when she met,
married, and teamed up with the
song-and-dance man Jack Norworth.
They wrote their own theme song,
"Shine On, Harvest Moon," and sang
it all the way to the Ziegfeld Follies.
But "The Stage's Happiest Couple," as
they were billed, was threatened by
Jack's philandering and Nora's
jealousy. On one occasion, she insisted
on their being billed as "Nora Bayes,
Assisted and Admired by Jack
Norworth." He ultimately left her and,
to make things worse, teamed up with
her competitor, Trixie Friganza.
Thereupon, Nora changed her billing
to "The Greatest Single Singing
Comedienne in the World."*

ABOVE:
The dancing Hungarians, Janszieka and Roszika Deutsch, better known as the Dolly Sisters, headlined in the Ziegfeld Follies *as well as in Broadway revues and operettas.*

BELOW:
The creative and original Bert Williams, shown here in the Follies *of 1910*

two graveyards to get to it. One night last week I was coming home kind of late and I got about halfway home when I happened to look over my shoulder and saw a ghost following me. I started to run. I run till I was 'most ready to drop. And then I looked around. But I didn't see no ghost, so I sat down on the curbstone to rest. Then out of the corner of my eye I could see something white, and when I turned square around, there was that ghost sitting alongside of me. The ghost says: "That was a fine run we had. It was the best running I ever saw." I says, "Yes. And soon as I get my breath you're going to see more."

According to Eddie Cantor, Williams was "close to genius . . . the greatest comedian I ever saw," but "comedy" doesn't seem to describe his act precisely.

> *I ain't never done nothing to nobody*
> *I ain't never got nothing from nobody, no time*
> *And until I get something from somebody, some time*
> *I'll never do nothing for nobody, no time.*

This was "Nobody," Williams's theme song, his own composition. In a hobo's sentimental ballad he conveyed the bitterness of a black man forced to grin and play the darky. Yet there was no talk of anger in the act. Had there been, it would have been disastrous. Even offstage, Williams was circumspect about bigotry, though he had constant cause for anger (the white Ted Lewis had developed an act so similar as to involve

As both singer and dancer, the beautiful Marilyn Miller was adored by Follies audiences. She starred in two editions.

a battered top hat and tails and even a lonely theme song—"Me and my shadow/All alone and feeling blue"). Racial slurs seemed to be a normal part of life. On one occasion, Williams was complimented backstage by a fellow performer who added, "And what's more, you know your place." By chance, John Barrymore and Spencer Tracy were watching the show from the wings and overheard the remark. Williams nodded to the two great actors and whispered, "That's right. I know my place. Dressing Room One."

Ziegfeld was ultimately encouraged by Williams's popularity to include him in a racially integrated sketch. It was a minstrel number, hardly a daring choice, but it was one with such minstrels as Eddie Cantor as Tambo and the fabulous singer-dancer Marilyn Miller as the interlocutor. Yet implicit in even so classy a routine was Williams's color, for the all-star cast had to be in blackface if he was in it. Even Booker T. Washington's accolade was condescending. Williams, according to Washington, had done "more for the race than I have. He has smiled his way into people's hearts." Small wonder the great comedian was bitter. One evening after a performance, Eddie Cantor suggested that they meet at his hotel before setting out for an evening's partying. "Okay," Williams replied. "I'm on my way to the back elevator." He paused before adding, "It wouldn't be so bad, Eddie, if I didn't still hear the applause ringing in my ears."

Williams's achievement was more than rising above racism. With stardom so casually bestowed nowadays, it is difficult to grasp the extent of his fame, or for that matter, the success of his fellow *Follies* stars. In an era of tough competition among many entertainers, the performer had to preserve the unique notion of himself that had first motivated him; had to keep generating the power that he had first produced onstage; had continuously to refine the craftsmanship that had been developed over the course of thousands of performances. And, not least, all his new material had to meet the audience's expectations of him.

The down-home style of Will Rogers so charmed and disarmed audiences that they forgot how much talent, expertise, and experience had gone into his act. Starring in seven editions of the *Ziegfeld Follies*, he too was at the pinnacle of the entertainment world. The one-quarter Cherokee Indian had come to New York in 1905 as a "dumb" act with a Wild West show, silently performing rope tricks. There were fifty of them in his repertoire but the best one turned out to be unrehearsed: Rogers lassoed a nervous steer that was aiming to charge the audience at Madison Square Garden. It put him in the newspapers, and the publicity resulted in a booking at Keith's Union Square Theatre. Within a week he was playing Hammerstein's Victoria, where one night he impulsively said, "I am going to throw two of these ropes at once, catching the horse with one and the rider with the other. I don't have any idea I'll get it but here goes." Once the audience laughed nobody could shut Rogers up until he died in a private-airplane crash thirty years later. By then he had become one of the most popular and beloved entertainers ever to appear on an American stage, transcending show business to become a national hero. Rogers would write a nationally syndicated column of political satire and even address Congress.

"All I know is what I read in the papers" was his tag line, and the newspapers were where he got his material. Rogers would amble on stage wearing a ten-gallon hat and riding chaps, twirling his rope and drawling about politics and economics or whatever events of the day interested him. The costume and routine were suited just so to his down-to-earth style and common-sense humor. Congress was "the house that

OPPOSITE, ABOVE:
The "Great White Hope" prizefight was reenacted in the 1910 Follies, with Billy Reeves as ex-champion James Jeffries and with Bert Williams, in blackface makeup, as Jack Johnson.

OPPOSITE, BELOW:
The Ziegfeld beauties were divided into three categories: the tall "show girls," who were displayed in elaborate and sometimes outlandish costumes; the "ponies," who did the dancing; and (shown here) the "mediums," who did a little of everything.

jokes built," the "national joke factory." If Prohibition was good for anything it would at least put an end to snake bites, because "no man is going to let a snake bite him after liquor goes out." His was a gentle twitting, social criticism that deflated without the sour taste of malice. "The woman who used to faint and be revived by a nip of brandy will just have to struggle along without fainting."

Rogers knew humor and vitriol are not good for each other. When he

Will Rogers managed to be showmanly without compromising his intelligence, and he demonstrated that audiences can follow a humorist's lead to rather high comedy levels.

chose to express himself with feeling, he cut the comedy. "Here is what Washington missed out on by not living to be 199 years old. . . . He would have seen our great political system of 'equal rights to all and special privilege to none' working so smoothly that seven million are without a chance to earn their living. . . . He would see 'em handing out rations in peace time that would have reminded him of Valley Forge."

Just as Rogers gradually replaced his cowboy costume with a crumpled business suit, so, when he died, he had transcended show business to become a part of American lore, and yet he never pretended to be anything but an entertainer. For most people in the world of show business, vanity and phoniness come with the greasepaint and the spotlight. The only ones who seem to escape this are the stars.

Could Fanny Brice have possibly been more different from Will Rogers? A tall, slender, elegantly plain Jewish girl from Brooklyn, she haunted amateur contests until at seventeen she landed a chorus job in burlesque, at the Columbia Theatre on Broadway. At the turn of the century, burlesque was raunchy but not lewd. There were certainly chorus girls and low comics but the show consisted mainly of brief musical sketches with a variety show in the middle.

On the night that Brice was asked to substitute for the soubrette (the leading lady), another of the chorines recalled: "You never saw a performance like it. Think of a one-man show with thirty people onstage. Fanny rolled her eyes, she winked, she kicked, she sang loud enough to wake the whole state of Ohio. She was all over that stage and they brought her back for seven encores."

Incongruous costumes are a staple of clowning, and what could be more incongruous than the folksy cowboy Will Rogers in drag? Brandon Tynan is spoofing David Belasco, the producer who affected a priest's habit, in this sketch from the 1920 Ziegfeld Follies.

After that, the management gave her a singing part in the variety section of the show. Irving Berlin was working for the Columbia Theatre at the time and he wrote "Sadie Salome" for her, spoofing with Yiddishisms the ongoing rage for Salome dances. Berlin suggested that Brice make the song funnier still by singing it with a Yiddish accent, and that started a career routine of hers.

After two years with the burlesque show, the nineteen-year-old was discovered by Florenz Ziegfeld himself, and he put her into the 1910 *Follies* singing a "coon" song written by the show's musical composers (themselves black) Joe Jordan and Will Marion Cook.

> *Lovey Joe, that ever lovin' man*
> *From 'way down south in Birmingham,*
> *He can do some lovin' an' some lovin' sho'*
> *An' when he starts to love me*
> *I jes' hollers for mo'.*

Twelve encores.

Fanny Brice was somehow able to combine serious singing with comedy. Most comediennes are sexless parodies of women, raucous and vulgar, perhaps trying to prove they are not women at all and thus are admissible to the all-male club of comedians. Yet away from the stage, humor in a woman can be very sexy. Brice's clowning was broad but not unfeminine. It seems to have been extemporaneous, a giddy urge. She could go from torch singing to clowning without a jolt. In one *Follies* she began to sing "You Made Me Love You" with total earnestness, then did the second chorus in Yiddish dialect. Singing the same song in London, she found the audience restless and so,

grabbing the curtains, Fanny began to swing on them while she sang. Swinging, she kicked her long legs, she winked at the orchestra leader, she leered, she rolled her eyes, she beckoned to the men in the audience to join her upstairs. She didn't stop grimacing or kicking or clowning until the audience was hers. (Norman Katkov, *The Fabulous Fanny*)

Despite such antics, she could spellbind an audience with a song, and it was invariably "My Man." Ziegfeld had commissioned an English translation of the French "Mon Homme" just for her, and when Channing Pollock wrote the new lyrics Brice rehearsed it for the 1921 *Follies*. Her notion was to look French while singing it. Her idea of French was a black silk dress and a red-fringed scarf drawn around her shoulders. And a red wig. Stark and somber in this melodramatic costume, she stepped out of the upstage shadows and stalked down the Winter Garden stage to rehearse the song. A pianist waited at the upright. Somewhere in the darkened auditorium, Ziegfeld sat and watched.

Now in the lone spotlight, Brice leaned against the piano. She pulled the red scarf tightly around her arms and with a pat made certain that the wig was in place. Then, just as she nodded for the rehearsal pianist to begin, Ziegfeld loomed out of the darkened rows of seats. He climbed the short flight of steps leading to the stage. He walked silently and purposefully toward her and without uttering a word he snatched the wig from her head. Then he pulled the scarf from her shoulders. He tossed it off into the wings. Then he took hold of her dress at the neckline and yanked it until it ripped. He shredded that dress until it hung in tatters and then said, "Sing it."

Oh my man I love him so
He'll never know . . .

Fanny Brice as "Baby Snooks" with
Bob Hope in the 1936 Follies

Her private life was public. The tabloids were reporting every detail of her marriage to the gambler Nicky Arnstein and lately the details had been grim. He was in Washington, out of prison on bail between trials.

She stood on the bare stage with the lights turned down low and the piano softly leading her on. She stood without moving once, holding her bare left arm with her right hand. She sang it straight, with no frills and no flounces and no invention and no tricks . . . she sang it ten thousand times after that . . . but she never sang it without caressing her arm and closing her eyes.

> *What's the difference if I say*
> *I'll go away*
> *When I know I'll come back on*
> *My knees some day.*
> *For whatever my man is*
> *I am his forever more!*
>
> (Norman Katkov, *The Fabulous Fanny*)

It was Fanny Brice who encouraged the fledgling Eddie Cantor. There have been stars so unique as to seem positively peculiar, and Cantor was certainly one of them. The little fellow was a comedian-singer with a tenor so light it was nearly soprano. According to Brice, "He couldn't dance a lick," and she told him so on the opening night of his first *Ziegfeld Follies*, the 1917 edition. According to Cantor, "We laughed so hard we had to hold each other up. . . . I relaxed and lost my fright and tenseness."

But she had probably meant it, because he *couldn't* dance a lick. In Cantor's own words, "It is hard to explain in cold type what audiences consider funny. Gestures, subtle inflections of voice, fleeting changes of expression, an upward roll of the eyes may turn a dull line of material into sparkling stage humor."

That was the main thing he did, roll his eyes. And clap his hands. He had made his stage debut one amateur night at Miner's Bowery Theatre, after a pal had said, "Look, even if you get the hook you get a dollar along with it." As Cantor recalled, "Two players had already been yanked in by the huge iron hook and the audience let out a bloodthirsty howl."

He was exaggerating. The hook was neither huge nor iron. It had been devised one amateur night in this very burlesque theater when a young singer worked vainly to amuse the boisterous crowd. Backstage the manager came across a prop cane with an unusually large crook in its handle and was inspired to lengthen it by attaching a long pole. He extended the pole behind the tyro so that it was in the audience's sight but not the performer's. Then, hooking the already despairing fellow by the neck, the manager yanked him off stage. The audience roared.

The cruel hook became part of theatrical lore, a reminder of the entertainer's risks in appearing alone onstage before the savage audience. The hook symbolizes the constant threat of rejection that the entertainer must deal with.

Eddie Cantor avoided the hook that amateur night by stealing Walter C. Kelly's "Virginia Judge" act and playing a series of characters in various dialects. Then he joined one of Gus Edwards's kiddie groups, "Kid Kabaret" with George Jessel and Lila Lee. He finally worked out his own act for a vaudeville debut on a small circuit owned by two ex-furriers, Adolph Zukor and Marcus Loew. The two future movie tycoons suggested he do a sketch, but instead the nineteen-year-old Cantor went blackface. By his own admission, he hadn't an original idea in his head and Jolson was the rage.

Fear of getting the burnt-cork makeup in his eyes led Cantor to leave great circles of skin unblacked, and he covered these with white-rimmed spectacles. The look was to become his trademark and he used it in his first *Ziegfeld Follies*, skipping across the stage, rolling his eyes, clapping his hands and singing

If you knew Susie
Like I know Susie
Oh, oh, oh, what a girl . . .

But he felt that a crucial decision he had been pondering was now inevitable and wrote about it with an articulateness and eloquence unusual in star memoirs.

Eddie Cantor would prance across the stage as he sang, clapping his hands and waving a handkerchief, and in this peculiar way he became a star of the Follies.

I had made my resolve that the old black face must die. This dark mask had helped me to success. Now the audience knew only this cork-smeared face while I stood hidden behind it, wondering what would happen if the blacking came off. . . . I had made my mind up . . . I was not going to be a slave to a piece of burnt cork for the rest of my acting days. For the *Follies* of 1918 I prepared a scene in white face. My agent asked Ziegfeld to let me try it and he agreed, but in an evasive way. . . . On opening night, Ziegfeld refused to let the scene go on, saying there was no room for it. . . . But this change meant more than my job to me. It meant my future and freedom from the black label. The second night I gave him an ultimatum, "Either the scene is in or I am out." Ziegfeld gave in and it was the first time I felt revealed to the audience and in personal contact with it." (*My Life Is in Your Hands*)

Cantor would don blackface only a few times after that. He didn't know it at the time but he had taken the step that would make the difference between his dying with vaudeville as a blackface singing act and thriving in the radio era as a personality comedian.

> How you gonna keep 'em
> Down on the farm
> After they've seen Paree?

Cantor sang this World War I song in the 1919 *Follies*, a show that he

Eddie Cantor's trademark was black makeup, and it made him famous in the Ziegfeld Follies *of 1917. But in the 1918* Follies *Cantor refused to go on in blackface, seeking to rescue his own identity, and in the process he rescued his career. It was this integrity that suffused his stage personality and made him popular, for Cantor's talents were not in themselves spectacular.*

considered "the greatest of its kind." He co-starred with Bert Williams and Marilyn Miller, and they introduced such great Irving Berlin songs as "Mandy" and "A Pretty Girl Is Like a Melody." Said Cantor, "If you were a hit in a show like that, you were a hit!"

The zest and ringing honesty of Cantor's recollections are the best possible clue to solving the mystery of why this apparently undistinguished and often even silly entertainer went so high. Surely he communicated in his work this selfsame enthusiasm, high spirit, and benevolence. That is what witnesses recall. Through sheer good will he maintained amiable relations, on- and offstage, with otherwise difficult and unpredictable stars, for if the act is the ego, a hugely successful act makes for a huge ego. Solitariness and powerful self-definitions are natural to even such unspoiled stars as Cantor worked with—Fanny Brice, Will Rogers, Bert Williams, and W. C. Fields.

Fields recalled a charming practical joke that he played on Cantor and Rogers during a performance of the 1917 *Ziegfeld Follies*. The prank began when Fields visited Rogers backstage not long before curtain time. Lounging idly with nothing seemingly on his mind, Fields puffed on his cigar and with some relish told Rogers a new joke he'd just heard. The Germans, it seemed, had let loose a new cannon that was so powerful it could shell Paris from thirty-five miles away. This did not frighten the always patriotic American military. "That's nothing," was the reaction of the brass. "Uncle Sam's now got a gun that can shoot everyone in Berlin, right from Staten Island, and all those Germans it don't kill it takes prisoner!"

Rogers enjoyed poking fun at American jingoism and said he would use the joke that very evening at the end of his monologue. Satisfied, Fields left cheerfully and strolled over to Eddie Cantor's dressing room. He told the same joke and got the same response. Cantor said that it was such a good joke he was going to close *his* monologue with it.

Fields had a busy time of it, that show, keeping Rogers distracted and away from the wings while Cantor (who went on first) was onstage. The joke went over wonderfully and an unsuspecting Rogers clapped Cantor on the back as the little fellow trotted into the wings after his final bow. Soon Rogers was himself onstage, doing beautifully as usual. He then launched confidently into the joke about the new German cannon.

"Well? How did it go?" asked the tickled Fields with a bright grin as Rogers strode into the wings after his act. The cowboy looked irritable, which only amused Fields the more. "Strange," Rogers muttered. "It sounded like a funny line to me but nobody laughed except the musicians."

The Ziegfeld Follies *did not have a monopoly on elaborate revues. Eleanor Powell, considered by many the best of all female dance acts in vaudeville, worked without her taps in George White's 1932* Music Hall Varieties.

W. C. Fields—William Claude Dukenfield—is the beloved bad boy of American entertainment, one of the great favorites of both audiences and professionals. Like Bert Lahr, he sought out burlesque when low clowning went out of fashion in vaudeville. Billed as "The World's Greatest Juggler," he had quickly learned that juggling wasn't enough. "Somehow, even though I was a kid I had sense enough to know that I must work with my mind and not just my hands. If I hadn't realized that, I'd be laid on the shelf today. People would be saying, 'Bill Fields? Oh yes, he used to be a juggler, didn't he?'"

He used to be the best juggler of all, it's still said, at a time when the stages of vaudeville were crowded with great jugglers. They juggled knives, flaming torches, and bowling pins while Fields worked with hats, cigars, bananas, and even white mice. The comedy of this aside, jugglers will tell you that their great challenge is not just the number of objects tossed together in the air but the diversity of their weights.

Fields's comic style was misanthropy delivered in a stewed literary style, and the combination of clowning, acid, and education was bracing. Groucho Marx's mixture alone is comparable. Additionally, Fields had struck upon so comic a stage persona that, like Jack Benny, he could skip the jokes and mine the resources of the W. C. Fields image. All he needed to do for a laugh was mention a child (he could not bear kids) or

ABOVE:
A Ziegfeld showgirl

OPPOSITE, ABOVE:
After the regular Follies *performance was over, a late show called a "Midnight Frolic" was sometimes produced in the roof cabaret atop the New Amsterdam Theatre. This scene is from the 1915 edition, featuring Oscar Shaw and the Dolly Sisters.*

OPPOSITE, BELOW:
Sybil Carmen and the Kidder Kar Girls in a Ziegfeld "Midnight Frolic"

booze (he could not get enough of it). In his delightful decadence he surely influenced the nightclub comedian, Joe E. Lewis.

Though the following anecdote may be apocryphal, Fields amusingly recalled the time when he was asked to stand in for an indisposed burlesque actor. The role was as the heavy in a sawmill melodrama. The heroine, as usual, was tied to a conveyer belt that was advancing her writhing body toward a fiercely whirring buzz saw. This particular actress, it seemed, had been repeatedly rejecting Fields's romantic advances. Now, as the conveyer drew her nearer to the buzz saw it suddenly became clear that this villain was not kidding. Her shrieks, as Fields gleefully recalled, were rattling the rafters of the theater when he finally called the moving belt to a halt. It had brought her perilously close to the saw. "One of my most superb performances," he said. "From then on, ingenues treated me with respect and fear, which is as good as love and usually ends up in the same place."

Even among originals, W. C. Fields was striking, and that was necessary if one meant to be a star in an era so abundant with entertainers. His special ability meshed with a special performing personality in a way that magnetized an audience and disarmed its hostile defenses. By transcending juggling, Fields became a comedian, but by making an artistic creation and an ongoing character of his comic sensibility, he became an immortal entertainer. To greater or lesser degrees, the other stars of the *Ziegfeld Follies* were in his class: Bert Williams, Will Rogers, Fanny Brice, and even, in his own sweet exuberant way, Eddie Cantor.

OPPOSITE:

Before coming to the Follies, *W. C. Fields headlined as a comic juggling act.*

ABOVE:

W. C. Fields occasionally resurrected juggling bits from his youth.

The Ziegfeld Follies

97

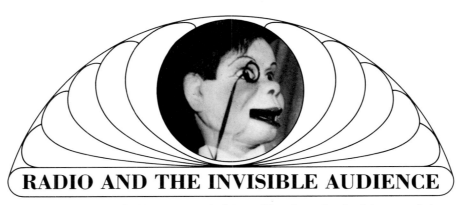

RADIO AND THE INVISIBLE AUDIENCE

In 1922 DeWolf Hopper made himself a place in the history of show business by agreeing to perform his rendition of "Casey at the Bat" on radio. Most stars considered the budding medium beneath them, and lesser performers who were tempted by it were frightened off by the Keith circuit's terrible-tempered Edward Albee and his threats never to hire any vaudevillian who ventured into a broadcast studio. Albee was wise to be fearful, for radio and the movies would prove vaudeville's undoing. More was at stake, however, than mere vaudeville. Moving pictures, radio, and phonograph records were threatening the very nature of the live entertainer as a physically present performer confronting a physically present audience.

Hopper found performing on radio unnerving. "It was a peculiar and dramatic sensation," he said, "speaking to thousands upon thousands you couldn't see. It was the hardest thing because I couldn't gesticulate." He spoke for a generation of vaudevillians who would be confused and even destroyed by the microphone and the unseen, unresponsive audience. The distance between the entertainer and the entertained, chasm enough when merely the size of a nightclub floor or an orchestra pit, was now infinite. Radio broadcasters tried to comfort their performers by inviting spectators into the studio, but this audience was not the target audience. *They* were at home. (*What* audience? *Where* at home?)

In 1926 the National Broadcasting Company inaugurated the first network, thereby creating a coast-to-coast home audience. This national radio hookup produced a sense of national community that had never existed before. Radio shows happened for all of America at the same time.

The earliest entertainment broadcasts were musical shows, fifteen-minute variety programs with orchestras and comedian-announcers. Such a program was "The Coo Coo Club," originating in Cleveland, which featured a seven-man band playing such favorites as "The Little Clock on the Mantel," "The King with the Terrible Temper," and "The Three Trees." Art Herske introduced the songs, spicing his announcements with humor:

I heard your mother-in-law was dangerously ill.
Yes, but she's dangerously well again.

It was not until "The Happiness Candy Stores," however, that network radio was truly launched. This immensely popular show was aired on Friday evenings from seven-thirty until eight o'clock and featured Ernie Hare and Bill Jones. It ran for almost six years, and, when the run was through, radio had become a national habit.

Musical shows were the programing of choice because they were essentially aural. They generated radio's first home-bred stars, the crooners. These new romantic singers were products of the jazz and dance bands, whose hotel and casino engagements were popularly broad-

LEFT:
The comedian DeWolf Hopper, a longtime associate of Weber and Fields, found radio "unnerving" because he "couldn't gesticulate."

OPPOSITE, ABOVE:
The first network radio program to become a national rage was the "Clicquot Club Eskimos." Named for its sponsor, a manufacturer of club soda and other mixers, this musical program established radio in 1926 as a medium for vaudeville to reckon with.

OPPOSITE, BELOW:
Every new mass-entertainment medium needs a star, for it is not technology that generates audience enthusiasm but a performer. The public buys the technology to reach the star. For radio, the new star was Rudy Vallee and, in turn, the "Vagabond Lover" reaped the rewards of novelty, drawing vast crowds of adoring women wherever he appeared in person.

cast by remote hookups. Microphones and the inherent intimacy of radio led the crooners to tone down from the more full-bodied voices of vaudeville stars Gene Austin, Nick Lucas ("The Singing Troubadour"), and Arthur Tracy ("The Street Singer"). The radio singer's audience, after all, was but a few feet from the loudspeaker.

The era of the crooner began when Rudy Vallee's radio program achieved national popularity, and from that day, vaudeville's star singers were finished. The top American singers for the next decades would be male romancers, performing in a soft-voice style popularized by Russ Columbo and Bing Crosby.

With radio proving itself quite able to manage without the vaudevillians, Albee lost his power to keep the comedians off the airwaves. By that time, however, the broadcasters no longer wanted all of them. Many of the great clowns were considered too visual, and others simply felt uncomfortable in the blind medium. Bert Lahr, perhaps the greatest clown in the legitimate theater, told his biographer John Lahr, "In those days, I was a fellow who was always moving. When I got in front of that microphone and had to hold a paper in my hand, I had fear. . . . I was always ahead of my script. I couldn't read it because I wanted to move all the time."

BELOW:
This photograph was taken purely for promotional purposes since Charles "Andy" Correll (left) and Freeman "Amos" Godsen hardly had to blacken up for a radio broadcast. Theirs was not a blackface act but a black-voice, or dialect, act—and for many years "Amos 'n' Andy" was among the most popular of all radio shows.

ABOVE:

Al Jolson failed in radio for the same reason that he had succeeded on the stage: his performing style, which had electrified theater audiences, was outsized for the fireside medium. His show did poorly, and not even such guest stars as Cantor could rescue him from the oblivion into which he was slipping.

BELOW:

Singers are ideal supporting acts for comedians because they don't compete for laughs and, even better, because they soften up audiences for comedy. Thus, radio comedians often worked with vocalist protégés. Jack Benny promoted Dennis Day. Edgar Bergen introduced Jane Powell. Here is Eddie Cantor with his discovery, Deanna Durbin.

Another great clown who had his travails was Ed Wynn, "The Perfect Fool," although for a couple of seasons, as the "Texaco Fire Chief," he too was successful on radio.

Announcer Graham McNamee: Say, chief, I read in the papers that you had an explosion on the farm.
Wynn: Oh, I had a terrible explosion on the farm . . . my pet hen ate some popcorn and then sat on a stove.

This was a merry madness, but Wynn, like Lahr, had sight gags in mind and would even wear costumes for his studio audience. This did not bode well for radio success and his show faded quickly.

Other funnymen made the radio plunge only to drown in the attempt, unable to cope with the medium's idiosyncracies. The most startling failure was Frank Fay's—startling because he was considered vaudeville's supreme monologist. George Burns analyzed it this way:

The reason [Fay] didn't make it on the radio was that he did the whole thing himself. He did a radio show for a half hour where he did the commercials, he sang the songs, he did all the talking. And he wouldn't pay for writers. That would be beneath Frank Fay. He didn't think anybody could write.

Like other reproductive media, radio reproduced indiscriminately. In performance, entertainers try to re-create themselves, but movies and radio (and later, television) short-circuit that, the lens and microphone transmitting every word and expression. Audiences want their performers to be not only entertaining but *nice*, and radio revealed Fay for the conceited and mean-spirited man he was.

Frank Tinney was another top monologist whose career was destroyed by radio. An understated and intelligent raconteur, he not only needed laughs for timing and feedback but couldn't even bring himself to believe that anyone out there was *listening*. He returned to vaudeville a demoralized and defeated man. Even his theatrical audiences sensed this and turned away.

Yet there were others who thrived in the new medium, and some were even inspired by its idiosyncracies. For if presence and visual impact no longer mattered, then of sudden new importance was personality and the quality of one's voice. Indeed, these characteristics often seemed more significant than the material itself. The comedian didn't have to be a funnyman.

With appearance irrelevant, a group of average-looking, rather than funny-looking, comedians rose to prominence, their humor based on vocal personality. They were dryer than vaudeville's clowns, but their speaking styles were more colorful than vaudeville's raconteurs, and also more personal, as befitted the intimacy of the new medium: Jack Carson, Jackie Gleason, Freeman Gosden and Charles Correll ("Amos 'n' Andy"), William Bendix, Danny Thomas, Joan Davis. They did not address the audience directly but performed in half-hour sketches that would come to be known as "situation comedies." And this was the start of the end of solo entertainers in radio. The showman was becoming an interpretive artist rather than a creative one, performing the material of others instead of doing his own act, an actor playing a part in a show rather than *being* it.

Radio needed more than musical and comedy shows to fill the hours of its days. New forms of programing were devised: quiz shows, dramatic anthologies, mysteries, discussions, news programs, game shows. All of these suited because, unlike stage entertainment, they could be enjoyed unseen. And yet the entertainer would not die; radio continued to be dominated by those vaudevillians who had been able to manage the transition from the variety stage: Jack Benny, Milton Berle, Fanny Brice, George Burns and Gracie Allen, Eddie Cantor, Fred Allen, and, of all things, a ventriloquist. In 1938, according to the Hooper ratings, the Edgar Bergen–Charlie McCarthy program was the third most popular in all of radio, behind only the Jack Benny and the Fred Allen shows.

The idea of a ventriloquist on radio was positively surreal. The premise of such an act, after all, is to create the illusion that a doll is alive. Diverting the audience's attention to the colorful dummy, supplying it with a voice and personality, the ventriloquist completes the effect of life by seeming to listen, with lips compressed, while the doll (the funny one) does most of the talking. The result is a one-man comedy team, the ventriloquist playing straight man to himself.

Radio obviated the technical feats of ventriloquism since it hardly made any difference whether or not the artist's lips moved—nor did he

have to drink water or smoke while his dummy talked (to mention but two stock routines). Indeed, with no dummy to be seen there was no need for a dummy at all: a voice would do. Edgar Bergen's genius, then, lay in the creation of a character so vivid that the home audience could visualize "Charlie McCarthy" and accept him as totally human. This made Bergen the ultimate ventriloquist, a creator of life. He was so complete, magnificent, and perfect in the execution of his act that he left the competition behind. Nobody ever came close. He was not a ventriloquist but *the* ventriloquist.

Charlie McCarthy's features had been modeled on a newspaper boy spotted on a suburban Chicago street, but Bergen's stroke of genius was Charlie's costume: top hat, white tie and tails, and a *monocle*. No explanation was given for all this finery. This was simply Charlie, dapper, neurotic, sassy, vulnerable, an ageless adolescent, a teenage bon vivant with urban complexities and anxieties. With his silky city toughness, he was sardonic and bitchy, even campy, and yet palpably sensitive.

Bergen (coming upon a humming Charlie): Charlie?
McCarthy: Bergen, you frightened me.
Bergen: I'm sorry.
McCarthy: Lately, I'm just a bundle of nerves.
Bergen: What brought all this on, Charlie?
McCarthy: Oh, it's unquestionably overwork. Schoolwork, homework, tests, and examinations. Oh, I tell you, it's simply driving me mad.

Fanny Brice's adaptation to radio was successful but sadly limiting, because, in order to achieve it, Brice replaced her wonderful mixture of burlesque clowning and torch singing with the silly, one-dimensional "Baby Snooks" character.

The average adolescent does not complain about being a bundle of nerves; he doesn't cultivate world-weariness. But Charlie McCarthy's character was based on a tension between sophistication and innocence.

Like most comedians of the era, Bergen could not resist insult humor. It was certainly appropriate and irresistible when the notable child-hater W. C. Fields was a guest on the show.

Fields (singing): Give me my boots and my bottle.
McCarthy (to Bergen): Here comes W. C. You're a walking ad for black coffee, Bill. Hello, Mr. Fields, hello.
Fields: Hello, my little chum. I was thinking about you only yesterday.
McCarthy: No! You were!
Fields: Yes, I was cleaning out the woodshed. Reminded me of you.
McCarthy: Mr. Fields, is that your nose or a new kind of flame-thrower?
Fields: You'd better come out of the sun, Charles, before you come unglued.
McCarthy: Do you mind if I stand in the shade of your nose?

Drier still, by consensus, was the work of Fred Allen. Born in Boston as John Florence Sullivan, he had developed a juggling act that carried him through the lesser wheels of vaudeville under the billing "Paul Huckle, European Entertainer." When Huckle added jokes to the act, he became "Freddie St. James" and then, "Freddie James, World's Worst Juggler," a joking reference to W. C. Fields's billing as "The World's

Edgar Bergen was the ultimate ventriloquist. He did it perfectly, succeeded absolutely, and there really was no point in anyone else's even attempting to be a ventriloquist after that. In fact, when Bergen added a second dummy, Mortimer Snerd, to his radio act, he proved that he could not improve upon what he had already done. Snerd, seen here with his creator, was amusing, but he was no Charlie McCarthy. For Charlie McCarthy lived.

BELOW:
When W. C. Fields, who seemed as much of a caricature as Charlie McCarthy, got together with him on his immensely popular radio show, even Bergen disappeared, as if he felt out of his depth with those superbright smart alecks. The ventriloquist's act is to disappear. How much suppressed cynicism and sarcasm, one wonders, was Bergen able to release through McCarthy?

*Fred Allen, who played the Palace
with his wife, Portland Hoffa, described
that famous theater as "the towering
symbol of vaudeville . . . a Palace
program with an act's name on it was
a diploma of merit . . . an act that
played there was booked unseen by
any theater manager in the country."*

Greatest Juggler." By 1920 he was "Fred Allen," working steadily in the
big time and then graduating to the legitimate theater.

Radio, however, proved Allen's true métier and, given his own show
in 1932, he used it to showcase his unique style of topical, bone-dry
skepticism. The program's format was conventional: a company of stock
players in half-hour situation comedies designed to set off the star's

sense of humor. The following segment from a typical Fred Allen program satirized the advertising agencies that packaged most radio programs, as well as the Hooper and Crossley rating services that had recently emerged as the virtual arbiters of which shows would be continued or canceled. Allen played an adman worried about the "Kenny Dank Show," now down to a minus rating.

Allen: Not only every radio listener in America isn't listening to Kenny Dank. Two hundred thousand people who haven't got radios aren't listening either.

Secretary: But how can people without a radio not listen?

Allen: Don't question statistics, Miss Yuck. The entire advertising business is founded on surveys. The first man who questions a survey will topple the advertising game like a house of cards. (To Dank) Figures don't lie. Here's the Crossley report. Here's the Hooper that checks to the Crossley. Here's the Dooper that checks to the Hooper. And the Booper. According to the Booper, Hooper, Dooper you are down to minus two point two.

Dank: Well I was on opposite two [of FDR's] fireside chats last month.

Allen: You can't blame him for everything.

Allen conducted an ongoing "feud" with Jack Benny, much as Bob Hope did with Bing Crosby. Mere references to the other fellow could draw laughter and provide an outlet for good-natured insult humor. Benny and Allen were certainly a disparate pair. Benny presented a benign character and made himself the butt of the jokes. Allen was a faultfinder, a carper—and however sagacious his satiric thrusts, they made him seem crotchety. Benny was downright *maternal.* His humor, in contrast to Allen's, was forgiving and therefore endearing, dealing, as it so often did, with his own vanity and ego, punctured. It avoided the topical, which inevitably dates. It was also better written.

The clown element in Jack Benny's work went largely unnoticed in radio because it went unseen. But Benny could still express this comic impulse for the benefit of the studio audience, as here, with Ralph Edwards as a guest, on the popular "Truth or Consequences."

Announcer Don Wilson: Mary [Benny's wife] told us that Warner Brothers were going to make a picture about your life.

Benny: Yes, sir, the same studio that made the life of Emile Zola, the life of Louis Pasteur, the life of Mark Twain and now the life of Jack Benny. [A pathetic fanfare, two shabby trumpets] *Now cut that out.* Smart-aleck musicians.

Bandleader Phil Harris: You know, Jackson, I can't understand any studio wanting to make a picture of your life.

Benny: What do you mean?

Harris: *I'm* the guy. Color, glamor, excitement. That's what they should make: the life of Phil Harris.

Benny: Phil, the story of your life wouldn't pass the Hays [censorship] office. So don't be ridiculous.

Harris: All right, so what's interesting about your life?

Benny: Mine is a story of adventure and courage. The real true life of Jack Benny. [Once more, a pathetic trumpet fanfare] Now stop with that. Enough's enough.

Jack Benny was the Mozart of comedians, elegant and perfect. Yet his success in vaudeville had not been immediate. Audiences had to acquire a taste for his deadpan style. Mack Lathrop, a fellow performer, recalled that "onstage in the hinterlands . . . the audiences didn't understand him. And he would be out there dying. And he would look off into the wings and make comments that would have us hysterical with laughter, but the audience wasn't laughing."

Radio seemed created just for Benny, providing a private, intimate audience that could concentrate on subtext—on what Benny did *not* say (he needed only to be asked about vanity or miserliness to get a laugh). Relying on the continuity and exposure, he patiently impressed a com-

Youthful Mickey Rooney and Judy Garland. Late in the 1930s, both Hollywood and vaudeville lowered their guard and allowed their stars to perform in the new medium of radio.

plete character upon his audience. He was able to spend a career capitalizing on this awareness of his foibles and quirks. At the end, a mere silence ("Your money or your life . . .") was all that was necessary for a laugh.

If Jack Benny was the happiest example of a vaudevillian adapting to radio, Bob Hope was the ultimate radio-bred comedian. The archetypal stand-up, he was probably more concerned with being funny (or afraid of not) than any of vaudeville's monologists. This may have been rooted in a terrifying awareness of how easily a radio-station dial could be turned. Hope's was the comedy of jokes, gags, one-liners, and wisecracks— as compared with the monologist's anecdotes, inference, and subtext. Shunning the traditional sober precision of the vaudevillian delivering a monologue, Hope rattled away, ignoring the traditional discipline of sequence and logic. Vaudevillians would denigratingly call him a "comic" rather than the loftier "comedian," but he would, in fact, become the

ABOVE:

George Burns and Gracie Allen were radio naturals because their routines were almost entirely verbal and because there was a pleasing natural contrast between Burns's gravelly baritone and Gracie's warbling alto.

BELOW:

Bud Abbott and Lou Costello were a burlesque act whose low comedy worked well in movies, less so in radio.

most popular comedian in the history of American show business. His brashness and energy were natural to the America of the twentieth century's middle decades.

Bob Hope made his stage debut at twenty-one, with Fatty Arbuckle's comeback vaudeville act of 1925. Within three years he was starring on

Broadway in musical comedies. He would seldom again work before live audiences, except for his celebrated troop tours. His career would be spent in radio, the movies, and television. Doubtless it was because of such media performance that he came to seem so cool and distant in his work, but he mastered these fields as did nobody else, for he devoted his career to them.

Hope began his radio career on September 27, 1938, and, just as he continued to sing his theme song,

> *Thanks for the memory*
> *Of this our opening spot.*
> *Oh! I practically forgot*
> *You'll love the show next Tuesday.*
> *There's a scene where I get shot*
> *You'll like that so much...*

with various lyrics, his style would remain virtually the same for the next fifty years.

My uncle just left town... he was here with the American Legion. It was a nice, quiet convention. The second night, the boys at the hotel gave the house detective twenty-four hours to get out of town. But I want to thank the American Legion for getting me a half-day off, last week at Paramount. They came over to the set I was working on, and took the camera with them as a souvenir. Paramount didn't mind that so much, but they'd be very thankful if the fellow from Texas would please bring back Dorothy Lamour. And the parades were wonderful. One thing I noticed, the women look different this year...

It was the rapid-fire style in full force. "American Legion" and "Texas" were catchwords for laughs, along with the idea of naughty boys abducting movie star Dorothy Lamour. None of this was based on character, situation, or comic logic, and as a result the writing showed. Hope even reduced the familiar connective "but speaking of" to the token "I want to tell you," and on occasion to a mere "but." He would never endear himself to the intelligentsia because his style was so aggressive. Too, his material had no point of view, though it was topical. There were no teeth in this satire, and a joke about one political candidate could as easily have been made about another. Yet Hope's popularity was immense, his success stupendous, and there is a weight and approval in that which must be recognized. However, among his colleagues, perhaps Hope's only champions have been the brainy Woody Allen and the fast-witted Johnny Carson. There are few comedians sharper than Allen and Carson, so perhaps that is a minority worth listening to.

It is a pity that Hope so rarely faced the challenge of the live audience. It might have saved him from the complacency that later marred his work. There is no way of knowing how different his career might have been had he plunged into the crucible of in-person performance. Surely no faster comic mind ever worked before a microphone.

America's transition to television was a comfortable one. Many of radio's familiar stars made the switch as smoothly as a monologist changing subjects: Jack Benny, Burns and Allen, Groucho Marx. Others, like Edgar Bergen and Fred Allen, could not manage it, their momentum irretrievably geared to the spoken word and the mind's eye. Although television at first seemed to promise a resurrection for vaudevillians, it only provided temporary work for the variety entertainers. The medium was even more dehumanizing than radio. The performer was now a mere picture of himself, dancing on the face of a cathode-ray tube.

By 1938 Bob Hope had developed the wise-guy style and the machine-gun delivery that would give his career an astounding fifty-year momentum.

THE SEX QUEENS

I t was the priggishness of vaudeville that launched American burlesque, for as variety entertainment was being sedated for the family trade, the rowdy comedians and their equally rowdy audiences were forced to find new homes. They found them in such burlesque houses as the Comique in Washington, D.C., Boston's Old Howard, Philadelphia's Olympic, and New York City's Miner's Bowery Theatre. There, entertainment remained cheerfully unpretentious and lowdown.

By 1905 the Chicago-based Sam T. Jack was touring burlesque shows south to Texas and New Mexico, and soon afterward there were two full burlesque wheels, the Columbia in the East and the Empire in the West. On these circuits could be found many of the clowns who had been displaced by vaudeville's refinement—Weber and Fields, Clark and McCullough, Jack Pearl, Gallagher and Shean, and the great Bert Lahr.

While there was plenty of bawdiness in the early days, there were no striptease dancers. Burlesque consisted of one-act plays that lampooned current comedies or melodramas and, between the acts, an "olio," or variety show. This would include not only comedy teams and pratfall clowns but also many of the other acts continuing in vaudeville, such as contortionists, magicians, and jugglers. So there was a certain amount of overlap between the two stages. Because of burlesque's later identification with strippers, some of the fine performers who played it were subsequently embarrassed by the connection and disowned it.

Burlesque became the arena for broad and boisterous comedy. The props to be found backstage would likely include slap sticks, fright wigs, pistols, and all manner of baggy pants. Onstage, there were countless courtroom sketches with slammed gavels and spritzed seltzer bottles. Cheating wives were familiar figures, concealing their lovers in armoires while comedian-husbands sputtered in impotent jealousy.

Primitive musical theater came to dominate these early burlesque shows while lampoon went out of style. A typical production of 1910 might begin with a blare from the pit band as the curtain rose and the chorus girls burst energetically from the wings. After this opening number of song and dance, the leading lady (or "soubrette") would be introduced, and then the comedian would barrel on stage. The plot might have the chorus girls coaxed into trying champagne and getting tipsy, or offer other developments of similar moment. It made no difference at all because the audience was not demanding. And in this cheerful, energetic setting a series of musical and comedy numbers would be linked, helping to introduce Broadway's great era of musical comedy. Irving Berlin wrote for such shows and Fanny Brice got her start appearing in them.

The middle act occasionally offered its own surprises. For a time, a curious taste developed for "purring matches," in which one man kicked another in the shins until the fellow couldn't take it anymore and con-

OPPOSITE:
The young Ann Corio

ABOVE:
Little Egypt

ABOVE:

Burlesque in Boston centered on the Howard Atheneum, the "Old Howard." In other cities, pasties came about the diameter of a quarter, but in proper Boston they had to be at least half-dollar size.

BELOW:

Bert Lahr played a low comedian in the Broadway drama Burlesque. *In later times, the broad antics of the clowns would come to seem more artistic than the sharp-witted but flashy comedy of the monologists.*

ceded defeat. Otherwise, the variety entertainment in burlesque differed little from vaudeville except for the broad and leering comedy. That was all the sex there was in early burlesque, until the arrival of the girls from Chicago.

Cooch dancing, that infamous craze, was originated at the 1893 Chicago World's Columbian Exposition by a unique performer appearing on

the Midway Plaisance. Her name was Fahreda Mahzar Spyropolos, but she billed herself as "Little Egypt." Her costume consisted of a fringed and brocaded bolero jacket and harem pantaloons. Her face was veiled but not her abdomen. To an insistent and insinuating drumbeat, chains jiggling at wrists, ankles, and hips, she wriggled and gyrated and shook her belly and fanny until she rocked the country. At once, "cooch dancers," "hootch dancers," and "hootchy-kootchy dancers" were titillating audiences in burlesque shows across the country. Billed as "Extra Added Attractions," they were saved for the end (a) so as to keep audiences from leaving and (b) so they could be easily deleted should the authorities arrive unexpectedly. Police raids, of course, made for wonderful publicity.

Cooch dancers were not the first females to expose their charms on the American stage. As early as the 1850s there had been theatrical presentations of "Living Bodies" that on the pretext of replicating great works of art presented nude, but motionless, women in such *tableaux vivants* as "Adam's First View of Eve," "The Expulsion from Eden," or "Rodin's 'The Kiss.'" Modest as these sensualities were, some audiences could not be restrained. At one performance, a number of men came to the theater carrying, according to a slumming critic,

prodigious opera glasses and pocket telescopes. The audience as a whole was made up of sensual old rakes, scoundrels around town and, yes, a few bankers and brokers. In one instance, the gentlemen left their seats and jumped over the footlights, forcing the terrified models backstage and into their dressing rooms.

This surely was as nothing compared to the night in 1928 that a beautiful chorus girl named Hinda Wasau went on a Chicago stage to do her shimmy dance. She was having costume trouble and, unable to manage a quick change, found herself onstage with one costume half off, the other half on. A trouper, Wasau proceeded as best she could, trying to pull away the wrong costume while still shimmying. Unfortunately, or perhaps not, both costumes came off, piece by piece, and although Wasau stopped well before nudity, the audience (according to reports) was most expressive in its enthusiasm.

Here are two of the best in burlesque, comic Jimmy Savo spritzing the vivacious Margie Hart who, according to stripper Ann Corio, "had a yen to take it all off."

At roughly the same time in Cleveland, a hefty interpretive dancer named Carrie Finnell also discovered the suspense value of disrobing, one garment at a time. However, she announced her intention in advance. Moreover, she promised that the disrobing process would continue indefinitely. Carrie Finnell managed to extend that engagement for fifty-two weeks. The invention of the striptease dance is credited to these two pioneering women.

After Finnell had established her act and shortened its duration, she continued on her innovative path by inventing the fine art of tassel-twirling. It seems that the revelation of an entire breast was morally acceptable so long as the nipple itself remained unexposed—doubtless, because of its maternal connotations. To preserve the image of motherhood unsullied, the "pastie" was created, a small circle of sequins glued over the nipple with a tassel attached for decoration and emphasis. Bearing these badges at the tips of her pendulous breasts, Carrie Finnell promoted herself as "The Remote Control Girl," who could move her breasts while remaining otherwise still. According to one journalist who preferred anonymity, "She trained each generous bust to twitch on cue, jump to attention and do just about everything except sing 'April Showers' in Swahili."

From a more technical point of view, Finnell

would start one tassel on one bosom slowly, like a propellor revving up on a World War I plane. Faster and faster it would spin while its fellow tassel lay limp and neglected on the other bosom. Then the other tassel would come to life. It would start spinning slowly, while the first tassel was at full speed. . . . She would walk across stage with the tassels swirling in front of her and the applause would ring out . . . she could make one go slow, the other fast. She could spin the left in one direction and the right in the opposite direction. She could lie on her back and somehow keep the tassels elevated and twirling. (Ann Corio, *This Was Burlesque*)

Any performer has sex with an audience in a metaphorical way. A stripper is in the business.

Within a few years the Minsky family established a chain of twelve burlesque theaters in New York City. Louis ("Little Ziggy") Minsky replaced the voluptuous strippers with slimmer beauties, and in the thirties striptease dancing became standard burlesque fare. The showmanly Minsky even brought the girls into the audience, dressing his usherettes in Scheherazade costumes. Many gifted comedians would get their start on his and other burlesque stages—Phil Silvers, Jackie Gleason, Bud Abbott and Lou Costello, and Red Skelton, who began his act by strolling through the curtain with a grin on his farmboy face, saying, "Hello, everybody!" He would keep on strolling until he crashed into the orchestra pit.

While comedy bits like Skelton's were wonderfully zany, and while the sketches were sometimes rich and earthy, too often the routines were heavy-handed, parceled out to the comic and the straight man. As described by Ann Corio (*This Was Burlesque*),

The straight man was an elegant character in a seedy way. He wore the right clothes for a gentleman, but somehow they just didn't look right. Compared to the baggy-pants comic, however, he was a tailor's dream. His job was to dominate the comic, to scold him, to get the better of him with the girls, to try to take his money unfairly. When the comic won out, everyone enjoyed his victory.

The straight man also had to be master of the double take, which in burlesque is called "the skull":

In Person:
The Great Entertainers

118

OPPOSITE, LEFT ABOVE AND BELOW:
Burlesque at the turn of the century relied more heavily upon songs, broad comedy, and costumes than upon the enticement of nudity, but the aura of bawdiness invited disrepute, nevertheless.

OPPOSITE, RIGHT ABOVE:
Little Egypt started it all in 1893 at the World's Columbian Exposition in Chicago.

OPPOSITE, RIGHT BELOW:
In an unsubtle and surely uncomfortable pose, the redoubtable Carrie Finnell, noted inventor of twirling tassels

Straight Man: Without a doubt you are the most illiterate person that I have ever met.

Comic: That's right. Build me up.

S: When I say illiterate, I mean you're dumb. You haven't the intelligence of my youngest child.

C: You have a child? How long have you been married?

S: Three years.

C: That's good. How many children do you have?

S: Six!

C: Married three years and you have six children?

S: Yes.

C: That's damned good! How do you account for having six children and only being married three years?

S: I attribute it to the reading my wife did.

C: Reading? What's that have to do with it?

S: Well, the first year we were married, my wife read a book entitled *One Night of Love* and at the end of that first year she presented me with a baby boy. The second year, she read a book entitled *A Tale of Two Cities* and at the end of that year she gave birth to twins. The third year, she read a book entitled *Three Men on a Horse* and at the end of the third year she presented me with triplets. That makes six altogether. See?

C: Let me get this straight. The first year you were married your wife read a book called *One Night of Love* and at the end of the year, bang, there was a baby boy. The second year she read *A Tale of Two Cities* and gave birth to twins. The third year she read *Three Men on a Horse* and gave birth to triplets.

S: Yes.

C: I'll see you later. I have to rush home and stop my wife.

S: Why?

C: She's reading *The Birth of a Nation*.

Such material was less than brilliant. Despite much insistence by nostalgic fans, the comics were not burlesque's reason for existence. The sensationalism of the strippers gave burlesque its excitement.

Phil Silvers (center) in burlesque at the Apollo Theatre on Forty-second Street

A burlesque theater of the 1930s had a standing company that included a motley chorus line and a house singer who doubled as master of ceremonies and straight man. The star comedian and stripper would vary. The performance began with a production number featuring the chorus line, a group not to be confused with the Rockettes. Traditionally, one of these girls was clumsy, but it was hard to tell which one was working at it. A comedy routine followed, a simple one because it was early in the show. Comedians often became favorites in a particular theater. Mike Sachs, for instance, was identified with the Howard Atheneum in Boston, a house that was never called anything but the "Old

Howard." He did the same sketches so often that he continued to do them at the Old Howard for years after going blind.

The first stripper on the bill would generally be a novice, a girl from the chorus line who had apprenticed as a "catcher," hovering in the wings to snare the garments wafted offstage by the headliner. When the beginner had finished her strip, more elaborate comedy sketches would follow, tasty items about short-winded traveling salesmen and insatiable farmers' daughters. A typical sketch was "The Gazeeka Box," named for an invention that the straight man sold to the comedian. When the straight man demonstrated it, the big box worked beautifully. It produced the wonders that were promised, usually a beautiful blonde. After the comedian bought it, of course, nothing happened at all. Or else a cop came out.

No question, as strippers grew more popular, burlesque comedy declined, but the price may have been worth it. For striptease dancing, while it lasted, was a solo performance unlike any other. Dealing as it did with sex and arousal, it traded in feelings of the most intimate kind. The living presence of a willing, eager, hungry goddess could not remotely be approximated by the same act on film. For adolescents, a stripper was often the first experience of a truly sexual woman. Not unlike a virginal visit to a prostitute, this event was heightened by its theatricality and the permeating sense of private passion within a community of aroused men. There were also occasional women of nerve and independence who visited a burlesque house to know the heat of sex; to learn the bumps and grinds; to discover the secrets of passion from the only authorities there seemed to be.

The strippers of burlesque were erotic queens in an era of sexual cover-up. Unlike the moist-lipped but virginal sex goddesses of Hollywood, these women were present, they were forthright, they were available. No doubt about it, they would come through. The tease was fulfilled onstage in proud exposure of the female bodies of men's dreams.

As described by Ann Corio, one of the most beautiful and famous of all strippers, the striptease was truly a rite of sexual arousal. "The various steps," she explains in *This Was Burlesque*, "were known in succession as 'the flash,' or entrance; 'the parade,' or march across the stage in full costume; and then 'the tease,' or increasing removal of wearing apparel while the audience lusts for bed and body; and the strip to G-string and pasties."

There is no known origin for the term "G-string." It is a sequined triangle of cloth covering the pubes and fastened around the waist with a string. G-string and pasties were all a stripper wore at the end of her act. That was as inevitable as the death at the end of a bullfight.

The basic outline of a stripper's act was ritualistic, too. She would appear fully clothed in the opening "flash" (a term derived from vaudeville's costumed "flash acts") so as to establish her act's uniqueness, dressed as a Southern belle, perhaps, or a bride. She would almost immediately strip to a "panel" dress, which had strips of material in the front and back with the sides left open to allow quick glimpses of thigh and breast. The real excitement came with the strip down to G-string and pasties, not because of the nudity but because of the bumps (thrusts of pelvis) and grinds (twists of hips and fanny), all simulations of lovemaking.

In this was the essence of the act and the heart of the stripper's talent. Her job was convincing the audience that this was for each of them, personally; that they so excited her she lost her senses onstage; against her wishes and despite every ounce of her professionalism, she was helplessly and violently caught in the driving urges of passion. This was a wonderful pornography. Her temples would go pale and her cheeks

Gypsy Rose Lee at work

flush as she rubbed against the curtain or lobbed a sash or her hair or anything between her legs. Her eyelids would lower under the weight of desire as she slipped into a trance of throbbing hunger, body heat rising. To the darkened and dream-filled balcony, the stripper of burlesque offered the prostitute's hot lewdness in the magnificent body of a dream woman, not for a price but from heavy urgency.

Asoak in this passion, adolescents, young men, fathers, and grandfathers sat in shoulder-to-shoulder fraternity. They gaped at these aggressive seductresses so hungry for the shy, so available, so womanly. These throbbing queens who thrived on the fantasies of the frustrated, came to fulfill sexual longings and starvations at a time when wives and girl friends wore bathrobes until the bedroom lights were out, and then stripped down to pajamas.

In show business as elsewhere, golden ages become golden only when they are over. The golden age of striptease dancing lasted from 1930 until 1950. Gypsy Rose Lee was probably the best-known stripper of the era, projecting sexuality by performing a cool and aloof act. A beautiful and smart young woman, she developed a striptease that depended more on style and humor than on disrobing and gyrating. Although famed as a stripper, she did not actually spend many years in burlesque. She capitalized on her publicity to build a career in the legitimate theater.

Among the more committed strippers, Ann Corio rates Margie Hart as the raunchiest—"a knockout redhead with a yen to show it . . . the most daring stripper of them all." Hart went naked whenever she felt like it, which evidently was often.

Another star stripper of the era was Georgia Sothern, who roared on stage, bumping and shaking to "Hold That Tiger." According to Corio, Sothern "did an act that no one who ever saw it would forget. She was a cyclone of sex and she literally blew the walls down." Georgia Sothern was indeed unforgettable. She would sit back on a park bench, facing the audience. The music would beat. She would fix a warm and moist smile on her lips, her eyes half-closed. She would slowly, urgently undo a long silken handerchief from around her waist. I think it was green. With a firm thrust she would tuck an end of it beneath her G-string. It would drop from between her spread legs to the floor.

She would sit on the bench, gazing profoundly at every man in the audience. Her arms would extend on either side, hands resting lightly on the bench-back. The weight and substance of her flesh—flat and muscled flesh of a dancer—was full on the bench. The rhythm of the music increased and the handkerchief would begin to move. And then *it would wave in rhythm to the music.* Carrie Finnell might twirl her tassels, and every other stripper in burlesque too, but Georgia Sothern . . .

Other strippers had other specialties. Sherry Britton, Lili St. Cyr, Peaches LaVerne: glorious creatures with exotic, self-mocking names that conjured up illicit hungers. When Mayor Fiorello La Guardia closed down New York City's burlesque theaters in 1937, these sex goddesses were forced to take their exquisite feathers and veils and silky negligees to seedy theaters and strip joints on darkened streets in small cities unworthy of their incensed fantasies. They continued in such sorry circumstances for another decade.

It is difficult to appreciate what La Guardia accomplished. In hindsight, his moral zeal appears politically motivated, and his persecution of the Minsky family seems unconscionable. We have hardly benefited. Today, sleazy sex shows proliferate in New York City, where once these magnificent creatures quickened our pulses, transporting us with such innocent lust.

OPPOSITE, LEFT ABOVE:
Since there was no way of improving on the fine simplicities of stripping, gyrating, and thrusting, each girl sought to stand apart from the crowd by developing a gimmick. Sally Rand's was the fan dance.

OPPOSITE, RIGHT ABOVE:
The porcelain Rose La Rose, born Rosina de Pella, died in 1972 at the age of fifty-three, leaving an estate of two million dollars. She had been living in Toledo, Ohio, where, a reporter friend recalled, "she decorated her home beautifully and expensively but it looked like something from a Hollywood set." Rose La Rose had told him, "Burlesque is dead." Understandably among the last to admit it, she added, just in case there might still be a chance, "but I'm not going to be the one who says it." The reporter wrote to a friend, "It's kind of crazy, Rose dying here in Toledo. It certainly wasn't her town, even though she tried to be one of the girls. She never quite made it with the neighbors. She tried to be a hausfrau but she didn't know how." No initiate who had ever watched Rose La Rose from the balcony would have been surprised.

OPPOSITE, LEFT BELOW:
Tempest Storm

OPPOSITE, RIGHT BELOW:
Lili St. Cyr's gimmick was based on the sex appeal of not undressing but dressing. Her act opened in a bathtub.

OUT OF A HAT

Perhaps of all the lost entertainers, none are more irreplaceable than the magicians. To do magic, what an act! Their performances were so stylized as to be ritual. We can still see the ghosts —elegant and graceful, elbows high and white gloves poised like the hands of conductors—waving magic wands to produce roses and doves from top hats, glowing cigarettes from thin air, and coins from behind the ears of ecstatic children. How could we have let such wondrous creatures depart? Fantasy, drama, suspense, mystery, surprise, glamor, and high spirits were combined in the exotic person of a man wearing a Vandyke beard, dressed in white tie and tails, making miracles before our eyes.

Like acrobats, magicians have always seemed foreigners. There is something European about the calling. They traditionally took exotic names—sometimes a single word, like Blackstone or Mandrake (yes, there was a Mandrake the Magician); sometimes, in Barnum fashion, a more complex concoction—"The Great Lafayette," for instance. Italian names were always popular in magician circles: Dante, Cardini, Rosini. At the turn of the century, the most revered among his fellow magicians was Kellar, and his prestige carried over to a protégé mundanely named Howard Thurston.

A few of these performers earned lifelong reputations among their colleagues for originating classic illusions. There were but two requirements for a trick to rate this distinction, and unbelievability was but one of them; the other was showmanship. Although magicians are wonderful in making us forget that we are watching entertainers, not wizards, *they* never forget it. They can hardly afford to. The apparatus of their tricks may be painstakingly mechanical and tedious, but it must be perfectly concealed beneath an appearance of miracle. Nowhere in all of entertainment, including the theater, is the synthesis of illusion and reality so flawlessly maintained. And of course that is necessary; the reality of illusion is the magician's very act.

Horace Golden was the first to saw a woman in half. Sam DuVries introduced levitation. It happened on the stage of Hammerstein's Victoria Theatre. Some of us are still awed by the sight of a woman seemingly afloat in the air, a hoop being passed around her body to prove that no strings are suspending her. We murmur, "How did he do that?" and who among us knows? In our hearts we suspect that the woman is truly afloat.

Some magicians, trying to separate themselves from the crowd and carve out a niche on the crowded vaudeville bills, became hypnotists. Often presented as a scientific demonstration, their acts invariably fell back on audience volunteers, who were stretched across the backs of two chairs—rigid! The mind readers had themselves blindfolded and tried to identify objects held aloft by the audience. There were even comedy magicians, best-known of whom were Frank van Hoven ("The Mad Magician") and Carl Ballantyne ("Ballantyne the Great"), whose tricks always backfired.

OPPOSITE:
Poster advertising the great magician Kellar

ABOVE:
Doug Henning

Out of a Hat

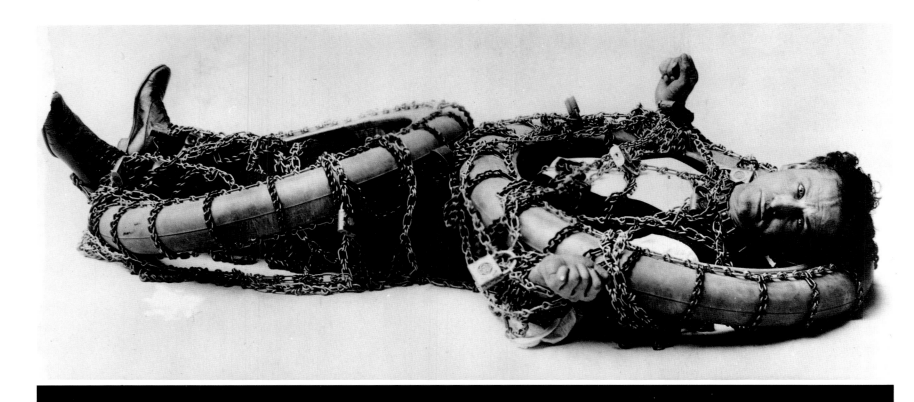

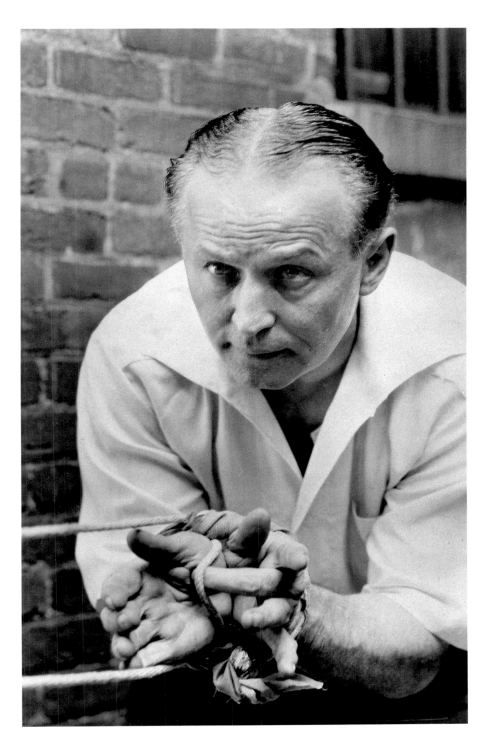

Mastery of illusion is not a guaranteed ticket to success as a magician. Houdini's tricks, marvelous as they were, dazzled the public because he decked them in showmanly trappings.

OPPOSITE, BELOW:

Milbourne Christopher's variation on the Sam DuVries illusion of levitation. His 1950s stage presentations, Now You See It and Christopher's Wonders, were the first Broadway shows devoted entirely to magic.

ABOVE:

Bound hands posed no problem to Houdini. He would reveal no more than what this photograph shows, aware that a magician's very existence rides on the most important illusion of all—that he is working magic.

Escapes were the novelty that established the most famous magician of all, Harry Houdini. Born Ehrich Weiss, in Budapest, he began as a trapeze artist, and it was his athletic agility that made possible his great feats of escape. At first he worked with his brother Theo in a conventional magic act called "The Brothers Houdini," taking the name from the French conjurer Robert Houdin. When Theo left the act, Harry devised an illusion called "The Metamorphosis." He would have himself tied up and put inside a trunk, which in turn was locked and bound. When the escape was made it was not Houdini who emerged but his wife, Bess. (The traditional presence of a lovely assistant in magic shows seems based not merely on the reliable appeal of beauty but also on the historic association of women with purity and honesty.) "Metamorphosis" has since been performed by many magicians, but by far the most inventive has been the young Canadian Doug Henning, who developed a career in magic long after magicians had become obsolete. As Henning has pointed out, the wonder of "Metamorphosis" is that "it has elements

of both escape and magical illusion. The fast escape is athletic and ingenious, but the showmanship of it lies in the switch of person and, even more crucial, the change in *gender*."

Houdini often performed his feats of escape as free public demonstrations until they had received sufficient coverage in the newspapers. This flair for publicity elevated him from performer to public figure and provided the leverage to demand extraordinary fees. In Manhattan on July 7, 1912, Houdini had himself handcuffed and his legs manacled. He was then locked in a box and tossed into the East River. Less than a minute later, he emerged from the water. When the box was raised and brought to the pier, it was still nailed shut. And when it was finally pried open (by a team of burly carpenters) the manacles were still inside. Several weeks later Houdini opened at Hammerstein's Paradise Roof and did the same trick, this time in a giant tank of water. "My Challenge to Death," as he called it, filled the house with curiosity-seekers who had missed the East River performance and were eager to pay top dollar to see it. Few entertainers have had such a genius for showmanship. Houdini proved that a magician is not merely a master of sleight of hand, distraction, and illusion, but primarily an entertainer, who must dress up his performances with effects and theatrics. Crafty illusionist and a brilliant escape artist he certainly was, but his showmanliness was what made Houdini the most famous magician of all. He never merely escaped from a trunk; it had to be immersed in a roaring river, or suspended above a deep gorge. Or he might have himself locked and chained in a jail cell, or tossed into the water strapped in a straitjacket. Gifted with a sense of what would thrill the public, he developed billing that read like circus posters. "Metamorphosis," for example, was subtitled, "The Exchange of Human Beings in a Locked, Sealed, Corded Trunk." Of course, this was only window dressing, but so much of theater is window dressing.

Houdini did not restrict himself to escapes. His feats of illusion were treated with similar dash. As he himself described one astonishing piece of legerdemain, "I swallow—if one's eyes are to be trusted—anywhere from fifty to one hundred and fifty needles and from ten to thirty yards of thread. Then, after a few seconds, I bring up the needles. All threaded." Allowing himself a showmanly boast, Houdini added, "In Boston, at Keith's Theatre, it was presented at a special performance to over a thousand physicians and they were never able to explain it." And if a *doctor* couldn't explain it . . .

When Doug Henning performed his version of Houdini's "Metamorphosis" on a 1975 television special, his own showmanship made it even more theatrical. As Henning described it, "The safety man who holds the ax, to chop the water tank in case anything goes wrong, wears a black executioner's hood. At the end of two and a half minutes, the curtains [dropped to cover the tank during the escape] are removed. The tank is empty and I had vanished! The executioner figure—who had been in full view through all the proceedings of locking me upside down in the water-filled tank—would remove his hood. And it would be me."

The magician is the only performer who should be called "incredible," and yet his astonishing illusions are produced by a series of quite practical exercises and some quite concrete and businesslike equipment, like hidden pockets, collapsing flowers, and false-bottomed pitchers. But compared to modern technology, the magician's tricks are as nothing. This is an age of space shuttles and microsurgery. We are too sophisticated now for rabbits and doves that emerge from top hats. With the primary exception of young Henning, a magician today cannot pull a career out of the air.

OPPOSITE, ABOVE:

The technique and showmanship Doug Henning displayed in his imaginative versions of traditional illusions made him a sensation first on Broadway and then on national television in an era when magic acts had become obsolete. Perhaps his best trick was success itself.

OPPOSITE, BELOW LEFT:

David Copperfield built his Broadway act on good looks and sensuality—that is, a modern version of the traditional, Mandrake type of magician. The Dracula-like sensuality of those moustached wizards was not lost on Copperfield.

OPPOSITE, BELOW RIGHT:

The magicians have abandoned their traditional costume of top hat and tails in an effort to modernize the profession and to redeem it. Most contemporary magicians, those that are left, work in dark suits, although some perpetuate the flamboyant taste of the past—and why not? After all, magic acts harken back to sorcery. Doug Henning wears colorful, hippie-style costumes, and in this photograph Siegfried (left) works in circus-ringmaster regalia.

THE STAND-UPS

Humor can be dissected but the thing dies in the process. It has a certain fragility, an evasiveness which one had best respect. Essentially, it is a complete mystery.

E. B. WHITE

The stand-up comic is a funnyman stripped of his baggy pants and makeup, denied the slapstick and the pratfall, laying his wits on the line before an audience of skeptics. The show he puts on is all talk—the mind as an act.

"Act," in its first definition, is a verb. The comedian is the only performer who doesn't *do* anything. What he does is himself, as we do ourselves in daily social intercourse; selves that cope, even charm, so as to get by in life, and in work, and in love. The comedian does himself-the-act as a public ritual. He claims that a funny thing happened on the way to the club; or that he was with no lady, he was with his wife. The audience understands that he is just joking but goes along with the conceit, accepting the fiction as its contribution to the entertainment transaction. Whether it continues to accept what the comic offers depends on his ability to keep what is nonsensical plausible. That is the equation of the humorous.

The comic is usually an ordinary fellow—neither good-, bad-, nor funny-looking, except for comediennes, who are traditionally unattractive. Audiences accept good-looking singers, acrobats, jugglers, and magicians. They are not threatening. A comedian dares an audience to keep from laughing and, when working in the nightclub style, he can be quite hostile. Were he good-looking, he would have almost no chance of success because audiences know that attractive people can hurt. Too, attractiveness would be inconsistent with an act that, at core, is attempting to prove that charm can win affection and attention. The idea is to amuse the audience and win it over without the use of anything but the mouth. That is the "look, no hands" of the stand-up.

The difference between a monologist and a stand-up comedian is the difference between a theologian and a Holy Roller. The concern is the same, but one approaches it with dispassion and the other with headlong hysteria. Vaudeville's monologist was devoted to sobriety and eloquence because he was distancing himself from the low comics of the honkytonks. Dignity was his costume and formality his routine. His offspring, the stand-up in the saloon, however, was a desperado, a con man shot into the arena like a rooster in a cockfight. The fellow's aggressive-defensive stance could not have been more effectively designed to provoke resistance. The spotlight was there, he trotted into it and was *on*. The battle for survival had no preliminaries, no warm-up. At mere arm's-length from his audience, the fellow had to come out slugging, for it was either slaughter them or die, and silence was the dreaded judgment, the resonant and echoingly mute announcement that a joke was unfunny. Only a wisecrack like Jackie Mason's "I never saw dead people smoke before" could cut that tension.

OPPOSITE:
Eddie Murphy spectacularly demonstrated the volatile nature of modern show business as he shot in only a couple of years from the Comic Strip, a beginners' club in Manhattan, to the "Saturday Night Live" television show, and then to head-rattling stardom. Despite his success in movies and his popularity as a television sketch comedian, Murphy is at heart a stand-up and has regularly returned to concert stages for the invigoration of performance before live audiences.

ABOVE:
Alan King

Vaudeville's monologists had been raconteurs. They told leisurely anecdotes and outright jokes. The stand-up in the saloon was part of a newer, faster world. He had to create patterns of humor, spin comic filigrees in the smoky air, play upon the audience until the smiles could be parlayed into heady and uncontrollable laughter. This might involve weaving the most bizarre narrative tapestries, but if the comic was rolling, then for the length of his routine the audience would roll with him. Before absurdism became familiar in drama, stand-up comics were trad-

"Sam, you made the pants too long,"
rasped Joe E. Lewis, ever the
irresponsible and irrepressible imp,
at his headquarters, New York's
Copacabana.

Jimmy Durante was neither a stand-up nor a sketch comic. His singing was funny, his looks were funny, and his act was simply to be adorable. From the start he was a legend.

ing in it. Without any pretentions to art or culture they were night-flying to fancy in wondrous and scary solos.

These kamikazes of show business were bred in the saloons while radio was in the process of eliminating the vaudeville monologists. Those elegant raconteurs had escaped the ethnic comedy and fright wigs of early vaudeville only to stand unwanted by this new and ironically *verbal* medium.

In 1935 no less a monologist than "The Great Faysie" was reduced to hosting an amateur night at Hollywood's Trocadero nightclub. "Frank Fay and His Undiscovered Stars of Hollywood," it was called, but the main attraction was neither Fay nor his undiscovered stars. Rather, customers came in hope that such moviefolk as his ex-wife, Barbara Stanwyck, would be in Fay's audience. Trouble was, those who had suffered from his arrogance and cruelty were rather enjoying Fay's sorry times, and there wasn't much of an audience in the Trocadero on the landmark evening when Joe Lewis strolled on stage to introduce the era of the saloon comic.

Lewis's history was melodramatic. Ten years earlier he had been a singer-monologist nicely launched on the speakeasy circuit. In 1925 he had summoned up the nerve to quit the first steady job he had ever enjoyed as an entertainer—a year spent as master of ceremonies at a Chicago club called The Green Mill—for a run at the competitive New Rendezvous that not only included more money but provided a chance to escape the mobsters who were his employers. Accepting the offer did not endear Lewis to those gentlemen, and he was warned, "You'll never live to open."

The New Rendezvous was jammed for his opening night, November 2. It was the kind of audience that watched suicide leaps. Word of Lewis's imminent demise had obviously gotten around. The room was ringed with Chicago police as the comedian walked on stage, a red carnation in the satin lapel of his tuxedo. He would always work in formal clothes.

ABOVE:
Nightclub entertainment was personal. As when jesters played for kings, the experience was nose-to-nose. Doodles Weaver's act involved eccentric singing voices. Up close it was odd.

BELOW:
In 1932 at Harlem's Cotton Club, Cab Calloway sang and pranced in front of his orchestra, anticipating the bandleader-as-performer by a decade. Working musicians tend to be quiet, letting their instruments speak for them, and Calloway's extroversion would remain unusual.

Later, all comics would. The waiters tiptoed through the room, cringing in anticipation of sudden gunfire. Lewis began his monologue. Everyone in the room seemed to flinch whenever a dish was dropped. It was not an atmosphere conducive to comedy, yet nothing untoward happened. In fact nothing happened for a week. Then, Lewis's throat was cut from ear to ear and he was left for dead.

Ten years later, his face scarred and twisted into a permanent grin, his voice a croak, he was trying again, but strictly as a comic, for he could hardly sing. He was trying to make a comeback at that shabby amateur night run by a demoralized Frank Fay, who was not getting many laughs with his torch songs for Barbara Stanwyck.

Lewis finally came on for his spot, on visibly quaking legs. It had been years since he faced an audience, and the things he used to do no longer were working. He fidgeted, put a hand in one pocket and then took it out, leaned against the piano. He lighted a cigarette. All of this, designed to create a casual impression, instead revealed a man patched together with bravura, and audiences do not laugh at nervous comedians. They prefer their martyrs brazen.

After the show, the owner of the Trocadero spared the distraught Lewis none of these observations and yet insisted on the completion of the full week's engagement. Lewis went on to play the Trocadero for fifty-nine consecutive weeks, taking over the master-of-ceremonies assignment from Fay. Unerringly he seemed to choose the most gifted amateurs—Deanna Durbin, Martha Raye, Tony Martin, Judy Garland, Mary Martin. His voice grew stronger, the rasp no longer interfering with his intelligibility. From the handicap he created a unique stage persona. He would later say, "I'm a lucky bum. If I hadn't been cut up I would have been just another comic. The knife sharpened my brain, made me slow down too, improved my delivery."

As the entertainer in the image of his audience, the scarred and vocally maimed Lewis reflected the wising up of America, its transformation from a naive and provincial society to a cynical, urban one. His philosophical acceptance of the assault reflected the hoodlum mentality that generally characterized nightclubs, lending them a heartless and illicit glamor.

This second career progressed swiftly. "I'm not Joe Louis the boxer," he would begin, "so stop fighting me already." They loved it. He moved on to the Chez Paree in Chicago and an audience attracted to late nights, bright lights, flashy girls, and famous names from sports, show business, and the underworld. Entering to his theme music, "Chicago (That Toddlin' Town)," he was the charming wastrel, a man-child happily wallowing in every working stiff's dream—a world of betting, broads, and booze. There were limits to his decadence, however. He never stooped to the sanctimonious hypocrisy that characterized later saloon comics. They might mutter about the good Lord after an evening of crudeness. Lewis would just head for the craps game.

His trademark was a glass of Ambassador's Scotch and the racing toast "It's post time," and audiences delighted in his amoral, cynical, and hedonistic tone. To them, there was a new and refreshing candor in Joe E. Lewis (he added the initial to distinguish himself from Joe Louis, although he would insist he'd borrowed it from the movie actress Lizabeth Scott). Thus originated not only the saloon comic but the saloon-style entertainer, the wise guy in the tuxedo who dominated floor shows for the next several decades, from Frank Sinatra to Sammy Davis, Jr. Where if not in Lewis would Dean Martin have found such happy inspiration?

Lewis's act was strictly of and for nightclubs. He seldom worked in radio, having a heartfelt contempt for its family style, which he considered unfit for adult consumption. On the rare occasion that he did accept a guest spot, his material usually misfired because it targeted the wrong audience and he could not bring himself to pander to the virtuous. Lewis would not work in the movie-presentation houses either. The grind at those screen- and stage-show palaces was unsuited to his sleeping habits and he didn't need the money. By war's end, he was the dean of stand-ups, the highest-paid entertainer in American nightclubs, earning five thousand dollars a week at the Copacabana, on East Sixtieth Street in New York City. Those were the golden years of American bistros. Concrete and neon meccas rose from the marshes and the deserts: twin El Dorados in Miami Beach and, in the West, Las Vegas.

Nightclubs meant more than drinking and watching a floor show. They symbolized what would later be called a "life style." "Cafe society" was now a metaphor for a middle class freshly released from wartime proscriptions and prewar class distinctions. The nation had entered World War II a farm-oriented, moralistic society intimidated by the culture of Europe. It was emerging as the watchman of the world. With our system triumphant, confident of our righteousness and strength, having attained a healthy standard of living but still without the culture or maturity quite to handle it, how could we not be brash, materialistic? Joe E. Lewis was this nightclub world incarnate, and, though ascent and eclipse lay ahead in Las Vegas, for the moment he held court in the Mount Olympus of saloons, the Copacabana. That was where every act in every tank-town club and provincial hotel aspired to. Comedians sweated through nasty audiences and miserable conditions with this one dream, and goal, and certainty in mind: the Copa was but a joke away.

In the years to follow, those acts successful enough to play the Copacabana would defer to Lewis: Frank Sinatra, Danny Thomas, Lena Horne, Billy Eckstine, Nat Cole, Eddie Fisher, Dean Martin and Jerry Lewis, Tony Martin, Sammy Davis, Jr., Peter Lind Hayes and Mary Healy. Only Joe E. Lewis could open the Copa's season in the fall, and he would get top pay. That was not mere respect. Saloon performers owed their very trade to him.

His style was recklessly cheerful but had an underlying hostility that would influence other cabaret performers. Lewis was perfectly capable of silencing a noisy critic with a modest comic device ("Please sir, watch your language. There are musicians present"), but more likely, he would be abusive ("Are you the victim of sex experiments?"); or he might even walk over to the offending customer, pick up a drink, and throw it in the fellow's face. Drunk or misguided hecklers could receive tongue-lashings far more severe than they deserved or than was necessary to silence them. Perhaps the explanation lies in the psychological profile of a typical comedian—a physically and mentally unexceptional person who has long felt inadequate and unloved; a person needing attention but lacking the conventional skills for getting it (academic, financial, artistic, athletic); a person with a lifetime of pain chits to cash in. Being funny can release and resolve this hostility through a burst of ego reward: the joke, the laugh. And since every laugh is potentially scornful (laugh with me? laugh at me?), the comedian is always abutting the self-contempt so close to home. His act, then, is thoroughly, and consistently, and brutally engaged with rejection.

"Please forgive me for drinking onstage," Lewis would say, "but it's something I like to do while getting drunk." There was a terror there, a comedy of self-destruction. "I know you're wondering about the cane," a limping Lewis once told his audience. "Yesterday afternoon I went

Phil Silvers, a sketch comic rather than a stand-up, graduated from the burlesque stage to the movies. He and another ex-burlesquer, Rags Ragland, had put together an act and got themselves booked into the Copacabana when Ragland suddenly died. Frank Sinatra stepped in as emergency comic.

over to Dean Martin's house to play some checkers. We drank some hot chocolate, then put on some Lawrence Welk records. That's when I spotted this spider on the ceiling. Without thinking, I stepped on it. That's how I happened to hurt my leg."

Lewis was to do for Las Vegas what Jack Benny had done for radio and what Milton Berle was in the process of doing for television: establish the franchise. He single-handedly gave the desert gambling resort status among high rollers. When he began playing the El Rancho Vegas Hotel in 1951 he brought cachet. By the time he was through, the strip of flash

in the desert had become America's Sin City. One hotel opened after another and hired top stars to perform in their great entertainment rooms at salaries that nightclubs elsewhere could not match, for the gambling casinos subsidized the floor shows and it was not necessary for the food and liquor receipts to carry the star freight. The Copacabana was paying Lewis five thousand dollars, while El Rancho Vegas was giving him twenty-five thousand. Entertainer loyalty could not be relied upon indefinitely, and it would only be a matter of years before the nightclub business went out of business.

Dreaming in the dark, a host of young comics was preparing for that business, a brazen and fearless brigade of tuxedoed, cigarette-smoking wise guys. These would-be Joe E. Lewises were to find other venues. Buddy Hackett would ultimately become a lewd panda rolling on stage at a gambling casino; Alan King, fit and handsome, would stroll out to confront his Westbury Music Fair audience with the aplomb of an insurance executive; the black sheep among these saloon tyros, Lenny Bruce would abandon the fast crowd to play to intellectuals, wearing jeans as pale as his troubled face. These and the other stand-ups following Lewis's star were not as diverse as first it might seem. They were New York boys mostly, and most of them, like Lewis, were driven by a street urge to be funny. They were sidewalk survivors living by their wits. "Funny" had streetcorner prestige because it was related to survival and bravado. "Funny" rode on wheels of attack.

The funniest among these fellows went to a curious school for comics:

Low comedy was not the nightclub crowd's cup of tea. The broadest any comedy act got was the Ritz Brothers, who were the smart money's version of the Three Stooges. Cafe headliners through the 1940s, they were a versatile team of zanies who could sing and tap dance and do fast-paced comedy routines.

a school tucked away in the Catskill Mountains of New York State. Most middle classes seem to be summer-swarmers. Parisians go to the south of France, Londoners to the beaches of Spain. In the decade before World War II and in the years to follow, the Jewish middle class of New York City went to "the mountains." The reference was not exactly to the Catskill Mountains, a range of gentle hills, the highest rising just above four thousand feet. More precisely, "the mountains" meant a sizable group of resort hotels, family camps, and bungalow colonies clustered around the towns of Liberty and Monticello about ninety miles north of New York City. The only topography significant to *these* mountains was the height of the waiters' chutzpah and the depth of the dessert menus, for such resorts catered to vacationing families in search of Kosher-style food and a Kosher-style atmosphere. The area came to be known as the Borscht Belt and it was said that the road leading there had a center stripe of sour cream.

Inevitably, entertainment was offered at these holiday resorts. It began on makeshift stages set up in the dining rooms after Saturday dinners. The audiences sat on folding chairs. The lighting and sound systems were primitive. The headliner was given ten dollars for a performance and a week's room and board. If he was already staying at another hotel, then he was paid a flat twenty-five-dollar fee.

As the area became more popular, some of the larger hotels built barn-like structures to house the shows. These were called "cassinos," after a card game played in the halls in the afternoons. By the outbreak of World War II, even the most modest bungalow colony was presenting a comedian at a Saturday-night show. After this casual start, the Catskills became a showcase for nightclub entertainers, the minor leagues for the saloon singers and comedians who would be the stars of the 1950s and 1960s.

Often these entertainers began as waiters or busboys, doubling as "tummlers" (a Yiddishism for someone who is playful, a clown). The tummler in a Catskill Mountains resort hotel was a daytime entertainer whose job it was to distract the guests between the gargantuan meals that were the hotels' main attraction. Most guests spent the days either anticipating or digesting them. Tummlers would make merry at poolside,

Alan King was the closest thing to a raconteur that the Catskills produced. Not unlike the gentlemen monologists of vaudeville, King appealed as a decent and intelligent fellow who could point out the humorous side of everyday life.

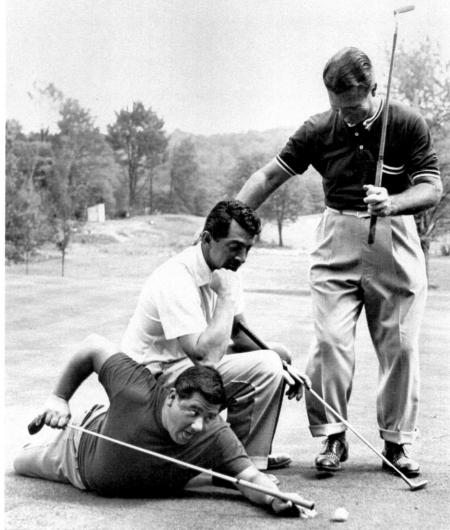

ABOVE:
Catskills resorts followed the lead of
Las Vegas hotels in replacing relatively
intimate traditional nightclubs with
large-capacity showrooms such as the
Imperial Room of the Concord Resort
Hotel.

BELOW:
A Catskills hotel publicity shot: from
right to left, golf pro Jimmy Demaret
with nightclub headliners Dean Martin
and Buddy Hackett

if necessary jumping in fully clothed. In short, they did whatever was necessary to divert the guests from the pangs of hunger or heartburn. This called for a manic energy that later characterized the antics of former tummlers Danny Kaye, Mel Brooks, and Jerry Lewis. Tummlers, the descendants of the minstrels and court jesters, are overdue for medical study.

In later and more pretentious times, the tummler, born again as "social director," would amuse the guests in more refined ways, but while games of Simon Says and finger-painting classes may have appealed to the more culture-conscious hotel owners, such diversions were unworthy of the true tummler, and his moment of glory was onstage in the nighttime show, introducing a comic or—dreams realized—as the comic introduced.

The comedy that worked in the mountains could not always be brought down to the nightclubs in the cities. Comedians can't resist tailoring material. Laughs, always torn from an audience, tear easier when the jokes are local, lewd, and ethnic. In the Catskills, a comic didn't even have to be Jewish to be *Jewish*.

A pair of black comedians ran into each other at the Red Apple Rest, which was the traditional lunch stop on the long drive to Monticello. "What are you doing here?" one asked the other. "Working the holidays," the fellow responded with equanimity, meaning the fall Jewish holiday season surrounding Rosh Hashanah and Yom Kippur. They sat down at a table and, over bagels and lox, one of these black funnymen asked the other what kind of act he was doing. "Well," the man began, "I open with 'Eli, Eli,' and then I go into 'Bei Mir Bist Du Schoen,' 'Joe and Paul,' 'Rumania-Rumania,' and 'Pincus the Peddler.' Then I do my tribute to Israel and the 'Hatikvah.' I beg off with 'Let My People Go' and do 'The Anniversary Waltz' for an encore." The other fellow stared in disbelief. "You son of a bitch," he finally gasped. "You stole my act." (Anonymous)

The ambitious comedian knew that such parochial material was undesirable in the nightclubs and that only those who developed general (meaning gentile) approaches would be able to join the world beyond this blintze Brigadoon. But the basic training had to come first: the development of the nerve to face an audience, and writing and practicing and rewriting (or buying) material that could get a laugh every ten or fifteen seconds and hold an audience for twenty-five minutes, the length of an opening act.

Borscht Belt audiences were tough. These vacationers were showwise New Yorkers who judged even the greenest novices by professional standards. A lackluster comedian might encounter restless and even brutal audiences who simply stared at him. But the fellow who was funny could count on club work in the fall because New York's booking agents covered the mountains like moss, and the word on a newcomer spread quickly. It was said that comedienne Totie Fields, for instance, had her contract renewed halfway through her first opening night in the Catskills.

As the hotels prospered, some became immense compounds that were open the year round. The most prestigious of these were Grossinger's Country Club and the Concord Resort Hotel. On only a slightly less exalted plane were such country inns as Brickman's Hotel, Brown's Hotel, the Evans, Kutscher's Country Club, and the Anglican hostelries, the Raleigh and the Windsor. Even this was but the tip of the mountains for, with war's end, a boom was on. Americans were climbing into their first new cars in years, to go out and enjoy themselves again. It was the dawn of the saloon entertainer's day, and no matter that this sun rose, with the early show, at 10 P.M.

The comics who sauntered down from the mountains must have seemed brash compared to established comedians like Jack Benny, Burns and Allen, Edgar Bergen, and Fred Allen, and to such radio funnymen as Bob Hope, Danny Thomas, and Jackie Gleason. These newcomers were certainly gaudier than their predecessors, but then postwar America was gaudy. Ruralism and Protestantism were no longer social imperatives. Vaudeville's Jewish comics had affected ministerial speaking styles, but war had freed the country's minority groups for diversity and the city boy could be himself. Joe E. Lewis's time had come. Thus were born the feisty, fast-talking saloon stand-ups, their punch lines adorned with rim shots from the drummer: Buddy Hackett, Alan King, Lenny Bruce; such hard-driving comedians as Jan Murray, Red Buttons, Jack Carter, Dean Martin and Jerry Lewis, Don Rickles, "Fat" Jack Leonard, Jackie Miles. They had been learning their trade onstage, from one hotel to the next, playing to a big or noisy crowd one night and a slow crowd the next. Some nights they did more than one performance—an early show in one hotel, a late show somewhere else, perhaps even another at dawn in a third hotel's lounge rather than the big room. Sometimes they opened for a singer or headlined in a bungalow colony. The occasional veteran was in their midst. A big hotel might, for the Fourth of July or Labor Day, engage Milton Berle, Harry Ritz, George Jessel, or Myron Cohen, but home-grown comedians were the rule: young and scrappy newcomers, fast-talking and sharp, honing themselves to professional smoothness by sheer backbreaking practice. They were the winking and finger-snapping imps, street urchins outfitted by Times Square haberdashers, pushy spielers in ruffled shirts and velvet lapels.

There was a future they had in mind, a long-range future in the big city nightclubs: Chez Paree in Chicago, the Latin Quarter in Boston, the Chase Hotel in St. Louis, Versailles and the Latin Quarter in New York, the Miami Beach hotels, and, at the end of the rainbow, New York's Copacabana. But even at first there was work available. These comics, already a notch above the "strips" (strip clubs) that were strictly for raw beginners, could move from the Catskills to the small clubs like Buffalo's Town Casino and Chez Ami, the Three Rivers in Syracuse, La Martinique in New York City, the Vine Gardens in Chicago, Blinstrom's in Boston, the Monticello in Framingham, Massachusetts, the Preview Lounge in New Orleans, the Triton Hotel in Rochester. Why, in Brooklyn alone there were clusters of nightclubs that hired mid-range comedians, clubs with such exotic names as the Capri, the Bali, and the Pink Elephant.

Comedians operate in a field of nervous energy. Abundant work only enriched the heady atmosphere, and the funnymen scrambling for this work were a sociable and rascally lot who dealt with their profession obsessively and compulsively, for in real ways they had made their work into a sexual rite.

The relationship between stand-up comedy and male sexuality is unmistakable. The singer gets the girl with his good looks, but the laugh extracted by the plain man is lustier. Funny-business has traditionally been a male occupation. The occasional female comic is usually impelled to make herself into a travesty of a funnyman, the performing equivalent of a tomboy, one of the guys—Martha Raye, Joan Davis, Imogene Coca, Joan Rivers, Phyllis Diller, Totie Fields. Such gifted comediennes as Fannie Brice, Gracie Allen, Mae West, Elaine May, and Lily Tomlin succeeded in remaining recognizably female but they have been exceptional.

The male comic struts for women's attention. If the men in the audience are not to be alienated, he must win their identification. Seducing

In the early 1950s Dean Martin and Jerry Lewis were the highest paid nightclub act in the country. Never before had a team so perfectly blended high (verbal) and low (physical) comedy. Their wisecracking appealed to urbanites, their pratfalls to provincials. When the team split up, Lewis's low comedy lost the balancing effect of Martin—and it showed.

with humor, after all, is nothing new ("Make me laugh and I'm yours"), and the grand tradition of dirty jokes reveals the basic tie between comedy and sex. The comedian is a homely peacock, a would-be frog prince, a hero in female eyes for having risked and won in the terrifying arena of the floor show.

The innumerable accounts of sex-on-the-run between comedians and backstage dancers, chorus girls, and strippers—accounts often puerile and sometimes pathetic—combine to create a professional image: comedians making love as fast as they rattle off jokes, grabbing girls in the alleys between shows; desperate for love—blind and groping, reaching, grabbing, much as they do for laughs. Their acts are sexual lures. Frank Fay, the suave matinee idol; Bob Hope a sharpie, the traveling salesman; Alan King, the paternal figure; Woody Allen, boyish and intellectual; Buddy Hackett, cute; Lenny Bruce as Peck's Bad Boy. All these are familiar seduction approaches and even when the ploy is one of helplessness, it communicates a machismo, for it is surrounded by the glamorous aura of show business. Comics get their girls. Funny has always been sexy and in the spotlight it is probably all but irresistible.

The sexual energy that impelled the performance of the fast-talking nightclub comedian (how far, after all, is a seduction line from a carnival spiel?) was short-circuited by television. A stand-up's aggressiveness and sexuality proved harsh and even frightening on the home screen. Television invited the lower-keyed performer, and better suited to this intimate medium were such understated monologists as Bob Newhart, Bill Cosby, George Gobel, and the dazzlingly weird Jonathan Winters. For the most part, they played Thurberesque family men—with amusing eccentricities, but family men nevertheless. They were not of the cities (a euphemism for Jewish) because television was a nationwide medium. They did not cater to the mood of the nightclub but, rather, to a split-level Middle American consciousness: formica over flesh. *That* was the real television network, a coast-to-coast mental suburb. The cigarette and highball glass of the naughty saloon gave way to the milkshake of the Eisenhower era, and there were no dirty jokes on television.

Following an initial flirtation with variety entertainment, television programmers—like radio programmers before them—discovered that soloists did not best suit the medium. Home audiences did not want to be confronted. They wished to be unobserved, to look in on something that was not looking back at them, and so television monologists did not endure unless (like Danny Thomas or Bob Newhart or Bill Cosby) they found a niche in situation comedies. Several sketch comedians of genuine artistry did develop on television: Sid Caesar, Jackie Gleason, Ernie Kovacs. But they could not work toe-to-toe with an audience—none performed successfully in person, or even just facing the studio audience. Among those monologists who became popular in the first wave of television variety-programing, only Alan King managed to extend his career to live performance, and he had developed his technique in the Borscht Belt and merely rubbed a goyish television patina on his satiny and professional nightclub technique. King, in fact, was probably the smoothest monologist since the heyday of Frank Fay and Jack Benny.

A recurrent theme of this book is the entertainer as a reflection of his time. The funnymen of the 1950s were products of a homogenized and wary McCarthy-era America. They were restrained performers who shrank from the stand-up's traditionally hostile challenge, his death-defying courage, his sexual energy. They were hardly the macho rascals of the nightclub floors. But the following decade was contrastingly active, hot, and energetic. That mood, too, found reflection in comedians' styles.

OPPOSITE:

Jackie Gleason was another brilliant sketch comic who had trouble with stand-up routines. He attempted to sidestep his discomfort by doing monologues in character, here for instance as "Joe the Bartender," an act he created for television. It didn't work.

ABOVE:

Like Will Rogers, Mort Sahl drew his material from the newspapers; in fact, he carried a furled newspaper on stage with him as a prop. Sahl spared neither major American political party his gibes. He was one of the first comedians to exploit the college market, playing university auditoriums, where his educated and sophisticated humor was likely to be appreciated.

RIGHT:

"My mother tried to kill herself with an overdose of Mah-Jongg tiles. Many members of my family are eccentric. My wife was an immature woman. I'd be in the bathroom taking a bath and she would walk right in and sink my boats." Woody Allen's stage persona— a lusty Jewish intellectual who is well-adjusted to his neuroses—was complemented by his stage style —restless and aggressively defensive. Through sheer funniness, Allen made an audience feel that it was on his own high intellectual level. As a movie director and writer, Allen keeps this stage character of his alive on film but he no longer works as a stand-up comic.

The Stand-ups

The John F. Kennedy years inspired idealism, respect for intelligence, and vitality in the country, and the energy flow continued after his assassination into the Vietnam years of unrest, protest, and rebellion. With the issues of war and race firing up the country, a group of thinking-man's comedians arrived, and their material was political, psychological, and socially conscious. Enough Americans were by then college-educated to support novel and bright comedians like Mort Sahl, Dick Gregory, Mike Nichols and Elaine May, Shelley Berman, Woody Allen, Robert Klein, and the Smothers Brothers. Lenny Bruce plunged down from the Catskills, surreal in his daring. Intelligence and wit came into style. Will Rogers, who had found that treating mass audiences with respect, as if they were intelligent, brought out their respectability and intelligence, might not have been pleased to find his successors scorning America's vast majorities and its traditional values. But then, the comedians of the 1960s and early 1970s were trying to be both rebellious and popular—quite a trick. They had to work on tougher turf than Rogers had known, in a show business that had been reconditioned by saloon entertainers; moreover, Las Vegas had wiped out the nightclub, and so these performers had to find new stages.

Of all the "sick" comedians who startled America in the late 1960s, none had a more deviant humor than Lenny Bruce. He satirized sacred cows from organized religion to presidents; he imagined Hitler in show business and stewardesses jettisoning infants from overloaded airliners. He used obscene language when other comics dared no more than "darn" and "heck"—and Bruce took off at them too. Yet if his material was radical, his delivery betrayed a schooling in the Catskills resorts, for he was as sharp and urban as any fast-talking stand-up. Then he became a cause célèbre. Intellectuals egged him on, and law enforcers rushed to protect the public from him. Possessed merely of a sensationally funny spirit and a need to make people laugh —and to be paid for it—Bruce was pushed to a sorry and dreadful end. Nightclub owners do not look for police trouble, and as they shied away from him Bruce's career collapsed. So did his front. Revealed was the frightened bravado of the essential comedian. Hounded, prevented from working until he was professionally destroyed, he retreated into narcotics and died of a heroin overdose. Not many years later, Eddie Murphy was using language and material that would have made Lenny Bruce seem an innocent—and that he had been.

Those new stages were college auditoriums (work pieced together in one-night stands—the "concert tour") or the handful of intimate clubs aimed at the college crowd, such as New York's Village Vanguard or San Francisco's Hungry i (*i* for "intellectual").

The thinking-man's comedians thrived on live audiences, and their comedy was not so recondite as to be ungraspable. After all, it is not in the comedian's interest to be obscure. As long as their audiences got the joke (and here they were no different from George Jessel or Bob Hope), Mike Nichols and Elaine May could joke about Béla Bartók, and Woody Allen about Kierkegaard. Their audience got it, and laughed in person. Theirs was a flesh-and-blood constituency, though a dwindling one, for America had, for the most part, turned to electronic showmen.

These wits opened doors for stand-ups who worked in original and even eccentric ways. George Carlin, Robin Williams, Eddie Murphy, Steve Martin, Lily Tomlin, and Richard Pryor introduced a personal comedy that met the highest standards of show business, and yet they

could deal with matters of substance or more adult whimsy. They found ways to combine fantasy and invention with sure technique. How the delightful and cockeyed Rodney Dangerfield fit into this group was both inexplicable and delicious.

Today, the shrinking market for live performers and the lure of movie and television money quickly removes the gifted from live audiences. The older saloon comics work the few remaining casino nightclubs, but the young and exciting comedians seldom face up to audiences. Soon face-to-face may be gone and the dreaded last laugh will have been had. There are many small comedy clubs around the country, clubs that allow young comedians to test their material and themselves, but to what end? These clubs pay virtually nothing and there are no paying clubs to move up to. Except for the almost extinct talk show there is only one place in television to aspire to—situation comedy, and that is no place for the stand-up. Was it symbolic that the gifted, weird Andy Kaufman went from stand-up, to a television series, to a premature death?

It may be that all our jesters are about to die, and that would be tragic. The mortal who teeters on the edge of disaster with just a mind and a mouth to keep his balance is speaking for all of humanity. More than the soldier or statesman, he is the hero of the mortal crowd, the symbol of human optimism, good cheer, and endurance. If this jester has in fact had the last laugh then that laugh will surely have been the worst.

ABOVE:
"Feuds" were good business in radio. They created continuity and provided a rich lode of harmless insult comedy in a medium that devoured material. One of the two most famous fictitious feuds in radio was Bing Crosby's with Bob Hope. (Jack Benny's with Fred Allen was the other.)

LEFT:
Rich Little is doing Richard Nixon. Impressionists were among the last of vaudeville's variety artists to go under. One performer seeming to be another is an act that has the appeal of wonder and an element of magic.

OPPOSITE, ABOVE LEFT:
Dick Gregory was a comedian with a conscience. As the era of black assertion began, he found it trivial to entertain in nightclubs. Instead, he devoted himself to marches and demonstrations and went on a hunger strike on behalf of black rights.

OPPOSITE, ABOVE RIGHT:
Vulgarity and toilet humor in Las Vegas: Charlie Callas at the Landmark. An opening act or lounge comic might resort to such gross business, but he had to be a desperate man.

OPPOSITE, BELOW LEFT:
Vulgarity and toilet humor in Las Vegas: Godfrey Cambridge at the Aladdin

OPPOSITE, BELOW RIGHT:
Richard Pryor was cheerfully sardonic from the start, dealing with the pimps, drug dealers, and winos who were fixtures in the world of growing up black. Pryor was unprejudiced in his disrespect, and behind his broad-reaching good humor was the mind of a disciplined performer and writer.

ROGER RIDDLE
Working Comic

You go on stage, you work the worst clubs, you live in terrible hotels, sometimes don't work at all. You're emotionally naked, you're psychologically rejected. Nobody goes through life like a comedian does.

ROGER RIDDLE

The stars are only a few of the working entertainers who carry on the torch, what is left of the flame. The larger group of this honorable breed does not plunge into stretch limousines; is not surrounded by flunkies; has no private planes, no bodyguards, no television specials. These are the fellows with a patent-leather shoe in the spotlight and a sandal on line at a Burger King, which was where I stood with Roger Riddle one warm September evening in 1984, on the way to a play-date at Brown's Hotel in the Catskills.

He handed the bandleader sheet music for "The High and the Mighty" and "Auld Lang Syne," the accompaniments he wanted toward the end of the act. He knew better than to ask for music earlier than that. Playing for dancing, the musicians expected a coffee break during the comedy routine. In fact, the bandleader's first question was how much time did they have for coffee?

Riddle has never appeared on television, in Las Vegas, or in Atlantic City. Virtually unknown except to the agents and managers who handle the day-to-day entertainers for the Catskills resorts, he is a professional who works almost two hundred engagements a year, almost all of them one-night stands, and who earns between seventy thousand and one hundred thousand dollars a year.

Scores of comedians like Riddle are supported by the Catskills hotels. The flashy euphony of their names does not (as intended) conceal but, rather, betrays their origins and their stations—and tells still more about them. The names suggest men who have bought a show-business dream: Dick Capri, Freddy Roman, Lee Allen, Lenny Rush, Marty Brill, Sal Richards, Vic Arnel, Roger Riddle. They are names without families, names born of nightclubs in Pittsburgh and St. Paul, Montreal and Fort Worth. Unknown, these fellows do not trot on stage to fanfares and applause. They are perennially up-and-coming, the journeymen of show business, flashy wise guys with savvy and street smarts, focusing their energies, their physical bodies, their wits, and crumpled bits of material upon the audiences of two hundred, five hundred, or even nine hundred vacationers spending saved money, vacationers who get a show with the price of a room and have nothing to lose by slamming an exit door in a comic's face. If being a comedian is the toughest and loneliest and most frightening thing a performer can do (and that is one thing virtually all performers agree on), nothing is tougher, lonelier, or more frightening than doing it as a journeyman. They are bruised but resilient, the gallant facing the lions with black ties and gags.

Riddle's dressing room is a bare cubicle the size of a monk's cell. He can hear the opening act vocalizing next door. Tonight it is to be a tiny, middle-aged, blonde soprano who can also belt from the chest. Her act is twenty-five minutes, as all opening acts more or less are. Riddle goes on at ten-thirty. He isn't nervous. At fifty, he has spent half his life in show business, the last six years doing the same act. He knows it works.

Roger Rosenthal (alias Riddle) was born in Manhattan into a troubled but well-to-do family, his father a Park Avenue surgeon. A college clown, he took a summer job as a tummler at a resort hotel and then, as "Jolly Roger," developed a kiddie act. Weeknights he emceed at strip joints until he talked his way into a four-month stint on a cruise ship. "I didn't know what I was doing, but I'd get away with junk," he remembers. "Polish jokes, gay jokes, ship jokes. Like, 'My room is so small I put the key in the door and broke the porthole.'"

After six years of such apprenticeship, he landed his first respectable booking in a New England hotel. Feeling that he was on his way at last, he brought along a current girlfriend, sat her in the front row, and then strolled on stage, beaming and quick. He had material. He had been developing it over the years in other strip joints, other cruise ships. Now he began. The Polish jokes, the gay jokes, the ship jokes. Elegant.

Out of the corner of his eye as he talked and grinned and gestured onstage, he saw the hotel owner walk out of the wings. He continued the act. The audience was dead silent. They stared at him. The owner approached and then, *apologizing* to the customers for the comedian, took Riddle by the elbow and walked him off stage. "You," the man said, "are the worst comedian I have ever, ever had on my stage. Ever seen on *any* stage. You'd better pick another line of work."

On the Catskills hotel circuit, Roger Riddle's dressing room was, more likely than not, a cubicle with a bulb-lined mirror.

As Riddle recalls, still cringing at the memory, "I wept when it happened. My girlfriend was there and I wept. Nobody can describe the pain, after working in a profession for six years (no matter *where*—I was working), and someone who is in a very class situation, with a middle-class audience in a hotel, tells you, 'You're the worst I've ever seen.'"

Actors flee their emotions, comedians show them for laughs.

"I decided he must have been right. That's when I started figuring out what the hell I was doing. To me, the true comedian is the one who can come out and have a character, an attitude, and a point of view. I decided that my attitude was, I was always in pain."

Riddle looks spruce in his mohair tuxedo with its white lining, his blue formal shirt, the crimson handkerchief flaring from his breast pocket. The 1,400-seat nightclub is three-quarters filled, a round room decorated in chandelier, mirror, and whorehouse-red flocked wallpaper. Asking for applause for the orchestra, he excuses the eight musicians and begins talk-

Roger Riddle at the Raleigh Hotel,
1985

ing about his birth, his childhood. "My whole life has been inundated with pain and, with your permission, I would like to share it with you. . . . Why should I suffer alone?"

"Pain," he says with a groan. "Pain" is the litany, and after a while the audience murmurs the word along with him. They are plain people, men in zipper jackets, women in slacks and sweaters. Elderly, undrinking. He pulls the microphone from its clamp and paces the stage.

Riddle is sympathetic toward his fellow comedians. The only one who annoys him is "the cuff-link comic. That's the guy who looks great in his well-cut tuxedo; he can do everything—sings a little, dances a little, he does impressions; he's learned an hour's worth of gags, jokes, *non sequiturs* and one-liners, some funny, some not; he has good timing, the mechanics are impeccable." Riddle goes on, "And the audience says to itself, 'He acts like a comedian and he looks like a comedian so he must be a comedian.' But they don't remember a thing he said."

A compulsive talker, Riddle has other theories. He has no urge to be funny offstage and shakes his head over the curiosity of that. Instead, he has an urge to be serious. He thinks that the difference between an ordinary performer and an *entertainer* is vast and yet simple. "I bet you one day Liberace was onstage, playing the piano as usual, when all of a sudden, for no reason at all, he turned around toward the audience and gave them a big grin and waved at them with one hand while he kept playing the piano with the other. And that was it. He was a showman."

He tells the audience about his mother marrying his stepfather and his father marrying his stepmother and nobody wanting him around. "I never learned to defend myself because my parents sent me to Jewish boarding schools. So nobody fought. They just sued each other." There are other outright jokes. This is, after all, a comedy act. He talks about a doctor "so young his surgical gloves were pinned to his shirt." But also, "I talk about the pain in my life and I even talk about with all the pain and all the sorrow I could die of it. And then I do die. And then not only do I die but after I die I prepare my own funeral. And then I envision somebody delivering my eulogy. I eventually go to heaven."

Delivering this routine is hard work for Riddle. He paces the stage, bending, turning, stretching. The physical strain leaves him awash in perspiration but the effort succeeds. The audience is attentive, even rapt. A stretch in mid-act exaggerates senility for comic pathos. This is risky business under the best of circumstances, and the audience at Brown's is an older audience, making it even riskier. Riddle gets a standing ovation.

He returns to comedy and is winning laughs about every fifteen seconds. After fifty minutes he gets to the funeral section. The band is back in time for "The High and the Mighty." Then he is off, having cut the eulogy and "Auld Lang Syne" because the laughs were steady, and better not to stretch.

The response is warm, the show went well. Nevertheless, Riddle does not stay to mingle with the audience. It pays off in wedding and bar-mitzvah dates, but Riddle can't bring himself to do that. Nor can he fawn over headliner singers who might make him their opening act. Instead, he scrubs off his makeup, changes clothes, and—it is nearly one in the morning—heads toward his car for the two-hour drive back to New York City. His tuxedo is in a garment bag slung over a shoulder. Guests compliment him as he passes. "You're original," one says. "I've seen them all but I've never seen anyone like you before."

Riddle has this repeated for my benefit. "I'm the best," he tells me. "Peerless."

INTERNATIONAL GLITTER

There can be no entertainers' hall of fame, no building with pictures and recordings and memorabilia, no museum with mannequins and preserved costumes. Not even film clips or videotapes can conjure up the vitality and magnetism of the top star in live performance. Such an entertainer is a legend of the moment, his very presence mythic. Every performance is, for every person in every audience, the event of a lifetime.

The greatest of the entertainers are not singers or comedians but showmen. They are the show themselves. Animate phenomena, they are raised to a higher scintillation than most humans; raised to glory and triumph as they come to life in the spotlight. They not only survive but emerge triumphant throughout careers that often endure for decades. In show after show, before infinitely diverse audiences, they prove themselves beyond vogue or nationality. Such stars have no generational boundaries, their styles no moments of fashion. In an era when a television series can create an overnight superstar who will be forgotten next season, we may well be reminded of this marathon of success, this grueling gauntlet. For if every entertainer faces his day of judgment anew at each performance, the international headliner must face it knowing that anything less than greatness will be a letdown.

Popular entertainment seldom travels well. Language is only one reason for its unexportability. Even in countries with a common tongue, communication with an audience can be hindered by slang, patois, even simple accent. But more crucial to communication than even language is a turn of mind, a cultural wavelength. This is at the heart of entertainment, and a turn of mind is usually untranslatable. *That* is why they don't get the jokes.

The international star is rarely a funnyman. Nothing is so parochial as humor. Sid Fields, an adored British music-hall comic, never attempted to work in America, and even those of our stand-ups who did perform abroad, such as Bob Hope or Jack Benny, never reached Englishmen as they did Americans (and Hope was *born* in England). The singer of songs is more likely to transcend cultural boundaries because music is truly universal, but even he must offer more than songs. Maurice Chevalier is a good case in point. His assets were modest. His singing voice, although musical and certainly agreeable, was a light and even raspy baritone. His stage movements and dance steps were slighter still. But in his manner—oh, and in his style—the fellow could not have been more endearing. The entertainer, then, as myth: Chevalier became, for his audience away from France, the epitome of Gallic charm.

He started out as, of all things, an acrobat. Injured in an early accident, he turned to dancing and became successful enough at it to perform regularly in the music halls of Paris. By 1904 he was appearing at the Folies Bergère and there he met the celebrated chanteuse Mistinguett. A romance began and after World War I Chevalier became her dancing

OPPOSITE:
Unashamedly derived from Elvis Presley's act, Tom Jones's blend of slick rock songs and sexy costumes made him a transatlantic drawing card. He was the alley cat of their dreams to older women, and they repaid Jones with flashing cameras and hotel keys tossed onto the stage.

ABOVE:
Judy Garland

partner, but by then he had greater ambitions and added songs to his dancing. "My influence," he would later say, "was the American music hall," by which he meant vaudeville. He came under that influence when he joined Elsie Janis in the 1919 London revue *On the Level, You're a Devil*. There Chevalier developed the manner and the costume that would become his career trademarks: a straw boater and tuxedo, an air of gay sophistication, flirtatiousness, and insouciance.

Within ten years, this French song-and-dance man was a generic "entertainer" on the international circuit. He starred in New York's *Midnight Frolic*, a sophisticated revue that Flo Ziegfeld presented on the New Amsterdam Theatre roof after performances of his *Ziegfeld Follies* had ended in the main auditorium below. Just as Harry Lauder had created the perfect Scotsman, so Chevalier was now the thing itself, the French troubadour. With his crumpled suit, his affectedly awkward pigeon-toed step, and a boater hat lifted in midair, he raised invention to archetype.

> *Every little breeze*
> *Seems to whisper, "Louise."*
> *Birds in the trees*
> *Seem to twitter, "Louise."*

Even his signature songs—"Mimi" by Rodgers and Hart and "My Ideal" by Richard Whiting—seemed singable only by him. He would translate American songs into French ("Isn't It Romantic?") and French ones into English ("Valentina"), and traditionally he concluded each performance with his theme song, "One Hour with You." Mistinguett said, "He put the song over as if he were humming it for his own pleasure, with a rhythm and sureness of touch that took my breath away."

Although Chevalier seemed French from his twinkle to his wink, "What I did," he said, "was mix the American novelty and the old French humor so that even to the French I was something new." But this sweetheart relationship ended abruptly after World War II. Not only was Chevalier accused of having been a Nazi collaborator because he had sung on Radio Paris for the Pétain regime; he was simultaneously criticized as being a Communist sympathizer for having endorsed the antinuclear Stockholm Peace Appeal. To be caught in such an absurd political sandwich would suggest not wrongness or opportunism but political naïveté. The America intimidated by Senator Joseph McCarthy was not, however, disposed to forgive, and the troubadour was denied a United States visa until 1955, when he made a comeback appearance on Broadway.

He worked on a big stage, unpretentiously accompanied by a lone pianist. He ran through his songbook between chats with the audience. Typically, at one evening performance he walked to the edge of the stage and, shielding his eyes from the spotlight, scanned the audience. "Oh," he remarked conversationally, smiling and waving as if at an old friend, "I don't know your name, but I have the impression you are my friend because the first time I sang here in New York, in the Fulton Theatre, you were sitting in the same seat." This was much the sort of thing that Jolson had done thirty years earlier. "And," Chevalier continued, "your wife—I remember her too. Yes. Oh, that's very nice to see you both here tonight. . . . You have not changed at all, you know. Oh, you have got a bit grayer over there—but so am I. I don't know anyone who gets younger each year."

It was an indefinable patter, not humor. It was Chevalier's act, confidential and wry. Producer Billy Rose was captivated. "There's plenty of

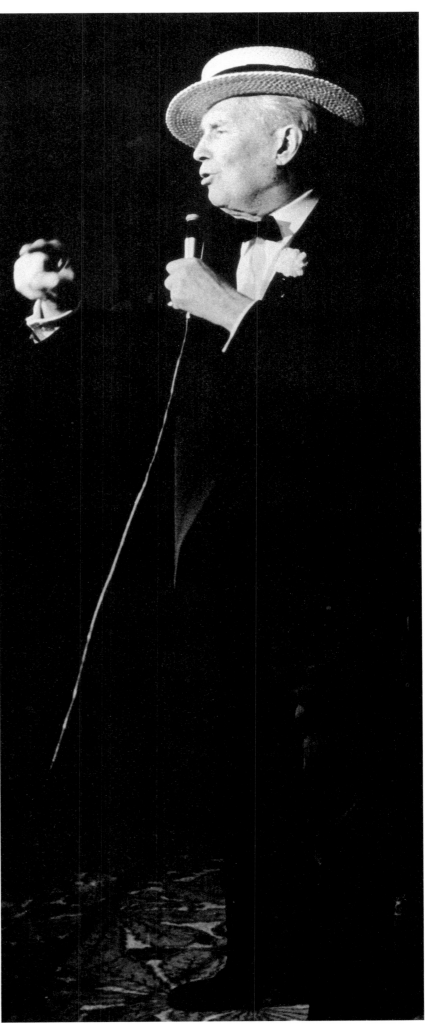

gray under that jaunty straw hat now," he said, "but when he begins to sing, he's still the gay young man of France . . . when Chevalier is on, the other actors might as well be dealing pinochle in the dressing room." But the *New York Times* drama critic Brooks Atkinson, a man of keener political sensibilities, could not in principle accept Chevalier simply as an entertainer. "There is something a little sad," he wrote, "in seeing him again. There are too many ghosts in the wings and backstage." The review did the entertainer no harm, however, and Chevalier played New York regularly and successfully for many years thereafter. Having begun as a romantic figure, Chevalier would conclude his run of fifty years on a note of nostalgia and grandfatherliness. Of all modern performers, only Frank Sinatra can match him in staying power.

Briefer by far was the cabaret career of Marlene Dietrich, and yet thinking of Chevalier calls her to mind both because they were friends and because she too was among the few Europeans to captivate American audiences. There was also a certain formality that they shared onstage, as if a courtesy paid to audiences by visitors from another country, although Dietrich kept her distance to the extent of being remote. She had developed this style as a film actress and it paid off handsomely as a stage manner. Whereas Chevalier was intimate and endearing, she was a figure of icy glamor. She loomed as if out of a mist—dramatic, cool, erotic—snubbing age in an evening gown that revealed every pulse beat on a death-defying youthful body that was well past fifty when she began her in-person career—a career that from the outset was on the international level.

Any great star develops an aura of legend. Audiences gather as if in appointment with history. A performance of Marlene Dietrich's had an even more solemn, ritual-like tone. The audience came to worship her, and without fail the final curtain of every performance brought flower-bearing admirers to her feet. Her biographer Sheridan Morley observed that

while Dietrich's Hollywood contemporaries drifted into elegant postwar obscurity, Dietrich took herself into the theatre, there to become not an actress nor precisely a singer but simply a solo star, able to command a minimum of $5,000 a week for an appearance which was to become one of the great recurring theatrical happenings of the 1950s and 1960s. (*Dietrich*)

She still had longish flaxen hair that tended to slip over one eye, framing her high cheekbones and setting off her alabaster complexion. Pencil-hard eyebrows arched over ice-blue, experienced eyes—but the core of the Dietrich allure lay in her brutally red lips, curling in the trace of a smile. Sneering? Cynical? Hers was the face of moral decadence, beautiful but arrogant and heartless. (Wasn't this a wonderful act?) Her beauty seemed total, her stance as intimidating as her face. Dietrich's costumes were probably more essential to her act than any other singer's, from her signature men's clothes to the famous creation she wore for her Las Vegas debut in 1959, a see-through gown of gauze, dappled with more than two hundred thousand hand-sewn beads, fitted to paint her skin. In a dispatch to the Paris newspaper *L'Etoile*, Paul Tanfield swooned: "She swayed to the microphone with that lubricated walk which is as old as Eve. Her hair was a cascade of spun gold. Her dress fitting closer than close, her figure like a debutante's. Age, Shakespeare said, cannot wither her. He was speaking of Cleopatra but the same goes for Dietrich, the soignée, the indestructible fifty-four-year-old butterfly."

Actually, she was a fifty-eight-year-old butterfly at the time of the Las Vegas debut. Born Maria Magdalene Dietrich in 1901, she was by then

Marlene Dietrich

known simply as "Dietrich" and, with theatrical flair she signed her autograph that way. Dietrich's second career as a performer was to last fifteen years, and her act remained virtually unchanged throughout. Whether at a Broadway theater, a Las Vegas hotel, or the Edinburgh

Danny Kaye had the gestures of a dancer.

Festival in Scotland, she did ninety minutes of songs without pause or intermission. When she spoke, she was brief and when she sang, she hardly moved. Her voice was a growly baritone, her appeal tantalizingly, voluptuously androgynous.

> They call me naughty Lola,
> The wisest girl on earth.
> At home my pianola
> Is played for all it's worth.

The other songs in her repertoire were similarly insinuating, a curious mix of American and European tastes: "La Vie en Rose," "The Laziest Girl in Town," "Falling in Love Again," "The Boys in the Back Room." Her musical director during the 1960s was the young Burt Bacharach, who, faced with developing a song program for a non-singer, framed and presented her with the skill of a true accompanist, sympathetic and supportive. The act was severe, as Dietrich herself was. There was none of the solo singer's usual patter or special material, none of the production values or back-up dancers. The show was Dietrich, only Dietrich, and it brought out the devotee even in intellectuals. The critic Kenneth Tynan, for instance, wrote with melodramatic ingenuousness, "It seemed as if whatever hell you happened to inhabit, she had been there first, and survived."

No performer was ever more an act than Dietrich. Audiences gave her that special tribute of the world-class star: the credit that she was onstage precisely what she was offstage. When Dietrich at seventy-three finally did stop performing, her audiences could not believe that age was the reason, even though the two nasty spills into the orchestra pit that did it were plainly age's fault. Until then, her gallant routine had been nothing less than the defeat of time.

To imagine Marlene Dietrich sitting down to dinner in Paris with Maurice Chevalier and Danny Kaye may seem a star-struck fantasy, yet that is exactly what she was doing when Prince Rainier of Monaco telephoned one evening. Seems a gala was being planned, a little party at the palace, at which, the prince hoped, a favorite entertainer of his wife's might appear. Princess Grace's choice was not Chevalier, nor was it Dietrich. It was Danny Kaye. As Kaye continued to decline the offer, perhaps in trepidation after many years away from live audiences, Rainier's offer rose from ten thousand dollars to twenty-five thousand dollars. And still he refused ("I am having too much fun in Paris to leave now").

Such conversations with such people would have seemed beyond all imagination in the lower-class Brownsville section of Brooklyn where, as David Kaniel Kominsky, Kaye was born in 1913. Kaye set his incredible escape in motion by becoming a tummler at a summer-resort hotel. Better than any other in recent memory, Kaye's international career illustrates the bloodline from the medieval gleoman—troubadour—wandering minstrel to the topflight twentieth-century entertainer.

Kaye's first winter work was as one of "The Three Terpischoreans," a dance act that did not get very far in New York but compensated for that by going all the way to the Far East on a seedy tour. There, an onstage tumble gave him his first laugh, and he was hooked on comedy. Instead of returning home, he went to London as a comedy-dance act, booked for eight weeks at the Dorchester Hotel. For this engagement he assembled special material from numbers he had developed as a tummler, including the song "Dinah."

Only it was not pronounced "Dinah." Oh, it was sung properly. It was even sung endearingly. But the title was pronounced "Deenah," as were all the rhymes, such as "feenah" and "Caroleenah." To compensate for a certain degree of limitation in this number, Kaye sang the second chorus in high-speed double-talk. Summer-resort audiences had enjoyed that somewhat more than did the Dorchester crowd. Another of his tummling numbers was Cab Calloway's "Minnie the Moocher," an audience-participation piece that in Kaye's version also led into double-talk. The Dorchester engagement was not a watershed in the annals of British entertainment.

Unsurprisingly, Kaye found himself back on the resort circuit that summer, and there he met Sylvia Fine while she was helping to write a show called *The Straw Hat Review*. It was brought to Broadway in the enthusiasm of summer, but what had been refreshing and delightful in the mountains in July proved amateurish on Broadway in the fall. After a ten-week run, the revue closed. Surviving were an enthusiastically received Kaye and his newfound writer-wife, Sylvia Fine. Kaye was the discovery of the following season, working at a New York nightclub, La Martinique, and singing his wife's clever and deft patter songs, such as the spoof of French hat-designers, "Anatole of Paris".

Kaye was, then, from the outset an entertainer rather than a mere comedian. His purpose was not to get laughs but to delight. He was unique, and his material would have been leaden in any other hands. Even though the La Martinique engagement was his last personal appearance for many years, he inspired writers to tailor material for him and in that way entertained in solo even while working in musical comedy. For the 1941 Broadway hit *Lady in the Dark*, Ira Gershwin gave him "Tchaikovsky," in which Kaye rattled off the names of scores of Russian composers. But he still had enough of the tummler in him to be restless doing the same show eight times a week. Eddie Cantor, engaged at the time in a musical version of *Three Men on a Horse*, recalled:

Danny played at a theatre next door. He had a break in his show at the time I did a number with six chorus boys. It would have taken Danny a little advance time to plot this one but one night [he] slipped out of his own show, made a split-second change into a chorus boy costume and pranced out on stage behind me. I was singing. As a grace note he took along a banana, which he ate during my routine. My number got laughs it never had before. What was up? I knew something must be happening behind my back. Every time I turned around the banana disappeared. I examined each boy sharply. Funny, I thought; that new chorus boy looks like Danny Kaye. The new chorus boy eyed me mildly with an affectionate look, the sort of look you get from a loving but not too bright cocker spaniel. I looked harder. Danny looked more lovingly and tossed first one foot and then the other, all in perfect timing with my own dance routine and the rest of the chorus. Finally I caught on—it broke up the show—it was too funny—it was a riot. Everyone loved it. (Kurt Singer, *The Danny Kaye Saga*)

Kaye had two distinct careers. His early fame and success rested on a series of movies (*Up in Arms, The Secret Life of Walter Mitty*), in which he played a bumbling innocent. These capitalized on his charm but not on his talents. The telephone call from Monaco may well have played a part in spurring Kaye into his second phase, which reinforced his original impulse to solo as a live entertainer. Simply by chance (or not) he

A rare photograph of Danny Kaye in drag, doing a takeoff of the ultrasophisticated Kay Thompson for a 1948 "Frolic" at the Los Angeles branch of the famous Friars' Club

was vacationing in nearby Cannes at the time of the Monaco gala and he impulsively stopped in at the palace on the night of the party. Recognized and admitted at once, he was introduced and called to the stage, where he performed impromptu and for nothing. Perhaps this reminder of the excitement of a live audience caught hold of him because soon afterward he accepted an engagement at the prestigious London variety theater, the Palladium.

The managing director of this famous house, Val Parnell, was going through a phase of booking American movie stars (Hollywood was suffering from the competition of television, and many famous actors were underemployed). The taste of the Palladium's audiences, unfortunately, was extremely British, and the American performers who ventured on that enormous stage did so at their peril. Just before Kaye arrived, for instance, Mickey Rooney had been unenthusiastically received and, before that, Rita Hayworth had played a calamitous engagement. Popular enough as a movie star, Kaye was virtually unknown in England, at least as a stage performer, when, on February 2, 1948, he stumbled out from the wings in a city where he had flopped only ten years before. (He stumbled out, as the story goes, because, frozen by panic, he had to be shoved.) As Kaye's biographer Kurt Singer describes it, that performance made him a cult figure.

He sang scat songs, told of his trip to England, lamented his fears and thrilled the audience with a voice of surprisingly good quality and a scintillating wit. He jockeyed the mood of the British to the point of seldom-experienced lunacy. He lured the audience to sing with him, to imitate his voices, noises and ugh-ughs. Without a pause for fresh air or sensible syntax he mimicked the Nazis and the Russians.

The audience was completely under his spell. The heartbeat of the performance gathered momentum. There appeared to be no way to break up the show. The audience stood clapping, smiling, laughing, stamping and refusing to go home.

The Royal Family came to see the show, as did Winston Churchill and even the archbishop of Canterbury. "With each new performance," according to Singer, "his popularity grew. A legend of enormous and almost embarrassing proportions was growing." At Kaye's last performance, the English were not about to part with him. He was to remain onstage for two hours, and the audience, at the end, rose and sang "Auld Lang Syne." Next day a newspaper headline lamented, "Our Danny's Gone Away."

In 1950 Kaye participated in an extraordinary benefit show in honor of the late Sid Fields, the beloved English music-hall comedian. The variety bill began at midnight and did not end until five o'clock in the morning. The fifty stars included Orson Welles, Judy Garland, Vivian Leigh, and Laurence Olivier. Even in such company, Danny Kaye was the main attraction. A series of annual visits followed and he became a British institution, a frequent visitor at Buckingham Palace, an intimate of Princess Margaret.

His prestige was now too great for conventional engagements. The showcase he sought was a New York equivalent of the Palladium. He found it in Broadway's Palace Theatre, and the entertainment "concert" he gave there—a solo performance in a theater—proved a pioneering concept, a way for entertainers to play to immense audiences without the distractions—food service, smoke, drunk customers—of nightclubs.

In 1956, when Kaye played an eight-week engagement there, the Palace had long since been abandoned to movies, but it was destined to be regularly rescued from oblivion because of its marketable legend as the stage for greatness. At forty-three, Kaye was still trim and youthful, and though he had never been handsome there was something of the willowy jester about his looks. His lithe, six-foot frame was topped with a head of golden red hair, and his movements were a dancer's, loping and graceful. Aging zanies tend to a barely concealed nastiness symptomatic of an awareness that what they do ill suits an adult. Kaye had little of that. At the Palace he seemed simple and charming. He dressed casually in a sports jacket and contrasting trousers, usually in shades of brown, his preferred color. He sang songs from his films, notably the recent *Hans Christian Andersen*, which many considered his best. With such enchanting Frank Loesser songs as "Inchworm" and "The Ugly Duckling," he reduced adults to children, lullabying them with his sweet and gentle, almost Irish, lyric tenor. A tummler to his fingertips, Kaye

Young, undamaged, and wonderful Judy Garland—never quite five feet tall. Of all the Hollywood stars, she most surely could have made it just as successfully on Broadway.

returned to routines he had done in the Catskills, organizing the audience into sections for participation. Now, with his reputation behind it, the material that had bombed years earlier in Britain worked beautifully.

He ambled to the apron of the stage and sat down, his feet dangling into the orchestra pit. Lighting a cigarette, he confided in the audience, chatting about his daughter, or the English, or (seemingly) whatever happened to pop into his head. He even reminisced about Harry Lauder, plainly aware that the casual act he had developed, with its confidences and anecdotes, and the bond with the audience upon which it rested, bore a startling resemblance to the working style of the great Scotsman.

Kaye had little patience with prepared and rehearsed routines. Even for the most accomplished ad-libber, the hour or so of a headlining act requires organization and polish. The seemingly most casual of acts are as carefully memorized, rehearsed, drilled, and timed as a full-length play. They leave very little room for the impromptu. For Kaye, however, having grown up on improvisation, "the written word doesn't mean a thing," he told biographer Dick Richards. "It's not till I start playing with the words, mouthing them, shaping them with my hands, kicking them around, winking at them, that they begin to excite me."

Kaye's engagement at the Palace was ultimately extended to fourteen weeks, but afterward a kind of retirement was inevitable. He toured the show around the world, but part of any performer's compulsive psychology is perpetually to top himself. Las Vegas hotels could pay his fees, and he played in them, but for Kaye, that was a step down from the prestige of the Palladium and the Palace. It was possible for exotic European stars like Marlene Dietrich and Noel Coward to play Las Vegas comfortably because there was novelty and humor in it, and because the stupendous casino salaries were irresistible to those underpaid and over-taxed Europeans. Danny Kaye, however, must have felt that he needed neither the money nor the nightclub environment. He then devoted himself to the United Nations International Children's Emergency Fund.

Kaye must have served as an example for Judy Garland when, in 1951, she too found her movie career in recession. Like Kaye, Garland had begun as a variety entertainer, in her case in a vaudeville act called "The Gumm Sisters." Her last stage appearance had been in 1938 at New York's Loew's State Theatre, a Times Square presentation house, where between movies she did twenty-five minutes of songs to promote her next release. Though her career problems were complicated by personal troubles, Garland now faced the same frightening question as had Kaye: had movie work drained her of performing blood? Did she still have the drive and energy and magnetism to attract and ignite an audience? Could she sing in person, sing to an audience and connect with them after thirteen years of recording soundtracks in Hollywood? What kind of stage personality would she project now?

America was not the place to find out. If things turned out badly, better badly far away. For Val Parnell of the Palladium, still reveling in Kaye's stupendous success, Garland's possibilities must have seemed limitless. What neither he nor anybody else could have suspected was that Garland's travails—the publicized battles with alcohol and pills and nerves that had broken her film career—would become *the very basis* of her stage act. Audiences were to gather not merely for Garland, the singer, but for Garland, the survivor. It was to be an emotional aerial act with the star risking nervous collapse onstage at each performance.

The audience's role was to be an active one: more than perceiving the risk that was being run, they would also respond to it, not as voyeurs but as participants. Suicide-watching was not a part of it, however, at least

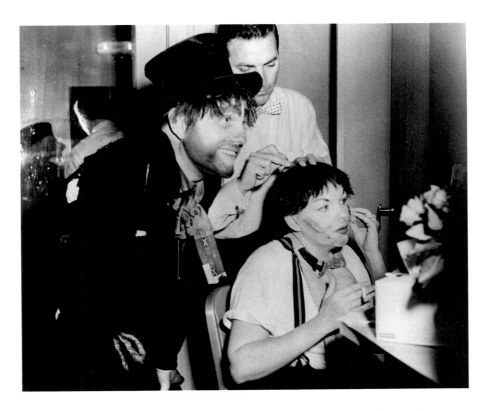

not at the start. At the start, the audience was survival-watching. It would cheer Garland on at every performance as she brought herself to the brink of breakdown. The very timbre of her voice conveyed past and present pain, and the unique gestures that she developed expressed an indomitable spirit transcending terrible agonies. This tightrope act, combined with high-powered songs and the volunteered emotionalism of her audience made for an electric atmosphere.

Garland brought her crisis-studded life to a London that had always been Tabloid City. Indeed, the newspapers had long been filled with stories of her demons, real and imagined. Now at the Palladium she was starting anew, and though it seemed as if she'd been a movie star for a lifetime, she was only twenty-eight. Parnell billed her as "America's Singing Sweetheart," but she was no longer the teenager lost in Oz, the Judy Garland who had so virginally co-starred with Mickey Rooney. She was a strange and striking mixture of ingenue and bag lady, a young woman brought low by circumstance and emotional ogres.

On opening night at the Palladium, the orchestra struck up the overture, a medley of songs associated with Garland. The volume and tempo and intensity of the music seemed to build as the star's appearance grew imminent. When the orchestra segued into "Over the Rainbow," the audience rose to its feet, reminded of the innocent girl, her promise, her broken dream—Garland's life story as movie script. Cheering and applause had built during the overture and now intensified. As Lorna Smith described the scene in *Judy with Love*, before Garland even appeared, the audience was in a state of frenzy, a state that fed on itself.

Making a nervous entrance [she] hovered hesitantly near the wings . . . clasping her hands in front of her and then behind her, standing first on one foot and then the other. She was clearly overcome as the applause continued. It was some time before she collected herself sufficiently. . . . Nervously she started to sing, and despite the crescendo of applause, she kept right on singing with hardly a pause between songs.

Then Garland *stumbled and fell down*. Was this the feared collapse? Was she drunk? Drugged? Dying? The pianist, the musician nearest

her, slid from his bench and stepped quickly to her side. He leaned down and grasped her elbow, whispering. She looked dazed but then smiled and nodded. He helped her to her feet. Pale, unsteady, smoothing her clothes, she reached for the microphone. The pianist touched her one last time, as if pushing a glass safely away from the edge of a table, and then stepped back to his place at the keyboard. She resumed her singing, the audience resumed its roar, if possible more intensely than before. "I wanted to cry," she later recalled. "But I laughed instead and the audience laughed with me."

The act was an ambitious one. The songs she'd been associated with in Hollywood were sweet and girlish: "For Me and My Gal," "The Boy Next Door." But the songs she added to her program were outsized and dynamic, such Jolson songs as "Swanee" and "Rock-a-bye Your Baby with a Dixie Melody." Even her quieter numbers were calculated to create emotional, if not musical, electricity in their implied references to her troubled life: Irving Berlin's "How About Me?" or Noel Coward's "If Love Were All":

> *I believe*
> *The more you love a man*
> *The more you put your trust*
> *The more you're bound to lose . . .*

The ambitiousness of her act, then, lay in the combination of whopping song and whopping emotion. Garland was attempting an emotional exhibitionism so intense, and a relationship with the audience so intimate, that the love would come through in waves, rush over her and wash away her griefs. The audience's participation was necessary in this and if, in the process, a certain hysteria was needed to convince her of their love, then she would do whatever was required to provoke it. Since some in the audience brought a need to be part of this transaction, and others arrived eager to be hysterical, Garland's slightest show of grief or panic was cue enough for roaring responses and accolades.

None of this can detract from her awesome talents as musician and entertainer. According to her Palladium conductor, Gordon Jenkins, she was a "tremendous musician, the whole band could tune to her pitch. Those electric crescendos are far beyond the scope of any mortal teacher." But Garland's stage power was more than merely musical. She instinctively made theatrical choices of songs, but then so did other singers. Was it her stage manner? Garland invented an entire vocabulary of gestures; her limbs became the supporting cast. She would reach and grope painfully for the rafters, or struggle to touch the wings, or wrestle one arm down with the other as if it were straining of its own will for some higher place of safety; or she would caress the microphone, crooning into the rhinestone sleeve she'd had it fitted with. This was real showmanship, but not just showmanship. To quote Jenkins again: "I believe that people cry at Judy for the same reason that they do at sunsets, or symphonies, or cathedrals. When one is confronted with greatness, it is impossible not to be touched."

The comparisons are embarrassing, and yet we do thrill at and are transported by such performances. Did she actually achieve greatness? The word is too big for mere entertainment but our responses to such performers do spill over. Our eyes well up with tears. We shiver. Whatever it means, even if it is a shallow response to stimulus, the performing energy is there to provoke it. Of course it is easier to respond to theatrics than to real life; easier and less costly in true emotion and depth of feeling. These tears are salt-free. But they are tears.

Judy Garland's last performance at Madison Square Garden

By the time Garland returned to America—again following Kaye's lead, to play the Palace—she had assembled the components of an act that she would perform for the next fifteen years. In a real way, the act and its audiences would, as promised, save her life. Although her career as a performer appeared to be based on her movie fame, she only *acted* as if her life were over, as if the present were but reminiscence and deathwatch. In fact, concertizing was to be the major part of her career in both duration and impact. Ironically, it was in concert that she kept her ingenue self alive, playing its artlessness and vulnerability against her taut and ravaged present self. Thus, the phenomenon of Judy Garland was no more attributable to her voice alone than Kaye's huge charm was to his comic sense, than the magnetism of Dietrich was to her singing voice, or than Chevalier's stage presence was to his songs.

Garland opened at the Palace on October 16, 1951. The Palladium story seemed to have preceded her because once more the applause began during the overture. Then the great crimson curtain soared upward and a chorus of eight male dancers stepped briskly into a number called "Judy" that had been specifically written for the occasion. Then the star appeared upstage, her hands cupped around her mouth. She strode straight toward the audience and then she grinned and yelled, "Hello!"

Her songs came in bunches. Some were plainly confessional: "I Don't Care," "Some of These Days," "My Man." Others conjured up her movie self: "The Boy Next Door," "You Made Me Love You," and of course "The Trolley Song." She changed into tights and a fedora for "Get Happy" and then teamed up with one of the chorus boys to do "A Couple of Swells." By the time she actually sang "Over the Rainbow," the Palace was hers, and she stayed there for nineteen weeks. The engagement established her as one of the top attractions in show business, but in dealing with her troubles as an implicit part of her act, the hook when all other love-lures failed, she made them the heart of her life. Her Palace triumph was jolted, four weeks into the run, when she collapsed onstage and had to be rushed to a hospital. So it was throughout the concert years: any Garland performance might be aborted because of physical-emotional collapse. That was the unwritten number on the program, the ghost part of the show. The main part?

In 1956 Garland returned to the Palace, giving the young comedian Alan King the opportunity of his career by making him her opening act. She would watch from the wings, already wearing the clown costume for "A Couple of Swells"—baggy pants, checkered coat, a fright wig. She would stand and cheer and clap her hands for him. When she returned to London the following year, the demand for tickets forced her to book a bigger theater, the 3,100-seat Dominion, and on closing night the audience simply would not let her go. "More! More!" the roaring crowd demanded. Back and forth she strode across the stage, finally so excited that she started singing without the microphone. Lorna Smith quotes Gordon Jenkins, her conductor, as having asked if they should begin "from the top."

"We will *not*," said Judy. "Six 'Swells,' four 'Swanees,' we'll be here all night." "We've got plenty of time," someone called out. "No," she grinned, "we'll take it from 'I loves ya.'" The closing ovations were shattering and Jenkins said, "That was one of the greatest performances of all time."

Garland's relationship with her audience was a mixture of need and fear on her part, love and threat on theirs. It was a grotesque exaggeration of the merely emotional relationship that exists between all audiences and performers. In her case, the audience's enthusiasm and friendship were laced with the menace of cries for more. What, we wonder, is the implied "or else"? How dangerous could this audience become, were it denied what it required?

Now Garland organized grand tours, following Danny Kaye's lead, but unlike Kaye, Garland was in financial straits and could not afford to remain aloof from nightclub work. When she played Las Vegas during the 1957 Christmas holidays, she walked out on the New Year's Eve show, blaming the noisy crowd. For a while a huge new Brooklyn club called the Town and Country made a run at matching the Las Vegas salaries, and when Garland played there the Copacabana's fate was sealed. Perhaps hers was too, for her appearances and condition were now unpredictable, and from time to time her young daughter Liza Minnelli was brought on stage to perform in place of the dazed mother.

The next year in Las Vegas, Sammy Davis, Jr., introduced her at the Sands Hotel as "the greatest entertainer in the world," but 1958 was to be a disastrous year for a Garland besieged by hepatitis, laryngitis, alcoholism, drug dependence, back taxes, back problems, money problems, and, because of all this, escalating emotional problems. Work was impossible, but essential. As she memorably remarked, "Wind up the Judy Garland doll. Get her on."

And the crowds grew bigger, noisier, even more threatening in their adoration. Writing in the *Chicago-American* in 1961, Maggie Daly said that as Garland's concert "reached its crescendo, the audience seemed incapable of absorbing any more emotion . . . that is, until she finished. They raced to the footlights by the hundreds to touch her foot, or her hand, or her perspiring face." She attracted fourteen thousand people to the tennis stadium at Forest Hills, Queens, and nineteen thousand to the Hollywood Bowl. She was playing giant auditoriums now, the opera houses in San Francisco and Chicago, the Shrine Auditorium in Los Angeles. An hour-long first act, a thirty-minute intermission, and then back for an hour and a half. Thirty songs in all. It was as if the point were not to celebrate performance but to survive it. The ordeal seemed devastating. The dumpy lady who had played the Palladium now weighed 103 pounds and less with every show. "By the time she reached the encores," as Lorna Smith tells it,

Judy was so totally winded and exhausted that she sometimes barely managed to walk to the wings between songs. Once there, she would mop up, square her shoulders, shake her head and take deep gasps for breath in much the same way a boxer does after a near knockout punch, then take a deep, deep breath before resuming a relaxed-looking smile and returning to face her deliriously happy audience who were calling for "More! More!"

"More! More!" The audience craves to mourn the *slain* gladiator, their martyr. "More!" Garland seemed to have sensed the perversity of their worship when she told a Chicago audience, "I keep having this terrible dream. I'm about eighty-seven years old and I'm wearing lots and lots of white beads and white orchids and I sort of creak onto the stage on my cane and I sing something like this." She emitted a few strangled notes. "And you're all there and you're just as old as I am and you clap and cheer and say, 'That's our Judy.' "

She toured the world. ("Adult men and women jumped on their chairs to applaud"—*Leicester Evening Mail*.) She played a command performance for the queen of England, kicking off her pumps while singing "Swanee," and she finished the number with the shoes in her hand.

ABOVE:

Victor Borge's "comedy in music" appealed to international audiences for decades. He exemplified the enduring professional who hones his materials to perfection. No matter how often Borge placed his sheet music upside down or slammed the piano lid by mistake, he made it seem as if he himself were still amused by it all. And if he was amused, so were we.

BELOW:

Noel Coward in Las Vegas

Financial pressures were unrelenting but they were not the only reason for her brutal schedule. She was probably only alive when onstage. She gave a legendary concert in New York's Carnegie Hall, a concert whose recording captures the fabled hysteria. Her usual costume was a sequined white or green pantsuit, but this time she put on a black Norman Norell sheath with a blue satin jacket.

Singing is a static act. Singers must invent their show, using patter and gesture to add a theatrical context. Garland's repertoire had taken on the Jolson style, and also like him she ruled the stage physically. She would rarely stand still before the microphone unless a moody ballad demanded it. Even then, her bony fingers might be spread before her face, or her hands would be thrust defiantly on her hips, the feet apart and flat on the floor. Or her head might be thrust back, her eyes closed, and the back of a hand to her brow. Or she might lean into the spotlight, hands raised to shoulder level and straight out in front of her, as if about to applaud. She might shoot an arm straight up, along a beam of light, as if reaching for the bulb and its comforting heat. She might snatch the microphone from its clamp and stride the width of the stage, great forceful steps from one wing clear across to the other. Others—Jolson, Cantor —had worked the stage with comparable energy, but Garland's act assumed an expressionistic vividness and unreality. She was a puppet, a stab of color with the tension of bottled explosives. How strange, such compression in someone ready to fly apart.

In 1964, skeletal and hollow-eyed, she toured Australia, momentarily triumphant in Sydney only to crash-dive in Melbourne, where she stumbled onstage to croak through several songs before calling an intermission. Thirty minutes later she returned to face the restless, excited, resentful, eager, angry audience. She stammered through a few more songs before concluding with Arthur Schwartz and Howard Dietz's "By Myself." Then she murmured into the microphone, "It's so lonely by myself. Goodnight," and hurried off in tears.

The audience snarled.

Her last five years were cruel. She concertized sporadically, fitfully. In London she unexpectedly sang at a midnight benefit for the Actors' Orphanage. She was supposed to simply sit at one of the onstage tables and watch the proceedings. The elite of British drama were the main attraction—Laurence Olivier, Edith Evans, Robert Morley, Richard Attenborough, Michael Redgrave, Flora Robson. But when Garland

Edith Piaf's growls and whimpers for lost love had an essentially sophisticated appeal. Her admirers comprised an elite international club.

made her entrance, the audience would not stop cheering until she said, "All right, what do you want to hear?" and then struggled through "Swanee," accompanied by an unprepared pianist. Her last concert was in Copenhagen in 1969, and three months later she died, ancient at forty-seven.

International stardom beckons only a small and elect group because the requisite talent, success, and durability are so rare and also because its logistics were fully developed only after World War II. Before 1945, it was extremely difficult for an entertainer to orbit the globe on performance tours, although some (Harry Lauder and Elsie Janis, for example) certainly managed it. Had Charlie Chaplin ever elected to return to personal appearance he would surely have achieved world success. Other performers likely to have appealed to audiences across national boundaries were Jolson, who was uninterested in travel, and Fred Astaire, who stopped dancing before live audiences in order to star in stage musicals and then in movies.

Among those American and European entertainers who have achieved international status is the honey-voiced Harry Belafonte, a balladeer with a magnetism in live performance that made him perhaps the sexiest man in show business. His counterpart in that respect was Lena Horne, whose international career—like Garland's and Kaye's—only began after the demise of traditional Hollywood. The sexiness and blackness of Belafonte and Horne undoubtedly contributed to their success. Much of the European world continues to see blacks as exotic figures, perhaps not quite as exotic as Josephine Baker seemed a half-century ago but still *earthy*, as if that were a genetic quality. However absurd the attitude, these entertainers wisely capitalized on it.

European performers who have crossed America's wavelength are not abundant because our arrogant provincialism has required that all entertainment be in our own language. Edith Piaf had but a limited success in America. Bea Lillie and Noel Coward achieved greater popularity, although they, too, played for only very sophisticated audiences, until Coward made sophistication a part of everyday life in Las Vegas. Among foreign entertainers, aside from Chevalier and Dietrich, perhaps only Victor Borge reached the mass American audience.

Of course there are international rock stars, and probably no act even approached the Beatles in popularity. At the arena- or stadium-level, the concept of live performance assumes new and awesome connotations, but the nature of an act performed before as many as a hundred thousand spectators belongs in its own category.

Today, the showman has less and less reason to make international appearances. The rewards of movies and television are tremendous. Why should Barbra Streisand or Bette Midler bother to undertake the hard work and constant travel of an international tour, even though it is safe to suppose that they would excite audiences everywhere and achieve tremendous success? In the past, vanity, ego, and ambition would have been reason enough, but today such qualities are considered naive and the money can be made in easier ways. Nevertheless, some showmen are still invigorated by the challenge of performance abroad. Frank Sinatra, Diana Ross, Peter Allen, and Liza Minnelli, for instance, continue to make such tours. But even when they do, they are physically so far removed from their audiences—think of Radio City Music Hall, the arenas, and even stadiums—that the "personal" quality of the appearance is insignificant. The entertainer becomes smaller as he gets farther away—less human as his voice booms out from scores of speakers —and finally he will be gone.

OPPOSITE, ABOVE:
In the 1940s pop singers aspired to movie careers, and Lena Horne found roles early in her career. The era's bigotry relegated her to cameos, however. It was not until much later that she was able to establish herself as a star act.

OPPOSITE, BELOW:
Harry Belafonte in performance at Madison Square Garden with singer Miriam Makeba. Belafonte's honey voice, his choice of catchy folk melodies and calypso tunes, his wonderful looks, and his radiant sexuality were the ingredients of international superstardom. Although he wore his shirts only modestly unbuttoned, the women in Belafonte's audience invariably left his performances convinced that the shirt had been open clear to the navel.

JOSEPHINE BAKER
and Exotic Harlem

"She resembled some tall, vital, incomparably fluid nightmare which crossed its eyes and warped its limbs in a purely unearthly manner; some vision which opened new avenues of fear, which suggested nothing but itself." This was Josephine Baker as described by the poet E. E. Cummings. Baker had traveled far from the Deep South. Having set out in show business as a teenage dancer with the Dixie Steppers on the black vaudeville circuit in the 1920s, she slithered and swiveled her way to the Plantation Club above the Winter Garden Theatre on Broadway. When the French painter Fernand Léger suggested to his friend André Daven, director of the Champs-Elysées Theatre, that a Negro show would excite Paris, they had the New York cabarets scouted for talent. Baker, according to biographer Lynn Hanley in *Naked at the Feast*, "kicked out of the line of hoofers shaking and shimmying . . . adding a touch of eroticism with a series of bumps and grinds." She was brought back to Paris, where she became the rage.

Josephine Baker was without a country rather than international, too American to be Parisian and too Parisian to be American. An exotic in France, where blacks were rare and romanticized, she exhibited her body as an artwork and sang her songs with the aura of sophistication that distinguished the popular culture of Paris during the 1930s. In the world of Cole Porter and Noel Coward it was chic to be ebony, to be a Negress.

Cummings went on to say with melodramatic license, "It may seem preposterous that this terrifying nightmare should have become the most beautiful star of the Parisian stage. Yet such is the case." Subsequently, Josephine Baker returned to America for brief appearances but she was more a legend in her homeland than a popular favorite. In an era of expatriates, she had become a European.

OPPOSITE:
After years as an expatriate, Josephine Baker returned to America and performed triumphantly at a Carnegie Hall concert.

ABOVE:
Josephine Baker, staying on too late in her career, as do many stars

POPULAR MUSIC AND POP STARS

*Unless you have a desire to live, to live a good deal apart from yourself,
from that overbearing self-concern, you can't play.*   ARTIE SHAW

Entertainers are poets of performance: they express the self through action. Like Shakespeare's fools, they not so frivolously mimic the tragedies of the times and in this way help make life bearable. They are mirrors that reflect the mood and style of an era, its human factor.

In the 1920s, music makers caught America's rhythms: the get-rich-quick fever of Wall Street, the machine-gun violence of Chicago's gangsters, the jittery exuberance of Prohibition speakeasies. Orchestra leaders became the magicians of popular music. They could wave a wand and set the world to dancing. The lyrics' sweet inanities made blue skies a nightly promise. There must have been an urgent belief that the dance could go on forever.

That was the time when it was important to know how to dance. There had always been light music for social dancing. Early in the 1800s, slave orchestras played for polite dancing and then the black musicians partied afterward, themselves dancing the cakewalk and the bamboula. In the 1860s dainty steps were set to chamber orchestrations of Stephen Foster's airs. Forty years later the elite syncopation of Scott Joplin's ragtime urged a quicker pace.

There were concert bands in the Midwest, and Dixieland jazz bands in the South. The circles and partners and whoops of country and square dances were accompanied by small fiddling ensembles, so the notion of an orchestra playing for dancers was nothing new. What was novel in the 1920s was an orchestra playing popular tunes for individual dancing, rather than patterned ensemble dancing. Americans replaced the rituals and group movements of the court or country dance with the improvising couple, and the music written for them was something all our own, something never heard before.

Modern American popular music did not exist until Jerome Kern wrote "They Didn't Believe Me" in 1914. It was a revolutionary song, coming as it did at a time when popular taste was exemplified by Harry von Tilzer's "Only a Bird in a Gilded Cage." A generation of songwriters was launched: George Gershwin, Cole Porter, Vincent Youmans, Richard Rodgers. Why, Irving Berlin was already writing about dancing:

> Ev'rybody step
> To the syncopated rhythm
> Let's be goin' with 'em,
> When they begin
> You'll be sayin', "Yes sir, the band is grand.
> He's the best professor in all the land."

The quickening pace of life was echoed in the fast dances of the 1920s:

the Charleston, the Peabody, the Black Bottom, the Castle Walk, the Negro struts, the tango. With the more sophisticated 1930s, a new step was invented to suit, and it was cheerfully called the "fox-trot." The times were depressed and gloom was masked by bravado. Weren't Fred Astaire and Ginger Rogers swooping and gliding in a lucite Venice? Wasn't Cole Porter's "Anything Goes" proof enough of American confidence? High-toned numbers swept out of Broadway's musical comedies, and the society orchestras played them for the Astaires from New Rochelle and the Rogerses who worked in Woolworth's—lightfooted couples who were even better escape artists than Harry Houdini. Depression could be danced away.

The sentimental syncopation of the fox-trot was the ritual rhythm of the bandstand Pied Pipers. In New York City, a fantastical palace arose in Central Park, built just for dancing. It was called the Casino in the Park. Located near the Seventy-second Street transverse, it featured the first true society orchestra, Leo Reisman's. Under his baton, those who would banish depression trotted, glided, and dipped to "You Do Something to Me" and "Life Is Just a Bowl of Cherries"—and they danced with an elegance and a freedom from care that would ever after set the standard for gaiety.

When Reisman's pianist succeeded him as head of the orchestra, the dance band became a star vehicle. The pianist was Eddie Duchin, and on Saturday nights in 1931 his performances were broadcast over the radio, making the debonair musician a favorite, for these broadcasts from dance floors—"remotes," they were called—became immensely popular. Radio transmitted not only the music but the shuffling of the dancers' feet, the buzz of conversations, the party atmosphere. Life itself seemed to be gliding along only because the handsome pianist-bandleader waved it onward from his keyboard, enticing fantasizers through radio's grille cloth with jaunty and irresistible rhythm.

I know that you know
That I go where you go . . .

Some of the bandleaders had higher aspirations than others. Jimmy Lunceford, Duke Ellington, and Fletcher Henderson took their jazz seriously. White orchestras adopted and modified this new "swing" for dancing. Paul Whiteman attempted to elevate the vaguely disreputable reputation of all jazz by commissioning concert pieces from George Gershwin and Richard Rodgers. Whiteman also featured a tight-harmony singing group, The Rhythm Boys, whose soloist was the young Bing Crosby, but star singers still lay in the future. In 1933 Benny Goodman organized the first swing band, and as it achieved national success, along came Tommy Dorsey, Artie Shaw, and Glenn Miller. A modern age of skyscrapers, industry, and autos was reflected in this streamlined white jazz played by "big bands," as they came to be called, and radio spread the news.

In 1936, Goodman played the Paramount Theatre in Times Square and drew his young audience out of their seats—out of the protective, passive, secure anonymity of spectatorship. They were up on their feet, in the aisles, dancing the jitterbug to Goodman's syncopating clarinet. By 1938 it must have seemed as if *everyone* was dancing to these orchestras' honey saxophones and toodling clarinets, their blasting trumpets and thumping bass fiddles. "Big band swing," the white, commercialized, danceable form of jazz, was what the country was stepping to, and although this was to be America's music for only a decade it would capture

OPPOSITE, ABOVE:
"Is everybody happy?" was Ted Lewis's tag line. A clarinetist and bandleader, he took the outcast-clown routine originated by Bert Williams. It enabled him to quit the music business and succeed as a vaudevillian. His comedy could be a bit strange.

OPPOSITE, BELOW:
Frank Sinatra sings with the Harry James band at the Roseland ballroom in 1939. Radio broadcasts of hotel engagements brought a sense of party into the home and helped establish popular music as entertainment.

and reflect a national sensibility—the mood, the tastes, the style and attitude of the country—as perfectly as any popular music ever would.

On the surface at least, the national outlook was homogeneous. As the 1940s began, America was a world complete in itself. Minority groups were unthreateningly in the minority, and, presumably, everybody was eager to be assimilated into the white, Protestant paradise. The big bands reflected the prevailing unity and harmony in tightly orchestrated arrangements that swung, but not too indecorously. These arrangements were muscular, straightforward, and, if it can be said of music, unneurotic. It is still possible to hear in them an American camaraderie, a national sense of moral certainty, and, as the war years approached, an open-hearted and quite wonderful patriotism.

> *Don't sit under the apple tree*
> *With anyone else but me*
> *Till I come marching home.*

Big bands and their singers and the popular music of the era marched us off to war dancing the boogie-woogie, the jitterbug, and the lindy hop. Because of this association with the arm-in-arm of war effort, there will probably always be something touching and valentine about our memories of Benny Goodman, Artie Shaw, and Glenn Miller; about the bobby-soxers of Frank Sinatra; about the crooning of Bing Crosby and the finger-snapping of the Andrews Sisters.

It was the bands that provided the basic *live* entertainment of the 1940s. Vaudeville had disappeared and nightclubs were subdued in the war years. Comedians performed on the radio or in the movies. Most star singers preferred radio, records, and, when they could get it, movie work to personal appearances. There was more money and prestige in performing for the mass media, and so except for armed-services tours, the stars seldom sang before the public.

By forfeit, then, the live entertainers of the 1940s were the big dance bands. They played not only for dancing in hotels but also as acts in the five-a-day movie presentation houses. From the classic brass of the Dorsey, Miller, and James organizations, and the reedy swing of Goodman and Shaw, to the bounce of Sammy Kaye, Guy Lombardo, and Freddy Martin, the greater and lesser bands appeared *live and in person* at the Roxy, the Capitol, the Strand, the State, and the Paramount theaters along Broadway, and in similar movie-vaudeville theaters across the country.

But with an occasional exception like Cab Calloway, the bandleaders were musicians, not entertainers. They had scant experience as showmen and little inclination to acquire any. What they did provide was music personalized so that the audience could identify the numbers with the faces. For instance, "Sleepy Lagoon" and "Ciribiribin" conjured up the handsome Harry James, while "Opus One" and "The Sunny Side of the Street" evoked the fatherly and academic look of Tommy Dorsey. Despite Dorsey's genial appearance, "The Sentimental Gentleman of Swing" had a nasty temper and tongue. Benny Goodman, another apparently amiable fellow, was known among musicians as "The Ray," a comic-book epithet inspired by the fiercely disapproving glare that Goodman directed at his band whenever his back was to the audience. (Symphony orchestra conductors, too, tend to the tyrannical. There must be something about leading a band that fosters tyranny.) These dance bandleaders did little onstage other than play their instruments and make perfunctory gestures conducting, but in popular entertainment audiences have a tremendous need to focus enthusiasm on an individual, and the bandleaders satisfied their need.

The band music could be heard on radio and records, but, just as with classical music, the listening experience was different when live. The physical proximity of the musicians, the ambience, and the social aspect of being part of an audience made attending a big-band performance an experience entirely different from hearing these songs on the radio or a record.

In order to make the event more of a show, dance bands developed companies of performers—boy and girl singers, a clowning musician (usually one whose instrument seemed funny and left his mouth free, like the drums or a ukelele), or small vocal groups, such as Glenn Miller's Modernaires or Tommy Dorsey's Pied Pipers. All of this made American popular music a genuine branch of show business, a branch that in the rock era would reach mammoth audiences.

During World War II, taste in popular music shifted from dance bands to singers. The psychology of this seems obvious. There were almost no boys left for the girls to dance with and there was a lot that needed to be expressed: "They're Either Too Young or Too Old," "Saturday Night Is the Loneliest Night in the Week," "I'll Be Home for Christmas."

There had, of course, been popular singers before the war: Al Jolson and Harry Richman, who played the legitimate theaters; Gene Austin, Nick Lucas, and Arthur Tracy ("The Street Singer"), who performed in vaudeville; and the various radio singers—Rudy Vallee, Russ Columbo, Bing Crosby, and Kate Smith. After the war, with the emergence of popular records as a mass medium of entertainment, solo singers began to dominate the popular music of America: Perry Como, Dick Haymes, Dinah Shore, Tony Martin, Nat Cole, Vic Damone, Peggy Lee, Jo Stafford, Doris Day, Margaret Whiting, and Gordon MacRae. Why, even the Andrews Sisters disbanded when Patti decided to go it alone.

The most individual of these singers by far, and the most representative of the era, was Frank Sinatra. Bing Crosby had symbolized the small-town, home-and-hearth, white America of the prewar years, but Sinatra, even in his travails—his fall from favor and resurrection—was emblematic of a new and young country, hard-bitten and feisty. Minority groups had come of age on the battlefields and in the army hospitals, and you no longer had to be white and Protestant and Anglo-Saxon to be American. Individuality had replaced assimilation as the ideal. Sinatra reflected the new ethos. This swinger was urban, not rural, and unashamedly Italian. He was off the streets and he represented the aggressive and confident mentality that was taking postwar America to prosperity. He also had the sweetest, most beautiful, and tender voice that had ever been (and probably ever would be) heard singing a popular song.

Like his contemporaries, Sinatra outgrew the bands, and by 1945 he was America's first pop star. Adolescent girls, honey-sweet in their innocent sweaters and bobby sox, would scream and sob and faint at his feet,

Young, impressionable band singers identified with the instrumentalists they traveled with and thought of themselves as musicians, too. Musicality influenced the singing styles of Frank Sinatra, Doris Day, Dick Haymes, and, shown here with Benny Goodman, Peggy Lee. Her launching hit with the band was "Why Don't You Do Right?"

setting a model for teenage fans ever after, and initiating a crucial change in American popular culture, of which adults had traditionally been the arbiters and consumers. Before the war, children had either observed or partaken of it obediently, and as a result mass entertainment remained at a relatively mature level. There was a real sophistication in our movies, radio programs, and popular music then. Inexpensive phonograph records arrived on the scene with a more permissive society, and the American popular-music makers became the first industry to perceive and respond to the youth market, and later to cultivate it aggressively. Ultimately, a plummeting age-taste quotient would deposit all of our popular arts at the preteen level.

Postwar prosperity was making America a cozy place. The war had necessitated Spartan restraint. The country had prospered, but there had been nothing to buy. Peace revived luxury and fun, and making it nicer was the savings account that could buy it all. This condition, historians say, created a mood of self-satisfaction and conservatism; a determination to hold fast to every gain achieved. So began the Eisenhower years—the 1950s, synonymous with complacency, which the popular music of the time reflected. The songs were spineless, the singers bland. This was musical carpeting for slow dancing, until the beat and the dancing disappeared entirely.

When the dancing stops, it is usually because the music has lost drive and vitality. American popular music between 1945 and 1955 was dominated by nonsense songs ("Mairzy Doats," "Ragg Mopp"), wimpy ballads ("Too Young," "Because of You"), sentimentality ("The Old Lamplighter," "Harbor Lights"), novelties ("Chatanooga Shoeshine Boy," "The Old Master Painter"), and listless versions of Broadway tunes such as Perry Como's "A Bushel and a Peck" (*Guys and Dolls*) and Eddie Fisher's "You've Gotta Have Heart" (*The Pajama Game*).

The world of popular music was now filled with sons of Crosby, milky crooners, and curiously assertive girl singers, but none of them sang in person because the prestige, the money, and the work remained in radio, records, and, at the end of the rainbow, movies. All of show business was now in reproduced media.

The big bands had returned from the war to find themselves as obsolete as the zoot suits with the reet pleats in which they'd enlisted. Once so virile and earnest, they were now forced to play musical mush in hotels that would soon decay like the vibrant inner cities, like the simplicities of wartime life, and like the bands themselves. Although its leader had died in a wartime air crash, the Glenn Miller Orchestra was

It was not rock 'n' roll that killed traditional American popular songs. It was musical decadence. In the 1950s a burgeoning music business looked for profit not in live performance but in hit records. Creative control was transferred from composers and singers to record producers, who created not songs but "product" and who condescended to the public rather than trusting to the appeal of good songs and good singers. The final generation of old-style vocalists was caught in this maw of gimmick music: Georgia Gibbs, Frankie Laine, Guy Mitchell, Patti Page, Kay Starr, and, shown here, Johnnie Ray.

resurrected to replicate the hits of a sweeter and richer time, and so a nostalgia for the 1940s developed. Nostalgia would ultimately become a national plague, choking off life's breath from the present as the dark mockery of camp replaced sincerity and enthusiasm.

The entertainer's performance is a metaphor for daring to live, for asserting individual character, for self-expression however frightening the risk. The studio-bound singers of the 1950s were not taking such chances; they and their music reflected the passivity of the time. They did *not* express themselves or assert any individuality. They sang the songs as written, and as directed by the record producers. They were obedient, and obedience was the tenor of the times. The record was the end product. Frankie Laine, Johnnie Ray, Guy Mitchell, Patti Page, Les Paul and Mary Ford—these popular singers would be used in the recording studios as elements in packages. Even Frank Sinatra and Perry Como were pressed and labeled like the discs. More records were being sold than ever, but there was less music on them. *Popular* music—music of the people, music that people sing—had disappeared. Who ever sang "How Much Is That Doggie in the Window" or whistled "Ghost Riders in the Sky" and "Mule Train"? The record machine had replaced the musical artist.

The beatnik movement of the 1950s rushed to fill the vacuum with jazz, and in the process restored the live musician to life. In bebop, jazz had evolved into a style so esoteric that few but musicians could appreciate it. But the high folk art that jazz is for blacks seems forever doomed to dilution and commercialization by the white music business. Thus the jazz that the postwar college generation embraced was "cool" (and white) jazz, as abstract as bebop but of a more accessible nature, easy and modal. It seemed to echo the sought-after personal style of the first hippies, the beatniks.

Jazz clubs cropped up from New York to San Francisco, from Birdland to the Blackhawk—and they featured such young and popular performers as Chet Baker, Stan Getz, Gerry Mulligan, and Dave Brubeck. Small clubs in college towns offered poetry read to jazz. Plainly, performance music still had appeal, and audiences still could be reached by musician-entertainers, but this jazz was so cool it had no beat. Rhythm remained the elusive factor in popular American music and teenagers fiddled with their radio dials, restlessly seeking a pulse. They found it in race music.

"Race music" was the term privately used to describe what the record business publicly called "rhythm and blues." It was, in fact, music for the Negro market, a gospel-derived popular music written, performed, and consumed by blacks. When white youngsters discovered this rollicking, popular style, they danced with the joy of those who believe they have discovered something new under the sun. In exuberant epidemic, the music swept across the lifeless landscape of American popular music. "Rock 'n' roll," it was renamed, a black slang expression for "sex," and sex was its unmistakable message. White America was appalled. Blacks were still superstitiously feared as reefer-smoking bacchanalians, unleashers of animal instincts. Scrubbed white American teenagers were shuffling, gyrating, stomping, and bumping to such non-Crosbys as Fats Domino, Chuck Berry, and Little Richard and to groups with improbable names like the Platters and the Penguins. Soon, inevitably, there were white imitations.

In every generation, in every era, parents fear their children's loss of innocence—that is, sexuality, whose development brings the end of dependency and childhood, the end of the joy of parenting. The fads and crazes of youth symbolize and herald the onset of puberty. A sexual

ABOVE:
Although rock 'n' roll ended the classic era of American popular song, an elite of sophisticated audiences and performers remained devoted to the music of Cole Porter, Rodgers and Hart, and the like. Perhaps no performer has been so closely identified with this genre as Bobby Short, the supper-club singer-pianist par excellence, who is seen here performing in 1983 at Maxim's in Paris.

LEFT:
Lena Horne still presented herself strictly as a singer when she toured with Tony Bennett in the early 1970s. But when she realized she was an entertainer, she could carry the show alone.

OPPOSITE, ABOVE LEFT:
"Good Golly Miss Molly." Little Richard was an audacious and exuberant rocker whose big songs were "covered" (imitated and recorded) in a diluted rock-'n'-roll style by singers like Pat Boone, so as to reach a mass (that is, white) market. Frankly effeminate in his outlandish hairdos and heavy makeup, Little Richard was willing to endure ridicule rather than change his outrageous style.

OPPOSITE, ABOVE RIGHT:
In 1959 Elvis Presley, fresh from the army, came home to Tupelo, Mississippi. He would not perform live again for ten years.

In Person:
The Great Entertainers

196

OVERLEAF, LEFT:
Dolly Parton's high spirits and
theatrical belting helped her break out
of the Grand Ole Opry circuit and move
onto cabaret stages.

OVERLEAF, RIGHT:
Steveland Morris began his career as a
precocious thirteen-year-old who
dubbed himself "Little Stevie Wonder"
and made a hit record called
"Fingertips." He grew up singing such
upbeat and uncomplicated songs as "I
Was Made to Love Her" and "My
Cherie Amour" and then matured into
an elaborately decked-out performer
and composer—one of the most
formidably gifted popular musicians
in recent decades.

harbinger and a sexual threat like the flapper fad, the jitterbug, and
Frank Sinatra, rock 'n' roll shook the foundations of Eisenhower America while the kids took to the dance floors, and small bands began to
play in local bars, and new dances called the "twist" and the "frug" and
the "monkey" set those youngsters to boogying. This touchless dancing
implied a physicality considerably more erotic than the prissy embraces
of the fox-trot.

Bestriding this pulsating and shaking world was the most shocking
image of all—truly greater than life-size—a jerking, twisting, thumping rock-'n'-roll cowboy in motorcycle leather, his hair greasy and his
sideburns dangerous. Was he not a father's nightmare? The classic bad
boy was Elvis Presley. He gyrated and he shook—and perhaps his lyrics were unintelligible, but his message was not. Presley's message was
sex, no different in this from Sinatra's or even Rudy Vallee's; but because the message was being delivered by a punk, a greaser, a rocker, a
poor white from the Deep South, the message was of course unspeakable, unthinkable, and irresistible.

The machine called the American entertainment industry has an ability seldom realized outside of horror movies: the ability to make products of people, the ability to ingest naive, vigorous, original, creative
talent and spew it out as homogenized, salable pap. The supreme achievement of 1950s materialism—the neutering and polishing of Elvis Presley
—began as soon as his commercial potential became apparent. He had

emerged from a musical ambience that had not yet lost its lusty vigor. In the South, from the roadhouses to the Grand Ole Opry, singers still sang on stages—before audiences—not as disembodied voices but as present performers who could set the blood to flowing. There, popular music was still a folkloric experience, a performance art—and Elvis Presley was a natural. His rich baritone voice hammer-tripped on syncopation, the counterrhythms jiggling in his shoulders and thighs. The young man put on a show. He would wind up and explode in the space of a chord progression while his hips swiveled and his knees did a hummingbird dance of their own. This display was what made him thrilling to watch, and it was the first thing he was deprived of. Much was made of Presley's television censorship, the networks' refusal to show him in action below the waist. It is not far-fetched to call this symbolic castration. With the rescue of twenty million virgins came the elimination of Presley's virility as a performer. Then he was whisked off to Hollywood to be taxidermized in celluloid. King Kong.

Of course that could not stem the tide of rock 'n' roll. According to Jerry Wexler, the musicologist and record-company executive, "Elvis Presley was the one person who changed the music. He was the apostle. In this vessel, black music came to white America." Like a Colonel Blimp at Armageddon, the entertainment establishment scoffed at the revolution in popular music. They and their audiences had an investment in the status quo. From Las Vegas to New York City, nightclub stages were denied to rock 'n' rollers, who, ironically, were the first live-performance-oriented singers in generations. The establishment was (insanely? audaciously?) trying to stem the changes of time. With the crisis-filled 1960s already on the way, the Nero-like club owners persisted in featuring the singers and comedians of a past they would not part with.

Meanwhile, youngsters were feasting on jazz, rock 'n' roll, even folk music. It was not the folk music of Pete Seeger or Woody Guthrie but a smoother, catchier, newly written kind of folk music. Guitar-strumming groups like the Limelighters, the Kingston Trio, the Tarriers, and Peter, Paul and Mary grinned and plunked about social issues. While the harmonies were sunny, the intent was to say something, *anything* but the inanities of 1950s popular songs. Theirs was exuberant folk music, and they were performers. They joked, they entertained.

Nightclubs employed *them*. They were white.

To this ferment was added something that changed the face of America: a bizarre war in Vietnam that tainted the Johnson Administration in the eyes of the country's youth, threatening the record-buying generation with the military draft. As rock 'n' roll developed into sophisticated "rock" music, a new breed of performer-songwriter sang of the new issues rather than of the romance of yore. The Haight-Ashbury section of San Francisco came to symbolize a youthful linking of idealism, mysticism, drug experimentation, and an ardent fury with the war. This was the era of flower children and hippies, an era expressed in the music of groups with image-drenched names like the Jefferson Airplane, the Quicksilver Messenger Service, the Grateful Dead, or Big Brother and the Holding Company. Rock 'n' roll had evolved into any kind of music that the creators chose to write.

Even though the Beatles assiduously avoided the political in their music, these English youths stood at the forefront of the American musical flowering. For in their experimentation and development they had opened all the musical doors.

Were the Beatles an act? Like all raw rock bands they began by playing in bars. The concerts they gave in the first flush of their fame were

ABOVE:
In the 1950s, Bill Haley and the Comets gentrified and broadened rock 'n' roll with his "Rock Around the Clock" and similar blockbusters. American popular music was being hit by its own version of the atomic bomb.

MIDDLE:
Possessed of a shining mezzo-soprano, Joan Baez was among the first of the popular folksingers to bring politics into performance.

BELOW:
Peter Yarrow (right), Paul Stuckey, and Mary Travers were among the top folksingers of the 1960s, along with Bob Dylan, Joan Baez, and Judy Collins. The trio's "folksongs" were actually new ("If I Had a Hammer," "Blowin' in the Wind"). Such songs of social protest were the door out of banal popular music, the door leading to the Woodstock era.

OVERLEAF, LEFT:
Rod Stewart at Jones Beach, New York

OVERLEAF, RIGHT:
The Rolling Stones started out as a scruffy alternative to the Beatles, but the band's lead singer, Mick Jagger, evolved into one of rock's flashiest showmen. Rock performers devoted much more effort to live performances than did their predecessors in popular music, whose media were essentially radio, records, and movies. Working live in concerts and clubs was a regular part of a rock performer's career, prompting the development of personal choreography, costumes, lighting, and showmanship. Mick Jagger's dancing style was modeled on that of the great James Brown, "King of Soul." Brown's act was based as much on dancing as on singing, and Jagger drew on that joyously funky bopping.

ABOVE:

Ray Charles was greeted by catcalls at a jazz concert given in Carnegie Hall in the 1950s. Purists considered any rhythm-and-blues singer beneath them. Less than a decade later Charles was hailed by jazz afficionados as the best of all soul singers and a jazz genius. Here he is with his band and the Raylettes at the world-famous Apollo Theatre in Harlem. It was a ghetto showplace for such entertainers as Ella Fitzgerald, Lena Horne, Billy Eckstine, and countless choreographed rhythm-and-blues groups, from Gladys Knight and the Pips to the Temptations.

BELOW:

Because of his showmanship on the podium as well as his television appearances as teacher and raconteur, conductor Leonard Bernstein transcended the hothouse of classical music and became well known to the general public. Other classical musicians, perhaps less extroverted than Bernstein, have also been world-class entertainers. Vladimir Horowitz and Van Cliburn do not merely play the piano; Isaac Stern and Itzhak Perlman do not merely fiddle; Luciano Pavarotti, Placido Domingo, and Joan Sutherland do not just sing. Their greatness, like any star's, lies in the sum of talent plus charisma and showmanship. Anyone who ever saw Maria Callas knows the difference between a singer and a star.

In Person:
The Great Entertainers

204

OPPOSITE, ABOVE LEFT:
Like Mel Torme, Bobby Darin was a musician-singer who could compose and arrange. Darin played guitar and piano. He was as comfortable singing primitive rock 'n' roll ("Splish Splash") as he was with theater music ("Mack the Knife") and jazz ("Bill Bailey, Won't You Please Come Home?"). As a solo performer he was ingratiating, clever, and magnetic. A brilliant talent, he died young.

OPPOSITE, ABOVE RIGHT:
Wayne Newton started out in show business as a chubby young man singing high and sweet on the Sunday-night Ed Sullivan television variety program. He was transformed by nightclub magic into the quintessence of Las Vegas machismo, and even though he was never a national star in concert or on records, he became box-office royalty in the casino showrooms, an attraction ranking with Frank Sinatra and Dean Martin.

OPPOSITE, BELOW LEFT:
Steve Lawrence and Eydie Gorme playing Atlantic City. Her voice was as good as any in pop music, with flawless pitch and sensitive phrasing. Lawrence's baritone was also a thing of beauty, and early on he relaxed and revealed an appealing sense of humor and a genial wit. A balance of brightness and musicality helped the two performers project a dual personality that made their act a routine of show-business and domesticity. They finessed rock 'n' roll to become a major showroom act.

OPPOSITE, BELOW RIGHT:
Sammy Davis, Jr., became a top-rank song-and-dance man long after such acts had gone out of fashion.

hysteria-driven rallies, where it was impossible to see or sense an act, if one was there. The charming personalities of Paul McCartney, John Lennon, George Harrison, and Ringo Starr emerged in their movies. The Beatles thrived in the record studio, where they spearheaded and exploited a revolution in sound techniques, capping it with "Sergeant Pepper's Lonely Hearts Club Band," the ultimate flower-era rock album. Their unpredictable songs spurred a generation of creativity. The music that resulted made for an era of rich artistic expression, and this rock music had an influence on public moods and attitudes on a scale never before approached. The era reached its climax with the Woodstock, New York, concert of August 16, 1969, when rock triumphed in all its musical, theatrical, communal, and political guises.

And so rock 'n' roll, which had begun as an illiterate drone justified by a lusty beat, became by 1970, rock—a cast of mind, a system of values, and, only incidentally, a musical medium limited merely by the imagination of the performer. Popular music was now restored to the creators who were writing it and performing it, and it was music to be heard in person and watched in performance. Rock records sold, but concerts were the main event.

The role that psychedelic drugs played in this creative explosion can easily be deduced from the band names themselves. Timothy Leary and Ken Kesey were the cult heroes of the day, proselytizing for LSD as the drug of choice, the doorway to nirvana. The rock bands buzzed and whined and spun out musical dreams reflecting the color drips and unfolding flowers of psychedelia. They wore elaborate hippie costumes and held forth in such rock emporia as the Fillmore East in New York City, or in the great dance halls of the West Coast such as Wonderland and the Fillmore in San Francisco. They performed in front of light shows that simulated hallucinations as patterns were projected on stage scrims and as stroboscopic lights were flashed across the audience. Amplification systems for the rock concerts made previous performance sound seem like the hum of transistor radios. Mammoth speakers were stacked one upon another, bellowing and radiating sound at ear-shattering levels, never too loud for the youngsters.

All of this created a theatrical experience that made the listener a participant, and roughly from 1967 until the early 1970s there was no entertainment in America that could compare to the rock experience in terms of creativity, productivity, and sheer energy. It was also frightening, as the energy expenditure and drug abuse destroyed such powerful performers as Janis Joplin, Jim Morrison, Jimi Hendrix, and, ultimately, Elvis Presley.

The entertainers who survived were perhaps the more conventional, certainly the luckier: Bob Dylan, Elton John, Paul Simon and Art Garfunkel, Mick Jagger, Paul McCartney. These reflections of an era's youth had matured into middle-aged professionals by the late 1970s. The smoothness of their performances could not obscure the tremendous energy they continued to radiate after *decades* of success. These people had learned how to perform before audiences the size of which would have addled ordinary entertainers. Or is it more difficult to perform for half a dozen people in a living room than for seventeen thousand in Madison Square Garden?

The question may be moot. By the 1980s, American popular music had once again submerged into a passive, reproduced form. McCartney and Jagger and the other elder statesmen of rock music seemed positively antiquated alongside new performers who seemed to be from outer space—performers who were working primarily on records and in the

OPPOSITE:
When they idolize performers, audiences often idealize them and credit them with qualities beyond the power to entertain. No performers have ever benefited from this tendency to the extent that the Beatles did. They were seen as summing up the best in humanity. Their music was, of course, catchy and sophisticated but it was the personalities they presented as their act that brought them an unprecedented popularity. The dynamic era of the late 1960s and early 1970s, with its powerful social and political upheavals, seemed distilled in them.

Although the Beatles started out as a club act, and performed the first of the colossal rock concerts, that 1965 Shea Stadium performance was their final live group appearance. During the rest of their reign as international stars, they performed reproduced— on records and in movies.

LEFT:
Paul McCartney, the matinee idol among the Beatles, wrote their sweeter and catchier songs, such as "Yesterday" and "Michele." His cheerful lyricism perfectly complemented the sardonic wit and toughness of John Lennon's songs ("Strawberry Fields Forever," "A Day in the Life"). The two wrote virtually the entire Beatles catalogue. Onstage too, it was McCartney and Lennon who set the style and tone of the group.

BELOW LEFT:
Singing with Big Brother and the Holding Company in 1968, Janis Joplin performed at a level so intense she could not sustain it. Joplin was one of a number of sensational rock stars who were self-victimized by drugs and alcohol abuse. Others were Jimi Hendrix and Jim Morrison.

OPPOSITE, ABOVE:
Romance was the essential subject of American song until the idealism of folk music merged with the drive of rock 'n' roll. Then a substantial kind of popular music evolved to reflect the serious concerns and the intensity of feeling that characterized America's cathartic Vietnam years. Among the most prominent singers of such songs was the team of Art Garfunkel and Paul Simon.

OPPOSITE, BELOW:
Flamboyance and showmanship were demanded of rock stars who performed in huge auditoriums with the competitive support of flashing light shows and gaudy simulations of drug hallucination. Elton John, one of the most musicianly of rock stars, was also among the most flamboyant and showmanly.

new field of musical videos. These musical television movies, with their bizarre imagery and synthesized sounds, became the prime launching pad for popular music. In many of them, the singer would not even be seen singing the song. Instead, the video movie would embellish, illustrate.

Such videos could hardly be duplicated in concert, nor could much of the electronically synthesized music, but it was the look that came to matter more than the performance or the song.

These new stars of pop music, with names like Duran Duran or Frankie Goes to Hollywood, embarked on periodic concert tours. The essential medium for their music, however, was the record or the tape cassette or the television set. The audience was listening. It was watching a screen. It was not singing. It was not dancing.

The world had turned electronic.

BIG BANDS

The leaders of the big bands were father figures, at least to their audiences. Glenn Miller, Tommy Dorsey, and Benny Goodman seemed humorless in their silence. They wore eyeglasses, their era's symbol of studiousness and wisdom. That they stood apart from and above their orchestras was always clear. Conducting, they would make the merest downbeats, tucking clarinet or trombone beneath an elbow, as if it were a teacher's pointer. Yet their musicians, their boys, wore costumes (matching tuxedos) and sat behind monogrammed music stands. Was this not an act?

In *The Big Bands*, George Simon writes, "Whenever the band played, the kids would scream for "In the Mood," and Glenn [Miller] always responded with quite a show, winding up with the trumpets waving their derbies [mutes] and the trombones whisking their horns high in the sky."

Of all the big bands, the one most closely identified with God and country was Glenn Miller's, and by 1940, two years after being organized, it was the nation's favorite, instantly identified by the "Miller sound." This musical signature was created by a clarinet playing the melody line and a tenor saxophone duplicating it an octave higher. Jazz men derided this as bland and monotonous, but the public never tired of it.

Major Glenn Miller disappeared over the English Channel on December 15, 1944, while flying to Paris to play in a concert celebrating the city's liberation. His orchestra had existed but six years and yet in that time it became a musical metaphor for the entire era, representing America's wartime harmony and determination. Miller's death created an impact of myth and for many decades after, the bandleader's records sold abundantly. He had conducted for a national prom that may have been the most sentimental era in American history. With no trouble at all, his enduring records of "Tuxedo Junction" and, of course, "In the Mood" made this era into folklore.

The Glenn Miller Orchestra was the archetypal big band. In the World War II years, it had an almost historic aura.

They danced in ballroom dreamlands beyond the cities, such exotic locales as New Rochelle, New York (the Glen Island Casino), and the suburbs of Chicago (the Aragon Ballroom). City ballrooms were less romantic but livelier: the Savoy in Harlem (Chick Webb and his orchestra, with vocalist Ella Fitzgerald) and Roseland, of course, where Woody Herman played. But the real places to dance in New York were the hotels, and each had its "room." Benny Goodman's band was stationed in the Manhattan Room of the Hotel Pennsylvania; Harry James and Tommy Dorsey played alternate engagements at the prestigious Astor Roof; over at the New Yorker's Terrace Room, Jimmy Dorsey's band played for dancing, along with the boy singer Bob Eberle and the girl singer Helen O'Connell. All band vocalists were boys or girls, there were no grown-up band singers. Doris Day was the girl singer with Les Brown and the Band of Renown at the Green Room of the Hotel Edison, and waltzers convened at the Hotel Roosevelt Grill to dance to "the sweetest music this side of heaven," played by Guy Lombardo and his Royal Canadians.

When Artie Shaw was in New York, he would play for dancing at the Blue Room of the Hotel Lincoln, but smooth and respected as the Shaw band was, its leader was troubled. "I'm cursed with a serious-mindedness," he said, an intellectual who might have been speaking for all entertainers distracted by brains. "I know that you can take yourself too seriously." Shaw's problem was like Hamlet's: to master his own complexity and inhibitions in order to *act* (that word again)—to become an extrovert single-mindedly devoted to performance. This conflict was reflected in his elaborately arranged swing music, which was sophisticated jazz pulled to tension between romp and self-consciousness.

Jimmy Dorsey at the Hollywood Canteen

BING CROSBY

For a long time, Bing Crosby was America. For fifty years he was one of its most popular movie and record stars. So powerful was his image as both a crooner and a film personality that often overlooked was the purity of his baritone and the musicality of his instincts. Yet once he had left Paul Whiteman's Rhythm Boys, he ceased being a live performer except on rare occasions, such as troop entertainments. Although his career was awesome in its duration and heroic in its reputation, it was bloodless and without human connection. Spending virtually all his working years isolated from audiences—in radio, records, and films —Crosby developed a performing style so private, so small in scale, and so removed from those who watched and listened to him that he evolved as a model of detachment. This is profoundly ironic, since no figure in American entertainment so well reflected the country's times as Bing Crosby.

In 1977 he embarked on an international tour to celebrate his fiftieth anniversary as a performer and he found that, although he was a giant among greats, he barely existed for live audiences. This proved most painful on the night he opened his New York engagement, the last stop on the tour. The Uris (later to be renamed the Gershwin) was a cavernous theater. There had been a desultory advance sale for the twelve-performance booking. Crosby simply was not a New York act. The city likes tough entertainers: Frank Sinatra, Lena Horne, Peter Allen. It is not laid back. It is not mellow. It is of the streets, whether those streets are Queens Boulevard, 125th Street, or Madison Avenue. And yet even for the New Yorkers who came, there was something out of the ordinary in the evening. Bing Crosby sang "I Surrender Dear," "Don't Fence Me In," "Pennies from Heaven," "Just One More Chance," "Moonlight Becomes You," "I'll Be Seeing You." The past was rushing by, brushing the cheek. "Accentuate the Positive," "South of the Border."

I'm gonna settle down and never more roam
And make the San Fernando Valley my home.

The audience sang along, uninvited, under its breath, sweetly. This was memory come to life, a childhood beside the radio. "You Are My Sunshine." Old songs bring the past into painful proximity. This voice was itself the past, and it was difficult to believe that the source of the sound so familiar, the *whistling*, was without a doubt that well-remembered face on the stage.

Yet what was there was not the man; it was a replica of a movie image. Crosby had no stage substance. He had refused to come and sing for the people and the people had become accustomed to it. They accepted him on his terms, media terms, the voice disembodied and the face a photograph. That finally became his legacy. His recordings and movies were the reality. Still, it was sentimental and nostalgic, even startling, to find that he existed in the flesh.

His show was amateurish, how could it not be? He was inexperienced. It was listless, under-rehearsed, and loosely written. The opening acts were embarrassing. Mrs. Crosby performed an interpretive dance. The theater itself was only three-quarters filled, and any show-business tyro knows that on the first night of an engagement, with all the press and television coverage, the appearance of a sold-out theater must be maintained, even if drunks have to be dragged in from the Bowery and propped up in their seats. But Crosby had been too proud to spend money on advertising. All the proceeds were being contributed to charity.

Crosby croons.

He had insisted that every opening-night ticket be paid for, which had effectively kept his publicist from ensuring a full house.

From Crosby's point of view, the world had waited so long to see him that it would break down the doors at the opportunity. From the world's point of view, it no longer cared. His years of distance had taken their toll. He was a myth, yes, but in show business even myths need promotion.

Still, when he sang "White Christmas" the audience hushed and became babe-like. There was no sing-along now. This wasn't just another nostalgic song. This particular song sung by this particular singer was linked with the past of anyone who had been alive in the 1940s, the 1950s, or the 1960s. "White Christmas" didn't recall merely a moment or a period but an entire era—for some, the best time of their lives. Bing Crosby singing "White Christmas" in person was the closest anyone could get to a time machine, and the hush of the theater reflected the awe at being hurtled back to so long ago—to a way of living, a way of thinking, and a trust in America, in religion, in moral absolutes and traditional values.

> *May your days be merry and bright*
> *And may all your Christmases be white.*

This was really something to give an audience. Crosby had finally developed an act.

Bing Crosby, shown here with the Boswell Sisters, followed Rudy Vallee into radio, where the studio microphones and intimate home speakers made crooning possible.

BOB DYLAN

Probably no entertainer has ever had so profound an influence on the lives of his audience as Bob Dylan. His power would have been calamitous had he been a demagogue, but Dylan was a preacher of idealism. His "Blowin' in the Wind" was the very anthem of a generation that would not only make a stand against fighting in a cruel and senseless war but actually drive a president from office. The valor of his conscience inspired a youth weary of parental cynicism and self-interest. When Dylan abandoned folk music for the electric guitars of drug-oriented rock, his followers might have been mistaken for powerful blocs warring over questions of international moment. During a 1964 concert at the tennis stadium in Forest Hills, Queens, Dylan was thunderously booed when he brought on an electrified rock band and sang such uncharacteristic new songs as "Mr. Tambourine Man" and "Like a Rolling Stone." This was the music of the folkies' rock-'n'-roll enemy, the brainless teenagers.

Dylan had sensed that rock music was developing beyond boogie-dancing and doo-wop lyrics. He pioneered the development of image-drenched, free-form lyrics that some academics compared to James Joyce (and others to the random typing of pretentious simians). With Presley kept under celluloid in Hollywood, Bob Dylan, a natural showman, became the most important and dramatic performer in American popular music. Like any star, he brought the quality of legendry to his concerts. Alone before a microphone that windy night in Forest Hills, he let his tuxedo jacket blow and snap against his lean frame, its crimson Broadway lining a punch line for his sexy jeans. He faced colossal rejection, yet he sang into the teeth of the hateful gale. The crowd strained to hoot out the despised rock sounds, but Dylan persisted and in that persistence rose to a showmanly stature from which he would never descend.

Like Garbo, Bob Dylan created tension by blending the heat and intimacy of celebrity with a personal, cool remoteness. The biggest of rock stars, and one of the first, Dylan became the political and social conscience of an era, and mythic figure was the role he played.

NIGHTCLUB CITY

*Frenzy in an audience can be worked up if you work in a frenzy yourself.
Al Jolson knew that. People want you to work, to give your all. They
want sheer exhaustion.*   LIBERACE

The last chapter in personal entertainment is being written on the concert circuit, the high-powered but final vaudeville wheel. At one time, acts gamely toured from one town and theater to the next. Then they moved up from roadhouses to strip joints, summer hotels, nightclubs. Today, caravans of production crews, like Egyptian slaves, bear limousine-throned superstars from stadium to arena, setting up and tearing down million-dollar technological extravaganzas. Here is the decadence of personal appearance, the ultimate stage for the live performer, and it is a tomb fit for a pharaoh. Leave it to show business —ever the flashy exit.

The last stars turn ghostly in these spotlights, the distinction blurring between the "live" of life and the "live" of videotape, for mere life size cannot deliver the thunderclap to dominate an arena or a football stadium. The audience, massed at a distance, must listen through arrays of loudspeakers and sometimes even watch on great television screens. Does anyone even know if that is the actual star who is being plucked from the darkness by the spotlight? Does it matter?

Simple multiplication suggests the immense revenues possible as abstract millions of magazine readers and television viewers materialize into tens of thousands who pay twenty or thirty dollars for a seat at a concert. No site can be too big when such profits are contemplated, and the audiences seem hardly to mind. This might be called the Woodstock Syndrome. No longer essential is the physical proximity, the magnetism that once lay at the heart of the in-person act. Frank Sinatra, it was said, seemed to make eye contact with everyone in his audience. That would hardly be possible in the Houston Astrodome. A modern solo performance for a very large audience is no longer a collective of such private communions but, rather, a social experience. The audience communicates with itself. Most are television children who have never experienced live performance and so do not miss it, and many know music only as records, radio, or tapes, heard only through speakers. In comparison, a gambling casino's four-thousand-seat showroom is intimate; it is also a penny-ante operation and hardly worth the effort of a star's appearance.

Only singers can play in sites bigger than concert halls because they need not be seen even clearly as long as they are heard. A comedian needn't be seen either, but who can be funny over a loudspeaker? That is why modern funnymen, if they wish to make a lot of money, abandon personal appearances for the movies. Steve Martin, Lily Tomlin, Richard Pryor, Robin Williams, Rodney Dangerfield, and Eddie Murphy rarely return to the audiences who first gave them recognition.

Those who can attract the crowd play the concert and arena circuit for fees that in 1984 for top stars climbed beyond one hundred thousand dollars for a single performance (see table). Michael Jackson's 1984 "Victory" tour traveled to arenas at guarantees of one million dollars a show. Sometimes these performers seem starbursts, novas with careers of the instant. At the end of Jackson's tour, his popularity was already waning. Next year, another star will rise for the crowd in the concert hall, the sports arena, the athletic stadium.

A few among these last entertainers are relics from the age of live acts: Frank Sinatra, for example, or Liberace. There are occasional new-comers who seem eager to project the charisma of the live act even in vast show sites. Liza Minnelli, for instance, or Willie Nelson. There is presence in these performers. As for the likes of Barry Manilow, Neil Diamond, and Kenny Rogers, they are the children of simulation and electronics. They have never had the chance to develop and project humanity. They are traveling television shows.

Mammoth-scale performing has outpriced and overshadowed Las Vegas, much as that city of nightclubs earlier replaced the country's saloons, cafes, and supper clubs. Las Vegas is today's Palace, a ghost theater once legendary for having played host to the great; but just as the Palace became a travesty of itself, so has Las Vegas. Today the gambling resort is a desert Disneyland offering midway entertainment to tourists. East of the Mississippi, it is easier for a high roller to go to Atlantic City to gamble. No excursion is involved. In a cool age, the casino itself is the attraction, and entertainment but a sometime distraction. Even at that, the Atlantic City shows are something with which the Las Vegas hotels cannot compete. For they can no longer afford to pay the biggest stars, and their own heroes have been overtaken by age and mutations of style. (Oh, beloved Buddy Hackett, Sammy Davis, Jr., and Shecky Greene —replaced by Julio Iglesias, Lionel Ritchie, Barbara Mandrell!) Will the newcomers have the staying power that once was requisite for simply *becoming* a star?

The nightclub sensibility was intimate, personal, and sexy. Hot. A modern concert or arena performance is neutered by distance. The per-formers project a video cool and a sexual absence. This, too, is a mirror of contemporary values. Nobody can be sexy on television, because the warmth of flesh is missing, and that has shattered traditional concepts of rugged masculinity and kittenish femininity, and has invited the androg-ynous manner we see in such vivid performers as Michael Jackson, Bette Midler, Peter Allen, and David Bowie. Theirs are gaudy and campy acts, often comments on the bogus sincerity of the nightclub floor. The sexy performers of Las Vegas, they imply, were frauds. Why pretend that there is romance and intimacy between performers and audience? Low necklines and tight pants are ridiculous. Only outrageous glitter, therefore, is sincere because it is frankly off the level. Innocently decadent, these campy stars of our time—inside-outs of Sophie Tucker and Al Jolson —are the final performers, last of the extroverts, bigger than life.

One courageous entertainer introduced flash and made it acceptable before the word "camp" became common parlance. In 1943 this twenty-four-year-old musician finished a performance on the Normandy Roof of the Mont Royal Hotel in Montreal. He sat down in his room and plopped a pile of picture postcards on the writing desk. Scrawling the same note on each, he addressed them to nightclubs across America. He was doing the secretarial work himself so as to save an agent's fee, and the message he wrote was direct: "Have you ever heard of Liberace?" It could have been the plaint of every performer who ever yearned to be heard of.

Liberace at the Café de Paris, London, 1956. And in Las Vegas, 1979.

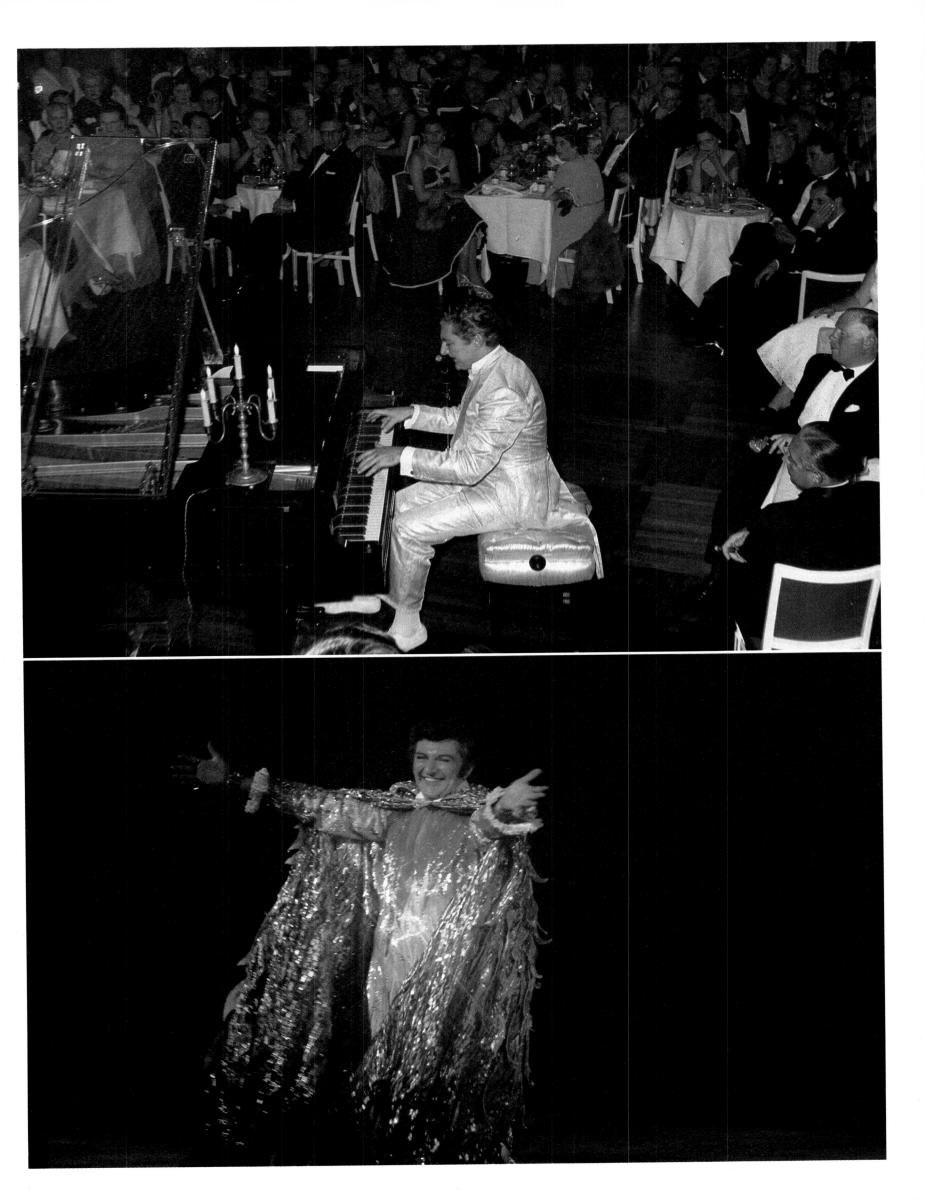

It was fair enough for him to ask. He had only recently shortened his billing from Wladziu Valentino Liberace, itself less than a household word. He was an intermission act, playing familiar classical themes and popular favorites between shows, one of a thousand such entertainers. His technique was respectable. Had he not made a youthful appearance with the Milwaukee Symphony? Other light pianists had similar credentials but Liberace's ambitions were greater than most, and he had imagination and originality as well as a pragmatic candor that would ultimately endear him to millions: "People say I'm prostituting myself by not sticking to the classics, but let's face it—there's more money in being commercial."

Soon after sending out the postcards, he received a telephone call from the entertainment director of the Last Frontier Hotel in Las Vegas, and within weeks was stepping off a train into a rural desert town with two rustic hotels on its outskirts, the El Rancho Vegas, built in 1941, and a few hundred feet of scrub away, Howard Hughes's brand-new Last Frontier. Liberace recalls these as little more than motels, yet the area would ultimately become the fabulous "Strip" of pastel-concrete hotels. In 1943, however, the only hint of that future lay in the entertainment offered, for improbably appearing in this remote outpost were Joe E. Lewis at El Rancho (show people abbreviate everything, as if having no time for mundane details) and, just closing at the Last Frontier, Sophie Tucker.

Liberace negotiated himself a $750-a-week contract and felt smug about it. He'd been paid but $350 in Montreal. On opening night the entertainment director felt obliged to confess that as Sophie Tucker had been paid $4,000 a week she would be embarrassed to offer less than $1,500. That would not be the last time anyone offered to double Liberace's salary. When the Flamingo Hotel opened in 1946, its managing director would try to lure him away. The owners, Al Capone and Meyer Lansky, were not folks to trifle with, but Liberace was spared the decision when the dealmaker Bugsy Siegel was shot to death for a New Year's present.

Definitely, then, the Las Vegas atmosphere was heady and the young pianist thrived on it. He was too restless to sit still on a piano bench. The strange circumstances of his birth seemingly prophesied that, for he had been born weighing an enormous thirteen pounds, while beside him, emaciated and dead, was a twin brother. "You see," his sister Angelina later mused, "my brother had taken all the vitality."

Vitality indeed. High spirits would be the key to his career. Inspired by a scene in a current movie biography of Chopin, he bought a second-hand candelabra and put it on his piano during an engagement at the Persian Room at the Plaza Hotel in New York. Finally, he moved up from intermission act to the show itself, where playing the piano became the least of it. He could as easily have been showing slides of table settings. The act was really the character he played, and it was daring: a sweet, virtually prissy matinee idol playing light favorites to the women in his audience. But it worked.

He made Las Vegas his headquarters. Its show-business aura was home to him. Like so many performers, the person he enjoyed being was too extroverted and in need of approval to operate at full throttle in ordinary society. Only on a stage was Liberace the self he needed to be. "Offstage," he once said, as if speaking for all performers, "I'm not too sure of myself but onstage I'm in command."

Yet it was television that was to launch him on a national stage. "The Liberace Show" began as a local Las Vegas program in 1951. The next year it was syndicated nationally, and then in 1952 something happened

OPPOSITE, ABOVE:
Caesar's Palace, Las Vegas

OPPOSITE, BELOW:
Casino showgirls

that changed the course of the pianist's career: he was signed to play the Hollywood Bowl, which was of course a most prestigious engagement for a cabaret performer. Because of his television exposure, the crowd he attracted was immense, some twenty thousand people. Preparing for the concert, Liberace confronted the problem of a mammoth audience and the distance that would separate him from it. How was he to be distinguished from an orchestra also dressed in black tie and tails? The solution was to decide his future. He would wear a *white suit of tails.*

All kinds of wonderful things began to happen and all kinds of semi-funny things were said about it. I was called "the new Cab Calloway . . . the hidey-ho man of the Hollywood Bowl." . . . The white suit didn't go unnoticed. And what's more, I noticed that it didn't. I saw the showmanship there is in daring to do something different, in challenging the conventional. I realized that just with the white suit I had lightning in a bottle. (Liberace, *Liberace*)

This remark clarifies the nature of stardom: it is not so much the product of superior talent as of a headlong drive to be different. *To be noticed.* No wonder reviews are called "notices."

By 1953 Liberace was a national craze, television's first, and sensing the importance of his discovery, he exploited its possibilities. He affected Edwardian clothes, with ruffles blossoming from cuffs and collar. Framed by candelabra and costumes, he smiled into the cameras and played to the housewives and grandmothers, bringing a kind and sentimental son-prince into their empty afternoons. Hardly handsome, he nevertheless was romantic, an unthreatening admirer dressed for daydreams.

Matrons were not his only audience, however. From the Cherry Sisters to Don Rickles and Howard Cosell, the performers people love to hate have been good box office. Nobody ever put this proposition to quite the test that Liberace did. His effeminate manner drove insecure males to frenzies of scorn. Unflappable, Liberace offered his classic rejoinder, "I cry all the way to the bank." The geniality of his cynicism won him widespread admiration, even from men. For not only did this fellow have the courage and the integrity to be what he was, he was also no fool.

The act now became a thing to be tinkered with, edited, honed, and polished. When in 1954 Liberace left the rebuilt and rechristened New Frontier for the Riviera Hotel, setting a Las Vegas salary record at $50,000 a week, his contract stipulated that he wear clothes topping anything he'd worn before. "From then on," he recalled,

it was Nellie bar the door . . . I was caught in a gimmick. I was a curiosity who had to come up with $50,000 of sensation a week. . . . Over the years I've used fur coats and fur trim, jewels of all kinds and diamond buttons that spell out my name. I've dressed as a hillbilly, a clown, a court jester. I've appeared in the styles of famous composers, worn hats, plumes and wigs of various eras. I even have a jacket that lights up and twinkles when the house is blacked out.

This was only an extension of national taste, for it was an era of tail fins and triple-tone superchrome cars, split-level ranch houses, and Cinemascope movies. When the Las Vegas hotels began to replace their nightclubs with theater-like "show rooms," Liberace made his entrance in a Rolls-Royce. A smaller car rolled out just to pick up his fur coat. Some years later, he appeared in star-spangled red, white, and blue shorts, twirling a baton. He might make an exit hoisted through the air on a wire, a sequined cape flaring and sparkling in the spotlight. His high spirits were indomitable, and when he billed himself as "Mr.

Showmanship," the title seemed deserved. He still played the piano, but it was really just an excuse for his costumes and patter. He would play a Gershwin medley, or selections from *My Fair Lady*, or a popular theme from a concerto. Winking at his audience, he would launch into boogie-woogie. Such humor was broad by sophisticated standards, but Liberace was not playing to sophisticates and knew that big careers are not built on small bases. Moreover, by this time his act had developed a life of its own.

He would lean toward those in the front rows and show off his diamond-studded, piano-shaped rings. "Heck," he would say, "why shouldn't you look at them? After all, you bought them." And he would chuckle, more amused than anyone by his frankness. As for his clothes, he would cheerfully concede, "I didn't come here to go unnoticed." Toward the end of a show, he'd admit, "I've had so much fun myself that honestly, I'm ashamed to take the money." After a pause worthy of Jack Benny or Harold Pinter, he would smile and shrug, "But I will." He used such lines for decades and yet his delivery always made them sound fresh. To most audiences, personal acts seem ad-libbed. Of course they are not. Acts are written, memorized, rehearsed, and practiced. The impromptu effect is dependent upon the writing, the direction, and most of all, naturally, the performance. If the routine sounds tired, practiced, or contrived, it will not work. Liberace's act grew smoother through the years, and four decades later it was a thing of beauty as he performed it for audiences of six thousand at New York's Radio City Music Hall during a week-long engagement in 1984. He played as personally to those in the faraway reaches of the upper balconies of that huge auditorium as he did to the people up front, and when he eased into "Let Me Call You Sweetheart" on the big concert grand, the audience sang along softly, without being asked. So, he had done what every super-showman does—brought the walls closer. Although he had once vowed that he would never play New York (perhaps in response to newspaper abuse, as we shall see), his warmth and star power took this audience as any. He put them in his pocket.

Then he was on his feet, attempting a few throw-away dance steps and panting, "I'm not good but I've got guts," and the audience adored the self-deprecation. Like any very great star he had about him the wrap of legend, and merely *seeing* him was the show; he could do as he chose.

It had not always been so. When he went to England in 1956, the *London Daily Mirror*'s pseudonymous columnist "Cassandra" called him a "deadly, sniggering, snuggling, giggling, fruit-flavored, mincing, ices-covered heap of mother love." Liberace sued for libel, perhaps feeling that as the highest paid act in the world he could afford justice. When the case came to trial three years later, he won a $22,500 judgment, but the price he paid was steep.

I'm No Homo Says Suing Liberace. (*New York Daily News*, June 9, 1959)

Twenty-five years would pass before performers could be flamboyant and campy without fear of insult. Liberace never made any declarations on the subject of homosexuality ("What am I supposed to do? Come out on the 'Johnny Carson Show'? "), but he grinned through much abuse to broaden general attitudes. As it's said, he paid the dues and took the heat so that others would not suffer as he had, and he did it with ability, pride, character, integrity, and good humor. "This is one of my sport coats," he would confide to an audience, the rhinestones positively blinding, "and don't ask me what sport."

Had it not been for this man of grace, who dared to be himself in an era of frightened conformity, Bette Midler would not have been able to go so easily from steam-bath performances to stardom, and Peter Allen could not have preened and wriggled and shaken his way to stardom with such delightful exuberance. "I'm just *this* far from a drag act," Liberace could finally say in 1982.

His forty years in show business had spanned a multitude of other changes as well, not the least of which was the rise and fall of Las Vegas as the self-proclaimed Number One Show Business Capital of the World. The neon oasis had come far from the scruffy desert town he'd found in 1943. Eleven years later, his switch to the Riviera Hotel made headline news in entertainment circles, for in that short time Las Vegas had become the main event. How long Frank Sinatra's contract ran, what was Dean Martin's salary, which performer played where—these were crucial matters in the place where the heart of America's nightclub life had been relocated, underworld aura and all.

Ever since Prohibition, cabaret performers had been linked with gangsters, for bootleggers had run the speakeasies. Repeal did not separate the underworld from show business. It was too profitable and too

All stars have a common denominator. It is the showmanly impulse, evident in this highly unlikely but irresistible team effort: the glamorous Dietrich and the earthy Louis Armstrong, seen at the Riviera Hotel in Las Vegas, 1962.

ABOVE:

After Gracie Allen's death, George Burns tried many partners. Here, in 1960, he dances with nineteen-year-old Ann-Margret at the Sahara Hotel in Las Vegas. He also teamed up with Carol Channing for a time. It was some years before he considered the possibility that he might actually be able to work alone.

RIGHT:

George Burns's amusement at Jack Benny in drag seems unfeigned—no surprise, since it is hard to even look at this picture without smiling. Benny had a priceless sense of absurdity and the wisdom to direct it at himself. Such clowning must be rewarded in heaven.

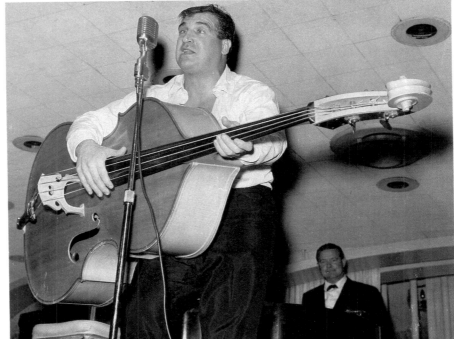

OPPOSITE:
Tony Bennett was a musicianly singer, celebrated for his ballads but inclined to swing and always looking for songs with jazz qualities. There have been few popular singers to equal him.

ABOVE:
A certain warping of perspective was required to bill a boys' club of entertainers as "The Summit at the Sands Hotel," but so enamored was the public of Frank Sinatra in 1960 that his pals' antics were major news. From left to right, Peter Lawford, Sinatra, Dean Martin, Sammy Davis, Jr., and Joey Bishop. They made a movie by day and entertained by night. Out of sight at ringside was young Senator John F. Kennedy.

CENTER:
Shecky Greene was one of the favorite comics in Las Vegas. He first played the lounges, later the main stages, but was never as popular elsewhere in the country.

BELOW:
Jan Murray, very professional and funny at the Riviera Hotel, Las Vegas, in 1967. Of all the stand-ups, he was the best-looking, the suavest, the most carefully modulated in his speech. Altogether a class act.

exciting. Now Las Vegas married nightclubs and gambling, one of organized crime's prime interests. In a sense, Fidel Castro had performed the ceremony. The baseball-playing, cigar-smoking revolutionary in military fatigues may have been a savior to the Cuban downtrodden and a threat to conservatives everywhere, but as far as show business was concerned, he was the man who made Las Vegas. When Castro shut down Havana as a playground for America's sharpies, the eyes of gamblers, swingers, and general fast-flyers turned to Las Vegas. From the mid-1950s through the 1960s, Vegas would be America's Sin City, show-business capital, and neon boom town. A flock of architectural spectaculars rose to form the glittering Strip. The Riviera set an altitude record at ten stories. It had gaudy neighbors in the Desert Inn, the Dunes, the Flamingo, the Stardust, the Thunderbird, the Tropicana, the Sands, and the Sahara hotels. America's biggest stars were on constant parade on their nightclub floors. Noel Coward, no less, played the Desert Inn, and so did Danny Kaye, Jane Powell, Gordon MacRae, and Eddie Fisher. At the Riviera, in addition to Liberace, the stable included Harry Belafonte, Tony Martin and Cyd Charisse, Juliet Prowse, and Louis Armstrong. The Flamingo had Mitzi Gaynor, Jack Carter, Pearl Bailey, Bobby Darin, Myron Cohen, and Ray Bolger. The Sands cornered the Copacabana alumni (its nightclub was called The Copa Room), and appearing there were Frank Sinatra, Dean Martin, Sammy Davis, Jr., Danny Thomas, and Lena Horne—but not Joe E. Lewis. The Flamingo had the dean of the saloons as well as Jack Benny, Judy Garland, Dinah Shore, and the Ritz Brothers.

Carol Channing's exuberant clowning was deftly transplanted from Broadway musical comedy to casino showrooms.

Even the lounges were star-studded. In these informal showrooms, where lesser acts played continuously and free of charge to come-and-go audiences, were the likes of Billy Daniels, Phyllis Diller, Vic Damone, Shecky Greene, Louis Prima, Harry James, Eartha Kitt, Sarah Vaughan, Della Reese, Don Rickles, Ella Fitzgerald, and Buddy Greco. Yet, though every well-known act in the country came at one time or another to Las Vegas in the 1960s, Liberace chose an unknown to open the show for him at the Riviera in 1962. It was a heady and daring thing to do.

His choice was a young New York singer and actress, Barbra Streisand, whom he had first heard in Manhattan's intimate Bon Soir cafe in 1959. She was eighteen years old at the time and earning $108 every week she was held over. A nearby bar in Greenwich Village had awarded her a one-week engagement there as a talent-contest prize, and that had paved the way to Las Vegas and her first professional booking. It would be extended for eleven weeks, beginning one of the fastest and most spectacular rises enjoyed by an American performer.

Barbra Streisand was a wise-cracking youngster off the Brooklyn streets, and her vulnerable confidence was engaging. "I'm a great singer. I always knew I could sing . . . I was given a sort of good voice," she said. "I suppose I'm going to be famous." A "sort of good voice," indeed. However sidewalk her speech, Streisand's singing voice was rich, accurate, powerful, and wide-ranging, and her use of it spanned the fast and slow, the loud and quiet. In 1961 she won a featured part in a Broadway musical and caught the critics' eyes, yet she insisted on moonlighting at

Barbra Streisand

New York's intimate supper clubs. "I never saw a nightclub until I performed in one," she told the *New Yorker*. "I'm doing this because I can sing the way I want to sing there. I can't do that in the show."

The next year she was working on a bigger and fancier nightclub circuit: Detroit's Caucus, Mr. Kelly's in Chicago, Basin Street East in New York, the Hungry i in San Francisco, and, in Los Angeles, the Coconut Grove, before going on to Las Vegas with Liberace. She seemed to relish the special nature of club work. "A great actress rides on emotion," she told a reporter. "She makes people feel the emotion behind the lines; a great singer does the same. You have to act to be a good singer. There's no trick in getting up in front of an audience and closing your eyes and singing. That's easy. But to get up there and keep your eyes open and look at your audience and make them feel what you want them to—that's hard."

Using a high stool as her only prop, she relied on dramatic numbers that could set off her soaring voice: "Where Am I Going," "Cry Me a River." She enjoyed resetting period songs like "Come to Me, My Melancholy Baby," or "If You Were the Only Girl in the World," and she had a taste for slowing down lively songs like "Happy Days Are Here Again."

Liberace went to Los Angeles for her opening at the Coconut Grove, loyal as well as professionally curious, and remembered with amusement:

She walked out onto the floor. She looked at the crowded tables in front of her. Then she looked to her right and saw still more tables full of people. To her left she saw another mass of tables and people. She took a deep breath and said, "If I'd known there were going to be people sitting on both sides of me as well as in front of me, I'd have had my nose fixed." (Liberace, *Liberace*)

By the time they opened at the Riviera, "her performance," he said, "was brilliant, electrifying." Ordinarily the entertainers in town had little opportunity to see each other perform since all show times were the same. To accommodate them, Liberace scheduled an occasional third show, late-late, "and the show people took her to their hearts."

Streisand was destined to abandon personal appearances quickly, perhaps successful too young to have developed loyalties to live performance. After her huge success at twenty-one in the Broadway show *Funny Girl*, she turned down offers to appear in gargantuan Shea Stadium and Houston's Astrodome. "As an artist," her manager said, "it wouldn't be right for her. All she'd make is money." But within the year Streisand was making money at Chicago's mammoth Soldiers' Field as well as at the 17,000-seat Festival Field in Newport, Rhode Island, and similarly cozy sites in Philadelphia and Atlanta.

Her concert performance had come far from the simple stool in a supper club. Now there was a thirty-five-piece orchestra onstage behind a scrim that was backlighted during the overture. She wore an orange and brown chiffon gown, with one shoe and one earring in each color, reflecting her early taste for offbeat, thrift-shop clothes. A short runway gave her the chance to stride into the audience, and for the second act she switched to a black, sequined evening gown and glossier songs ("I Wish You Love," "What Now, My Love?" "Autumn Leaves").

Already ranked with Frank Sinatra as not only the most popular but the best singer in America, Streisand was making a stupendous success with standard popular songs at a time when rock music was at its creative peak, and yet her drawing power was immense with all age groups. When she played the Forest Hills Tennis Stadium in 1965, the seven-dollar tickets were scalped at twenty-five dollars. Tickets to the Beatles'

performance at Shea Stadium that same summer fetched only fifteen dollars. Making this either amazing or explainable were her looks. Traditionally, singers are supposed to be good-looking, but as Norton Mockeridge wrote in the *New York World Telegram and Sun*:

Barbra Streisand is just about the darnedest looking female I ever saw. . . . She's ungainly, she has scrawny legs, angular arms, a flat facade and a face that sometimes looks as though it came right out of *Mad* magazine. Her eyes perpetually seem to be peering at each other, her nose proportionally shames Jimmy Durante's, her gaping mouth slurs and twists and contorts when she sings, and her hair is a squirrel's nest.

There was something about Barbra Streisand's plainness that made her unique, even brave. Perhaps the combination of homeliness and magnificent talent gave hope to ugly ducklings everywhere. She was an individual, and in 1969 she won a truly impressive accolade, the Friars Club Entertainer of the Year Award.

Regular attempts have been made by the award industry to create prizes for variety performers, prizes that would rank with the Oscars, and Tonys, and Emmys, and Grammies; prizes as excuses for network television shows. One such effort resulted in the Las Vegas Entertainment Award, which fizzled after five annual presentations. Another, untelevised but more enduring, is the Friars Club award. This historic fraternity of variety entertainers has managed to retain the prestige of its annual accolade, doubtless because the flashiest of entertainers continue to be loyal Friars and because the award dinner has become famous for its "roasting" of honorees. Some twelve hundred guests bought their way into the Waldorf-Astoria's Grand Ballroom in May 1969 to watch Barbra Streisand become the second woman to win the Friars' appreciation (the first had been Sophie Tucker; in 1973 Carol Burnett would be the third). Danny Thomas was the master of ceremonies and Don Rickles said, "Barbra, I want to say this publicly and from my heart: I never liked you." In short, the fraternity gave her the same treatment it did the male stars.

Streisand's last live performing to date was done at the opening engagement of the International Hotel in Las Vegas, in June 1969. A third generation of hotels had, with Caesar's Palace, made the desert resort a skyscraper island. The International, with fifteen hundred rooms in its thirty stories, was then the world's largest resort hotel, and it was spectacular. Like Caesar's (as, of course, Caesar's Palace was known), it replaced the conventional nightclub with a 4,000-seat showroom, naturally called the Show Room Internationale. It was actually a theater, complete with balcony. The audience, like drip-dry Vikings, sat on either side of long, narrow tables. A wide stage replaced the traditional nightclub floor (from which floor shows had originally taken their name). Indeed, there was no dancing, nor was food served. There were no chorus girls either, nor any of the other conventional trappings of nightclubs. The nightclub, in short, was dead. Live entertainment was becoming bigger and grander, relying on large orchestras, awesome sound systems, and elaborate production. The intention, obviously, was to play for bigger audiences.

Not only was Streisand engaged to inaugurate this spectacular new hotel, she was signed up for a then-astounding five-year contract at one million dollars a year for four weeks of performance each year. On the first night of the hotel's first show, she sang for an hour. Her independent concerts had offered two acts, forty-five minutes each, but no hotel-casino will have its gamblers kept out of action for that long.

Raquel Welch had been written off as a vacuous Hollywood sex symbol who would not survive a few exploitation movies. Instead, she developed a spectacular command of showroom musical stages.

Wearing "clouds of fuchsia chiffon" (according to a *New York Times* report), Streisand opened her act mocking the extravagance around her by singing, "I've Got Plenty of Nothin' and Nothin's Plenty for Me." As prop snowflakes fluttered down for a rendition of "Jingle Bells," she joked about the unfinished hotel: "That's not snow, it's plaster." But the brash humor that had been so disarming a few years earlier now seemed snide. One of the more unfortunate side effects of stardom is egotism. We accept that, but allowing it to show during performance is unacceptable. Performing, however, plainly did not hold the charms for Streisand that once it had, and so perhaps she had no reason for good behavior. She'd once said, "The exciting thing about being a performer, the really creative thing, is going onstage or stepping in front of a microphone in a nightclub and creating something special just for the people who are there. You may be great or you may be lousy that night but that's the exciting thing about creating it all over again each time. The emotional quality is the thing I'm riding on, reaching out to the audience." But after this opening night, all she had to say was, "Whew! Only thirty-nine performances to go."

At least her disenchantment was conveniently timed. In 1969 every traditional American value was under assault and nightclubs, as bastions of materialism, were hardly excepted. Las Vegas had already put most of them out of business by offering higher fees, and now Las Vegas was replacing its own clubs with giant showrooms. These eliminated the personal communication of floor shows. At the same time, high-steppers in New York and Los Angeles were exchanging the spectator sport of entertainment for the participatory pleasures of dancing in a discotheque, a chic variation on the rock-'n'-roll dance halls of San Francisco with the same raison d'être: instead of sitting and eating and drinking and watching, the customer was himself the show, costumed in gaudy clothes and drenched in multicolored flashing and blinking lights. America's historic urge to dance, denied by the casino showrooms, was being exploited by the Daisy and the Factory in Los Angeles, and the Electric Circus, the Cheetah, and Arthur's in New York. But not in Las Vegas, where the drive was on to preserve the 1960s forever.

Streisand fulfilled her International Hotel contract, and that was the end of her live work. She had given the hotel its money's worth. In a town where the spectacular is everyday, she had launched the International glamorously; she had gotten it widespread press coverage; and she had practically sold out the huge new showroom for her entire engagement. Only the balcony had stubbornly remained unfilled. Only one performer ever *would* fill it, and he would fill it every night of his engagement, an engagement in fact that immediately followed Streisand's.

The marquee soared high above the hotel entrance. At night it shone like a heavenly monolith. The letters were giant, stark, black, and bold against the white background. They spelled out a single name. The name was "Elvis."

Three images form a triptych on which the vivid and tragic career of Elvis Presley was painted, and even though his immense fame was spread by records and movies, these pictures are of live performances because, as was evident all too late, Presley was first and most of all a showman, one of the most exciting and original ever produced by America. Probably no other entertainer in the country's history has been to such an extent conceived, nurtured, energized, influenced, and destroyed by the social and theatrical forces of his time. Probably none better deserves the now trite epithets "legendary" and "mythic."

The central and most triumphant of the three images is of Presley in Las Vegas, reappearing in 1969 as a live performer after a decade's submersion in movies and records. The earliest of the three images is the freest and most rapturous: Presley at the start, raw and untamed, a white-hot youngster who could sing black. This was the punk, the greaser, the country's first rock-'n'-roll star who so alarmed adult America, the sexual revolution incarnate. The final, cruel image is of Presley as a bloated, robotlike grotesque being lugged into arenas like a leaden parade float and then found drugged dead.

A carcass in a bathroom.

Broadway and the personal stage have always been very different places. On Broadway, individual talent is subordinated to the needs of a show, even when the show is a star vehicle. In person, the individual is the whole show. Carol Lawrence proved to be the rare entertainer who could play both Broadway and the showroom, achieving stardom as Maria in West Side Story *and then making a career in the nightclub big time.*

My first appearance after I started recording in 1955 was [with a touring Grand Ole Opry company] in an outdoor stadium. I was scared stiff. I came out and I was doing a fast-type tune and everybody was hollering and I didn't know what they were hollering at. Then I came offstage and my manager told me that everyone was hollering because I was wiggling. So I did a little more and the more I did, the more I got. (As quoted in William Allen Harbinson, *Elvis Presley: An Illustrated Biography*)

Like Liberace and his white tails, Presley had caught lightning in a bottle and knew it. "Wiggling" was to be his gimmick and, like Liberace, he appalled buttoned-up 1950s America. The management of the Grand Ole Opry had in fact been hesitant in the first place about the twenty-year-old country singer; had rejected his original audition in favor of Pat Boone, who would make a career of being the upstanding alternative to Presley's tomcat sexuality. But it was the tomcat's day. Marlon Brando and James Dean were swaggering across movie screens with vulnerable bravado, sending waves of body heat crunching in jackboots and rumbling with motorcycle engines. Presley already quivered and shook to his rocking music. Eager youngsters shrieked with comprehending joy. So did his first reviewer, a Memphis newspaperwoman: "I don't know what it is but he's got it. He moves, he struts, he shakes, he's mean, he's sweet. He's Sex."

Playing the Mississippi-Alabama Fair that year, still in a cowboy outfit, Presley brazenly opened his act with the decidedly un-country "Good Rockin' Tonight," and there was no doubt about what the "rockin'" referred to. A year later at the Dallas Cotton Bowl a ten-foot fence and a police cordon had to protect him from the twenty-six-thousand screaming fans trying to get at him in his pegged pants and draped jacket.

Presley had begun billing himself as "The Hillbilly Cat," but when his record "Heartbreak Hotel" became number one on the national popularity listings—not the country category but overall—he too left the hills. He indulged a taste for costumes that were part greaser and part black dandy: pink suits with white shoes, or green jackets with black trousers, cummerbund, and creamy boots. As the first rock star, he had no one to learn from. Those to come would model themselves on him. There were, to be sure, other performers on the same scent and they influenced him, country rebels like Jerry Lee Lewis, playing the piano on his feet and sometimes *with* his feet; or equally exuberant black singers like James Brown or Little Richard, leaping and stomping and flopping all over the stage. Presley surely shared their style, and yet he remained an original. He was the white boy who could dance and move and wiggle with the best of the blacks.

His style was not so smooth as to be slick, and he would always retain an amateur edge to keep his greaser credentials legitimate. His self-absorbed passion was like a stripper's, and yet a laugh hovered about him, providing a certain self-mockery to leaven the abandon.

He growls just a little, flicks the hair from his eyes, lets his heavy-lidded gaze burn up the front rows, raises his left hand...sways his body, shakes a leg, rolls his groin....His hips begin to undulate, his head whips up and down and he seems altogether to be in some sort of trance....His eyes are pencilled in and his fair hair dyed black to add demoniac qualities to his rough, romantic good looks. He does "Heartbreak Hotel" when the main lights are turned down....He bends his left leg, supports himself on the right and then throws out his arms in appeal

> Well since mah baby's left me
> I've found a new place t'dwell
> It's down at the end of Lonely Street at
> Heartbreak Hotel.

It is more than they can bear—they are out of their seats—they are rushing for the stage and as the cops push them back he has already gone on to something else, crouching over, hands flailing. . . . He never fails to close with "Hound Dog." He falls to his knees, thrusts his groin in their faces, crawls

When Elvis Presley triumphed in Las Vegas, his white jump suit got as much publicity as most other entire acts.

over the stage like a snake, convulses, jerks upright, twists back to his feet.... And when he's finished he doesn't bow, never comes back for an encore, is just rushed away, shivering, sometimes crumbling from exhaustion. (W. A. Harbinson, *Elvis Presley: An Illustrated Biography*)

Presley's success was all but instantaneous. His records dominated American popular music—"Don't You Step on My Blue Suede Shoes," "You Ain't Nothin' but a Hound Dog," "Don't Be Cruel to a Heart That's True." The only hitch in this otherwise classic rocket ride to stardom was an engagement at the New Frontier Hotel in Las Vegas, where he was booked for two weeks in 1956 at $8,500 a week. The hotel had a reputation for offbeat choices. Liberace was one that had worked. In a couple of years, Mario Lanza would be one that didn't (failing to show up on opening night, then and there ending a tragic career). Presley's experience was almost as bad. Business was so poor that his act was nearly canceled. A hip-swiveling rock 'n' roller who symbolized a threat to the status quo was hardly what Las Vegas audiences, beneficiaries of the status quo, wanted in entertainment.

Presley struggled through his second week, and the rejection plainly stung. "I got no feeling from them," he later complained. "They just sat there and listened. They didn't respond." He was young enough to think that, given the chance, adults would like the same things teenagers did. He was also young enough to show his hurt. "I wasn't a flop," he insisted. "They don't keep flops two weeks, do they?" Later, in a more reflective frame of mind, he said, "I always wanted to play Las Vegas. So I did. Now I'll go on from here."

Liberace, once the reigning star of the New Frontier, tried to console Presley. Odd couple though these two might at first seem, they had their similarities. Both were nonconformists and both had a taste for the flamboyant. Presley, in his own way, was becoming as campy as Liberace. Both were blithely outrageous and both were sexual outlaws, threatening the traditional machismo symbolized by Las Vegas and embodied by such casino stalwarts as Frank Sinatra and Dean Martin. Liberace encouraged Presley to wear even flashier clothes than before, and they swapped gold lamé jackets for a backstage photograph.

There was something else that Presley and Liberace shared. Elvis, too, had been born with a dead twin brother, Jesse Garon Presley. That was eerie indeed. It was almost as if each of these driven entertainers had needed an extra life's energy, as Liberace said, "to work in a frenzy."

If Liberace's effeminacy was too much for the 1950s, so was the lustiness of "Elvis the Pelvis," as he had inevitably been dubbed. Both were too extroverted for the times, but despite all the indignation, they were extraordinarily successful. Plainly, the same suppressed sexuality that fostered public outrage prompted public adoration.

A great fuss was made over Presley's entering the army and having his hair cut short, particularly the infamous sideburns. Here, the castration symbolism and the parallels with the Biblical account of Samson's haircut and subsequent impotence are so apparent that it is embarrassing to take the opportunity to mention them. But, as Liberace says, I'll take it anyway.

Presley slipped unresistingly into a Hollywood maw of romantic musical comedies. It is not, I think, overly analytical to see in this a bargain struck, emasculation and dilution in exchange for the nirvana of movie stardom. His music and performance lost their hot sexuality, and with it their vitality and integrity. With the single exception of a 1961 benefit appearance for the Memorial Fund of the USS *Arizona*, Presley would not perform in person again for ten years. Had his movies not eventually

ABOVE:

*Like many singers, only more so,
Elvis Presley never developed a social
assurance commensurate with his fame,
and he virtually never went out in
public. He made an exception, though,
for Liberace's 1956 opening at the
Riviera Hotel in Las Vegas, out of
gratitude for the showman-pianist's
support during Elvis's disappointing
Las Vegas debut.*

RIGHT:

*Presley was the only star ever to sell
out the gigantic showroom of the
International Hotel in Las Vegas. And
he sold it out for every show.*

declined in popularity, he probably would never have been seen or heard from in the flesh again.

That is what made his return to the performing arena so suspenseful. It was not an elated Presley who arrived in Las Vegas in July 1969 to prepare for his opening at the Show Room Internationale. It was, rather, a somber Presley, who had reason to be uncertain about his ability to perform in person, uncertain about the appeal of his music—for rock 'n' roll had become white and sophisticated, dominated now by the Beatles —and uncertain about his ability to attract Las Vegas audiences, since he could hardly forget his 1959 debacle at the New Frontier.

Though a decade had passed, bringing rock 'n' roll to the forefront of America's popular music, none of its great stars had proved a popular attraction in Las Vegas. Ironically enough, Tom Jones, a slicked-up rock singer, had made a career out of what was essentially an impression of Presley in nightclub mufti. In turn, Englebert Humperdinck and Wayne Newton had drawn their acts from Jones. Yet as for the original "King of Rock 'n' Roll," the very continuation of his career was at stake, and he was too young to retire. Like all pop music stars since Frank Sinatra, he was struck by mid-career crisis when his teenage constituency grew up. If he was to continue, he would have to change.

Changed Presley had. It was an utterly new Elvis who showed up in Las Vegas that hot desert summer, a Presley designed to appeal to the fans who had (presumably) grown older with him and who (he hoped) were now the Las Vegas audience. He had always been a good-looking fellow but with a surliness through the cheek, an unpleasant sneer curling the lip, and a pasty softness about the face and body. Now, at thirty-four, he was broad-shouldered, slim-hipped, lean and taut. Maturity had given his features definition. His eyes remained soulful beneath the familiar lush eyelashes, and with long hair in style his sideburns seemed dashing rather than sleazy. Hardly a greaser, he was downright handsome.

The showroom's great golden curtain soared upward to reveal, dramatically silhouetted against a vivid red cyclorama, a fifty-piece orchestra already throbbing with rock-'n'-roll drive. The strings were massed and the rhythm section hefty—four guitarists and three percussionists beating out an opening vamp to set up the audience for show time. The vocal forces joined in this rhythmic overture, four white men singing back-up and a quartet of gospelizing black women, counter-clapping against the pulsating orchestra. The atmospheric opening that is so important to a showroom act was now rocking the big theater through the hotel's terrifying audio system, as out strode Presley in full black leather, his guitar a prop slung along his hip, to be thrust or jerked or hitched over his back.

The audience roared and the rhythm section delivered syncopating bursts of harsh trumpets against honking saxophones, propelling him through "I Got a Woman," a rhythm-and-blues song popularized by Ray Charles, but one whose momentum was pure Presley. Then "Polk Salad Annie," a country-and-western number with the classic Presley mix of Southern black and white. He crooned "Love Me Tender" to remind the audience of how rich his baritone remained, sweet as a choirboy's, which was where it had all started. Then back to the beat.

> *I'm proud to say*
> *That she's my buttercup.*
> *I'm in love*
> *I'm all shook up.*

He smiled into the resounding din and the big orchestra rocked behind him, pushing a wall of sound out at the audience. Then, as when young, he danced. The moves were not quite the same as when he'd first brazened it out before the nation. That had been thirteen years and the Beatles ago. Lately, he had watched Tom Jones sell stage sex in a style adapted, but updated, from his very own and he took the tip in return. His new moves, then, were up-to-date, yet characterized by his own vitality, and he was grinning with tremendous self-satisfaction—and then triumph. He was still the white boy who could dance with the blacks. He had survived everything that the forces of morality and conformity had contrived to make him a eunuch, and had emerged intact. The sexual electricity that had been the basis of his original appeal, and everything that had made him unique and special, had been suppressed but not eliminated. Like a butterfly wriggling and straining against its cocoon, he had won, bursting free to beauty and flight. It is neither romanticizing nor intellectualizing to call Presley's reemergence a triumph of individuality over a system.

The press did not miss the point. Presley's management made sure of that. It seemed as if half the International Hotel's opening-night audience was made up of invited media people. An airliner had been chartered merely for the East Coast rock writers. Restoring Presley's musical currency was a major purpose of this engagement.

And in that July of 1969, Elvis Presley was indeed restored. Not, however, by media manipulation. It is a myth that such things can be contrived. Our world may be fast and electronic, televised and publicized, but the artist must ultimately still do it by himself. Communicators may be flown in to spread the news, but the news must be made and the entertainer still has to go it alone to make that news.

Having exhilarated the entertainment world with his Las Vegas rebirth, Presley returned to the International Hotel six months later, this time wearing a spectacular white jump suit sparkling with sequins, brilliantly sashed, and slashed to the waist. This gaudy costume played a greater part in his act than even white tails had done in Liberace's. It was as if, in this costume, Presley had been reborn.

Movie work was more profitable than even the fanciest live engagement, but to Presley, playing Las Vegas meant much more. He was not only searching for validity as a live performer in the Beatles' era; he was not only revitalizing a sputtering career. A live act was the way Presley had begun. Audiences had all but conceived him, and plainly he felt at home with them, again sucking life and energy from them, vampire-like.

Alas, his triumph was to be short-lived. The "Elvis Presley Show" toured arenas across the country. Souvenir programs were peddled —pictures, posters, buttons, even replicas of the scarves that he tossed to fans in the front rows. The show would open portentously with the fanfare from Richard Strauss's *Thus Spake Zarathustra*, which had become a cliché in the wake of the movie *2001*. Presley would appear in an elaborate version of the Las Vegas jump suit, designed not quite artfully enough to camouflage the considerable weight he was gaining. In the huge auditoriums engaged for the tour he could only play to the eons of space surrounding him—without personal contact with the audience or feedback. The grossness of his body seemed to reflect a grossness in his work, as he postured grandiosely, as if to match his fame and reputation with the physical size of the arena. W. A. Harbinson, an Elvis enthusiast, described the resplendent decadence of his final appearances:

The drums begin to thunder . . . the strobe lights start flashing, the sound builds and builds, reaching deafening proportions and the stage lights pour down as Elvis slowly turns around, one hand on the mike, the other holding out the gold cape and it shimmers and flashes . . . and the BAM! BAM! BAM! Elvis' fist punches three times, the whole stage explodes and then, sudden crescendo, his right hand above his head, the incredible gold cape waving . . . and they've gone into the finale.

Glory, glory hallelujah
Glory, glory hallelujah

And as the last word builds, the stage lights come on full blast, the whole orchestra is standing and there, behind the band, stretching over the huge wall, lights flashing all over like the silver birds of truth, is an enormous and most garish Stars and Stripes. . . . And Elvis stands with legs parted, his head bowed, his arms outstretched and the lovely gold cape is a huge sun, burning up the whole auditorium, so they rise to their feet, their tears flow, their hands clasp and he falls to one knee, bows his head, crosses arms and wraps the gold cape around him like a shroud.

Shroud indeed. Audiences were appreciative, but the event was grotesque, its performer a bizarre parody of himself, no longer remotely the exuberant youngster with a jiggling leg and wiggle, or the glamorous Elvis who had survived to triumph in Las Vegas. Those, boy and man, were symbols of individuality and life; this was demonstration of commercial greed and ego crunch at work to subsume such individuality. He was a bronzed, dead pharaoh, hoisted on the throne and then borne to the arena where the fanfares and lights and blare might create the illusion of his existence. Dead-alive, he was displayed to the crowd.

In 1977, at forty-three, death came to Presley in a haze of madness and drugs, and it was followed by rumors and half-truths and speculations and investigations, but its basic meaning was not complicated. It merely made fact of a foregone conclusion: the vibrant, hot, dancing young man had not been able to handle the forces that attend immense stardom intellectually or emotionally, and so the entertainer had survived only at the expense of the individual. It was—was it not?—like one twin draining the life from another.

Stardom in show business invites an attention and a gratification for which the human ego is scarcely prepared. Emotional maturity, never common, is undermined by such forces. Is it inevitable that the self will crumble under such an assault as the public person becomes the only person? Is that why, in the modern show business of million-dollar one-night stands, the artist, ego inflated to the bursting, must die?

It is perhaps ironic that in these pages Frank Sinatra follows Elvis Presley, who could not survive the ravaging splendors of stardom; Presley, whose effect on adolescent girls and their aghast parents so resembled Sinatra's. "Rock and roll," Frank Sinatra said in 1955, "is phony and false—and sung, written, and played, for the most part, by cretinous goons." He had doubtless forgotten that Artur Rodzinski, director of the New York Philharmonic Society, blamed *juvenile delinquency*, no less, on the spell Sinatra had cast over teenagers in his younger days. Elvis Presley was doubtless the cretinous goon Sinatra had in mind, but the young rocker had his revenge. Upon Elvis's discharge from the army in 1959, Sinatra paid him half his television show's $250-thousand weekly budget for a six-minute appearance. Presley paid his own price: as a joke, he had to sing in white tie and tails.

The superstar is the individual distilled to legend. The crowd pays homage to that legend. Frank Sinatra became a star as a great and personal singer of popular songs, but it was not the voice or the songs that made him such a presence in our lives. Nor does the Sinatra legend rest on a unique personal quality such as Chevalier's gaiety, Dietrich's

glamor, Garland's emotionalism, or Kaye's charm. Frank Sinatra's legend is based on the tender heart we believe he has, consistent behavior to the contrary. Sinatra could sing like an angel and when he did, he *was* an angel. When he did not sing he got into trouble, and so he was us at our best, us at our worst; a man of confusion, inconsistency, and contradiction; cocky, vulnerable, pugnacious, classy, dangerous, and naive; an innocent with hoodlum tendencies; and the most attractive of singers, charismatic to distraction. Why do we think that someone who can sing (or dance or act or tell jokes) is also wise and informed, a great man (presidential material, perhaps)? Frank Sinatra's inability to handle power and fame suavely only made him seem as fallible as the rest of us. His melodramatic romance with Ava Gardner became the great and tragic love we all enjoy-endure at least once in our lives. His comeback from professional disaster was the ultimate show-business Cinderella story, and remember: Cinderella is a fantasy for the commoner.

Even were he not the finest singer of popular songs ever produced by America, Frank Sinatra's absolute presentation of self as show is reason enough to make him the closing act in this account of the great solo entertainers. As for his singing,

what few people, apart from musicians, have never seemed to grasp is that he is not simply the best popular singer of his generation, a latter-day Jolson or Crosby, but the culminating point in an evolutionary process which has refined the art of interpreting words set to music. . . . The secret of [his] technique lies in his uncanny gift for rephrasing a melody, his grasp of the nuances of lyric writing and his remarkably sensitive ear for a harmonic sequence. . . . Nor is there even the remotest possibility that he will have a successor. Sinatra was the result of a fusing of a set of historical circumstances, which can never be repeated. (Benny Green, *London Observer*)

Frank Sinatra's middle-class Italian family was not encouraging about his singing aspirations, but when as an eighteen-year-old he saw Bing

When Frank Sinatra played the Paramount in 1943, he discovered a new and powerful star-making market: adolescent girls.

Crosby in a Newark vaudeville house, in his own words, he turned a corner in his career. "I watched him. . . . He had such great ease that I thought, 'If he can do it that easily, I don't know why I can't.' That was one of the big turning points of my life." The next year, in 1934, Sinatra won an amateur contest in a local movie theater and with it an engagement across the river in New York at the Academy of Music on Fourteenth Street, where the early vaudevillian Tony Pastor had once reigned.

He joined a quartet, the Hoboken Four, and they came up winners on the "Major Bowes Amateur Hour," a radio program, going on to tour with a Bowes show. As a solo in the next few years, the slender young man with the lyric baritone and a startling clarity of diction plugged songs, performed in local clubs, and even sang for nothing on a New York radio station, just to be heard. Among the listeners was bandleader Harry James, who one June night in 1939 tracked him down in a New Jersey roadhouse where, as singing master of ceremonies, he was getting fifteen dollars a week. "I practically gave up," Sinatra later remembered, "because I felt I was getting nowhere. Someone said, 'That guy over there looks like Harry James.' I said, 'What would he be doing in a joint like this?'"

James had just left Benny Goodman to start a band of his own. He invited the skinny twenty-four-year-old to join him in an engagement at the Paramount Theatre in Times Square, the most prestigious of all the Times Square presentation houses. As James recalled, Sinatra accepted the sixty-five-dollars-a-week offer immediately. "We made a deal and it was as simple as that. There was only one thing we didn't agree on. I wanted him to change his name because I thought people couldn't remember it."

Once, observing Sinatra's nervousness in anticipating a review, James's band manager noted, "He wants a good write-up more than anybody I've ever seen." Sinatra's later imbroglios with the press may have originated in his need for approval and in his corresponding vulnerability to disapproval. In 1959, writing in the *New York World Telegram and Sun*, Scott Lawrence described Sinatra's retaliation against criticism as "swift and direct, whether [it] stems from a newspaperman, a heckler in a nightclub or the dissenting opinion of a friend. . . . When friends try to counsel, he will flare up. 'Don't tell me! Suggest! But don't tell me!'"

Any human being can be stung by criticism. The performer whose ego is exposed to the public seeks to prevent the considerable hurt which that can entail with a shield of bravado. Frank Sinatra never learned quite how to do that, not in fifty years of international stardom. Not learning made him famous.

From James's band, the young singer went to Tommy Dorsey's. As he remembered,

that night the bus pulled out with the rest of the boys at about half past midnight. I'd said good-bye to them all and it was snowing, I remember. There was nobody around and I stood alone with my suitcase in the snow and watched the tail-lights disappear. Then the tears started and I tried to run after the bus. There was such spirit and enthusiasm in that band. (As quoted in Robin Douglas-Home, *Sinatra*)

Despite Dorsey's reputation as "The Sentimental Gentleman of Swing," and his professorial appearance, he had a sharp tongue and a taste for fistfights. Sinatra had his share of scraps during this time, yet he always credited Dorsey's slide trombone as the inspiration for his own long-lined, swooping style. (Sinatra's musical expertise is considerable, and he has had a lifelong interest in opera, Puccini especially.)

His youthful distress at losing the security of the James band was doubtless allayed by a series of hit recordings with Dorsey ("I'll Never Smile Again," "My Prayer," "South of the Border"). Singing these songs in front of the band, on stands from New York's Astor Roof to the Hollywood Palladium, Sinatra established that his personal appeal—to women particularly—was obvious, instant, and amazing. After yet another hit record ("There Are Such Things") he quit the band to go it on his own. It was a daring decision in an era when singers were but appendages to orchestras, but his timing was perfect, for the big-band era was about to end; indeed, Sinatra would end it himself. He would become a phenomenon within four months.

His debut as a solo act came at the Mosque Theatre in Newark in November 1942, and it was there that Bob Weitman, managing director of the Paramount Theatre in New York, scouted him.

This skinny kid walks out on the stage. He was not much older than the kids in the seats. . . . As soon as they saw him the kids went crazy. And when he started to sing, they stood up and yelled and moaned and carried on until I thought, you should excuse the expression, his pants had fallen down. (As quoted in Arnold Shaw, *Sinatra: Twentieth-Century Romantic*)

Weitman booked Sinatra into the Paramount the following month as an "Extra Added Attraction" with Benny Goodman's band. "The King of Swing" was not a magnanimous man (in fact, it is beginning to seem as if few orchestra leaders are nice, whether popular or classical). Although Sinatra already had several hit records with Dorsey, Goodman claimed never to have heard of him. But the singer stayed on after the band's departure and business built. He was held over for four weeks and, according to Weitman, as quoted by Arnold Shaw:

During [that] first appearance at the Paramount, as the fever spread among the bobby-soxers, extra guards had to be retained to maintain order. Girls remained in their seats from early morning through Frank's last show at night. Some fainted from hunger, others from excitement. As his engagement lengthened, the windows of his dressing room had to be blacked out since the mere sight of him from the street below resulted in traffic jams.

The riot scenes were repeated during his appearances in Boston and Chicago. There had been matinee idols before, but as *Time* reported, "Not since the days of Rudy Vallee has American womanhood made such unabashed public love to an entertainer." There was, however, something new about these women. These "bobby-soxers" were adolescents. And he was "Frankie," "The Voice," the original pop star, the first teenage heartthrob, the first male singer to provoke plainly sexual responses from pubescent girls.

He was also nicknamed "The Swooner" (to Bing Crosby's "Crooner"), and the swooning might just as easily have been his as his fans', for, five-feet-ten-inches tall, he weighed only one hundred thirty pounds and would cling to the microphone as if for physical support. Seemingly burdened by the broad, padded shoulders of his draped jacket, he had only to smile, or adorn a note with a glide, to elicit shrieks of passionate despair from the hall. There were dark rumors that George Evans, his clever press agent, was paying some of the fans to instigate such demonstrations. Evans, in fact, once did rent an ambulance and park it outside the Paramount box office, but such stunts are futile if there is no show to back them up.

Sinatra's show was only beginning. In January 1943 he joined the popular radio program "Your Hit Parade." RKO Radio Pictures hired him to make a movie. Meantime, he performed in such night spots as New York's Riobamba. There, Robin Douglas-Home quotes him,

I had to open the show walking around the tables and singing. There was no stage and the dance floor was only as big as a postage stamp. I was nervous as hell but I sang a few songs and went off. Walter O'Keefe was the star of the show and he was to do his act last. That night he just walked on and said, "Ladies and gentlemen, I *was* your star of the evening. But tonight, in this club, we have all just seen a star born."

The real explosion was to come in October, when Sinatra returned to the Paramount for yet another engagement.

This appearance brought on the mightiest demonstration of female hysteria that any entertainment star had until then been accorded. When Frank arrived the first day for a 6 A.M. rehearsal, almost 1,000 girls were on line. By seven it stretched halfway down the block to Eighth Avenue. When the 3,000-seat theatre opened its doors at 8:30 A.M., enough youngsters were admitted to fill it to capacity. The picture preceding the stage show, *Our Hearts Were Young and Gay*, was utterly ignored. The bobby-soxers chattered, joked, exchanged Sinatra stories and intermittently sent up cries of "We want Frankie!" And after he was onstage, excitement reached such proportions that he had to plead for quiet or threaten to leave if the audience did not settle down.

The following day, a school holiday, was the haymaker. News reports spoke of "The Columbus Day Riot" at the Paramount Theatre . . . over 10,000 young-sters queued up in a line that, six abreast, ran west on 43d Street, snaked along Eighth Avenue and east on 44th Street. An additional 20,000, according to police estimates, clogged Times Square making it impassable to pedestrians and automobiles. . . . When the first show finished, only 250 came out of the 3,000-seat house. (Arnold Shaw, *Sinatra: Twentieth-Century Romantic*)

In this period of his career, the singer's image was boyish and even virginal. Occasional reports of tantrums were not played up in the inno-cent press of the time. The public Sinatra remained a frail singer of sensitive songs. "Try a Little Tenderness," "Put Your Dreams Away," "All or Nothing at All," and

> I couldn't sleep a wink last night
> Because we had that silly fight.
> I had to call you up this morning
> To see if everything was still alright.

He was a vulnerable young man with a floppy bow tie and a curl on his forehead, standing before the adoring audiences, smiling and hold-ing the microphone as if for dear life. That was his routine, and women repeatedly expressed the conviction that he was singing directly to them.

Face it, singing is an act with limited visual possibilities. Unless the singer does *something*, he is going to look boring, or even silly, since it is difficult to appear adult and intelligent while vocalizing. In the vaude-ville era, gesturing and dance movements made entertainers out of sing-ers like Eva Tanguay and Al Jolson. In Sinatra's era of slow songs, such movement was inappropriate, and records and radio studios made it unnecessary. Singers became static performers, all the more so for being bound to their microphones.

Like other vocalists of his era, Sinatra simply accepted this, smiling occasionally and gesturing perfunctorily as he sang his songs. He spoke as little as possible, although he was always thoughtful about crediting

OPPOSITE, ABOVE:
When Hollywood's fat years were over, many star actresses attempted nightclub acts. Among those successful at it were Mitzi Gaynor, Debbie Reynolds, Shirley MacLaine, Raquel Welch, and seen here, Ann-Margret. She assembled an elaborate show —but not to disguise any lack of talent. Among the movie stars, in fact, none was more gifted, or more vibrant onstage.

OPPOSITE, BELOW:
Johnny Carson's career was made and largely spent in television, hosting the "Tonight Show." His heart seemed to lie with stand-up comedians, and he devoted much of his television time to them, even educating his audiences about their working methods. Carson particularly admired Jack Benny and Bob Hope, not only for their humor but for their professionalism. He was a professional himself, one of the quickest wits in show business, and when television commitments permitted, he played Las Vegas. One classic Carson line on the "Tonight Show" was: "In keeping with the holiday spirit, why don't you all turn to the person next to you, shake his hand and say, 'Howdy, stranger!' And that goes for you people watching at home in bed."

composers, and lyricists, and sometimes even arrangers. Yet it was still his person rather than just his marvelous singing that made him popular. Was it in his looks? He was hardly handsome, although it was plain at the start that women responded romantically to him. Some theorized that the skinny young man who clung to the microphone was appealing to the maternalism in all women, even young ones. His explanation was, "It was the war years and there was a great loneliness and I was the boy in every corner drugstore; the boy who'd gone off, drafted in the war."

Perhaps so, for at war's end his career slumped and sales of his records were declining precipitously by 1948. The public was turning to robust novelties such as "Ghost Riders in the Sky" and "Come-on-a-My-House." Sinatra, a wolf boy reared by musicians, had no taste for such gimmickry and by 1950 found himself without a movie contract or even a recording affiliation. Given a television variety show, he was slotted at the same time as Milton Berle, "Mr. Television," for whom all America paused. Sinatra's bad luck had become laughable. Forced, now, to return to live performance, he sang to the painful accompaniment of thin applause from sparse audiences at the Chez Paree in Chicago and even New York's Copacabana, a club that as a performer he'd once owned. Playing a New York spot called the French Casino, he tried to appeal with songs currently popular, but they were either mediocre ("You Belong to Me") or ill-suited to his voice ("I've Got My Love to Keep Me Warm"). He sank still lower with parodies that made fun of "Ol' Man Crosby":

> He don't say nothin'
> But he must know somethin'
> For he just keeps singin' along.

It was as if he were blindly groping for the magic that made Crosby's success enduring, and then, surely in response to crisis, his voice went. The lyric baritone strained and then cracked as his vocal cords began to hemorrhage in the middle of a show at the Copacabana. He broke off, muttered a terse "Good night," and strode from the floor.

At the same time, his personal life was in disarray. Troubles somewhere, troubles everywhere. The tabloid newspapers scrawled his love life across their front pages as, not yet divorced, he romanced Ava Gardner. In the straight-laced 1950s, this was scandalous. For Sinatra it was also embittering. "Those newspapers," he said. "They broke up my home. They broke up my family. They ruined my life." And his life must indeed have seemed ruined, with his voice failing, his popularity fading, musical styles changing, and his marriage collapsing in the wake of a new romance that was itself rocky. Still only in his thirties, Frankie-boy was a has-been.

And so it was a fairy tale, a serial story, and altogether a show-business miracle that Sinatra was restored to wondrous fame and glorious fortune by a single stroke of his era's magic wand, the Academy Award. The story is inscribed in the holy writ of show-business press coverage: how Sinatra pursued a featured role in the movie version of James Jones's *From Here to Eternity*, how he was paid only eight thousand dollars to do it, and how a brilliant performance led to an Oscar, and a recovered voice, and hit records, and all things wonderfully golden. This was more than an ordinary comeback: it was to be the archetypal show-business comeback and the spine of the Sinatra legend.

That his renewed career was to outstrip his first was indeed marvelous, but, still more incredible, there was a critical difference between the two. The first Sinatra was a superb and magnetic singer. The second was, like all great entertainers, the one who brought his life onstage with him. He had been tested in the crucible and had emerged triumphant, manly, experienced—that was what he strolled into the spotlight with. Only with such personal revelation is performing greatness achieved. It is touching but absurd when such performers decry journalistic snoops. They want to keep the details of their personal lives private while offering the public their naked spirits. The gossip sought by the snoops is nobody's business, of course, but it is also small potatoes compared to the tremendous act of self-revelation that the great star performs on-stage. As Presley and Garland so tragically learned, transcending mere "act" to achieve an ultimate self-revelation can result in the onstage self dominating private life, character, and finally existence. That is always a risk as the entertainer takes the final step toward legendry.

Sinatra's 1952 Academy Award was heaven on earth and all God's blessings. Transformed, he was no longer Frankie-boy. He had seen himself in the character of Maggio in *From Here to Eternity*—an Italian kid off the streets. Now he was willing to be his own adult self onstage. As his voice came back, tougher and surer, he put on a fedora, lighted a cigarette, and sang of experience.

> *It's a quarter to three*
> *There's no one in the place*
> *Except you and me.*

Ironically, the popularity of rock 'n' roll forced him through a door that led to a receptive musical public. The market for single records was made up of teenagers who were uninterested in Frank Sinatra and traditional songs. But the just-introduced long-playing record created a new kind of product, an album that was one record. "Record albums," of course, were so called because they incorporated four discs in a book, or album. The long-playing record, which contained the same amount of material, seemed a much smaller investment. So Sinatra could record his kind of songs—classic American popular music—for an adult public, rather than futilely compete with rock 'n' roll. Sales of these new long-playing "albums" would become as important to the record industry as single hits. He was rolling lucky. Even long-playing records had been invented at the right time.

Resurrection was now his stock-in-trade. Because he was, after all, only a *singer*, his scrappiness and the rumors of gangland connections made him appealingly feisty, and newspapers doted on his every lapse. When he produced John F. Kennedy's inauguration show, the media even made his wardrobe a source of scandal because of reported quarrels with the designer. "This is the story of my life," Sinatra muttered with exasperation. "I buy some nice clothes and it becomes a crisis."

He occasionally reinforced his reputation onstage, and such moments were not pleasant. He interrupted a splendid concert to castigate a female gossip columnist with sexist slurs. Yet, in his increasingly triumphant career, even such mistakes made him seem human, and fallible, and all the more himself. He was one gritty customer, unsinkable, untamable, incorrigible. That was why he could sing the banal "My Way" and make it thrilling.

The decade following this rebirth Sinatra spent in movie and record studios, but even though records particularly let him be his best self, the musicianly singer, he was too much the child of live performance to live without audiences.

You know, I adore making records. I'd rather do that than almost anything else. . . . Once you're on that record singing, it's you and you alone. . . . Something happened [recording "One for My Baby"] which I've never seen before or since at a record session. I'd always sung that song before in clubs with just my pianist, Bill Miller, backing me up, a single spotlight on my face and cigarette, and the rest of the room in complete darkness. At this session the word had somehow gotten around and there were about sixty or seventy people there. . . . We had kept this song to the last track of the session. . . . [The] atmosphere in that studio was exactly like a club. . . . There was one take and that was that. The only time I've ever known it to happen like that. (As quoted in Robin Douglas-Home, *Sinatra*)

As television cut into Hollywood's popularity, reducing the number of movies made, he turned ever more to live performance. The times were his. John F. Kennedy was a show-business kind of president, and Frank Sinatra had the entree into the presidential circle. Las Vegas reflected his sensibilities, and he could appear there at whim. He was considered the ultimate attraction among high-rolling gamblers, and that made sense because he was a strong performer as well as a representative of the flash mentality.

When he was announced, a roving spotlight picked him up walking through the packed tables. . . . The deafening applause drowned out the music. A cool look at the audience, a snap of the fingers, a toss of the head and he was away into "The Lady Is a Tramp." Nobody in the audience moved—they just sat, staring with absorbed attention, at the man with the microphone whose voice rasped, flowed, blared, tiptoed, hovered and swooped through a score of songs from the poignant torch song with just a piano and a single spotlight on his face and cigarette to the exultant showstoppers with a full 40-piece orchestra and floodlights. His singing electrified that audience. (Robin Douglas-Home, *Sinatra*)

His love affair with the saloon and gambling set grew hot enough for him to acquire part-ownership in two Nevada casino-hotels, but when the Nevada State Gaming Commission revoked his gambling license in 1963, because of alleged underworld friendships, the romance ended. Sinatra was not to appear in Nevada until 1981, when he successfully won reinstatement of the license. In the years between, he entered the international concert circuit, triumphant across the country and around the world. He could appear whenever and wherever the fancy struck him and guarantee a sold-out house at exorbitant prices.

The golden songs of Tin Pan Alley, 1920 to 1940, were his personal territory as he became the musician's singer for all the world, master of the music of Richard Rodgers, Cole Porter, Jule Styne, Harry Warren, Harold Arlen, Jimmy McHugh, and James Van Heusen. With an instrumentalist's ear, he sought out the most inventive, surprising, and gratifying of popular songs, from the esoterica of Alec Wilder ("I'll Be Around") to the saloon-at-sunrise of Matt Dennis ("I Bought You Violets for Your Furs"). He was responsive both to the sense and to the poetry of lyrics. His uncanny sureness of phrasing forced a concentration on those words. But for all his success with classics, his alienation from contemporary popular music nagged at Sinatra, and he blamed his 1971 professional retirement on that. "Music was changing," he said. "There wasn't enough material around." As chance would have it, several years later he found a hit in Stephen Sondheim's beautiful new "Send in the Clowns."

Sinatra grew restless in retirement. When he resumed performing in 1974, however, it was not as an elder statesman, or even as the dean of entertainers. It was as star of stars. In 1978 he strolled on stage at the London Palladium to sing the golden classics he'd made his own: from

Cole Porter's "At Long Last Love" to Richard Rodgers's "The Lady Is a Tramp"—and more Rodgers ("My Funny Valentine")—and yet more Rodgers ("It Never Entered My Mind"). The same year he sold out eight consecutive shows at the Radio City Music Hall in New York. There may have been gaudier stars from moment (Bob Dylan) to moment (Michael Jackson), but for durable appeal and for his inscription of personal statement upon the sensibility of an entire era, no performer can equal Frank Sinatra. He came to be, at last, the ultimate solo performer.

It is tempting to suppose that he can go on forever, tempting to think that performers like him, because they say so much about our time, our bravery, and our survival, can so endure. But is not the "essential" repeatedly rendered obsolete? And do we not adapt and endure? The solo star symbolizes pluck and endurance, but if he goes under, why we will just have to change with life and get by without him.

Have not the jugglers tossed their last hoops while we watched other acts? Have not the magicians as a final trick made themselves disappear while we remained? The dancers no longer dance and the funnymen are funny only for the cameras. If the singers still sing in our presence, they do so at a vast distance. And so as Frank Sinatra mourns for lost lovers into the dawn of our transistorized and computerized age, it is plain that he is the last of the line. Who will ever sing "That Old Black Magic" again? Or "Night and Day"? Nobody, my friend. We watch this fellow, once so frail and young, now a prosperous man of years. He sings the thoughts and melodies of America's youth. Still bold and arrogant, he reminds us of cocky America. This live entertainer works as personally as our nation did in the time of the handmade, when our fortunes lay in ourselves, in our confidence, in our nerve, and in our ambition.

They were wonderful and brave, the solo performers, and so were we.

At the start, Frank Sinatra's act was his voice and the appearance of being in need of help, physical help. The floppy bow tie was his trademark.

ACKNOWLEDGMENTS

Not the last but the first to thank is the editor of this book, Robert Morton, who has tormented me on two books, now, with his regular and indispensable two cents worth. And while no writer would agree that a picture is worth even a single word, the glamor and excitement of this volume just would not exist without John Crowley's enthusiastic and exhaustive picture research or the stunning book design of Judith Michael. My copy was edited with tactful precision by Ellyn Allison.

As for expert help, there is no nonfiction without libraries, and this book could not have been written without the cooperation of Thor Wood, Chief of the Performing Arts Research Center of the New York Public Library, or of Dorothy Swerdlove, Curator of the Billy Rose Theatre Collection at Lincoln Center, New York, and their helpful staffs.

There are few professors of show business. The experts are the professionals. I am grateful to a number of them for having shared their expertise with me: on the subject of nightclubs, Lee Salomon of the William Morris Agency; and on saloon performers, Lee Guber of Westbury Music Fairs. Shelly Rothman told me about the Catskills resort casinos from the booking end, while Roger Riddle shared stageside with me. I heard about the golden age of burlesque from Morton Minsky, and Beverly Anderson recalled the modern era. What Jerry Wexler didn't tell me about popular music, Stuart Ostrow and Mitch Miller did. Milton Berle talked to me about growing up in vaudeville, and Fred Ebb described the business of writing modern acts for Las Vegas.

Some were willing to read and criticize early versions of this work, particularly a couple of swell Kates—my pal Katharine Hepburn and my dear Kate Carmel. Finally, memories of vaudeville were hardly the least that George Burns provided, but they weren't the most either, for —showman to the heart—he communicated the energy, the endurance, and the survivalism that give personal entertainment meaning. Indeed, Mr. Burns represents what this book is ultimately about—performing as an act of survival—and those to whom it is finally dedicated—all the performers who make the nightly high dive to prove it.

PICTURE CREDITS *Numbers refer to pages.*

Agron, Lawrence/FPG International: 149 above; Aliano, Ron/Neal Peters: 19; AP/Wide World: 105, 155 below right, 169, 178 above, 231 center; Baldridge, Robert: 8; Barr, John/Liaison: 11; Barr, Nancy/Retna Ltd.: 210, 211 above right; Bellissimo, John: 4–5, 7, 184, 202–3, 211 center left, 211 center right; Bensimon/Gamma Liaison: 196 above; The Bettmann Archive: 125 below right, 166, 215; Borsari, Peter C./FPG International: 205 above right; Boston Athenaeum: 116; Bridgeport Public Library Historical Collection: 26 above; Brown Brothers: 23, 34, 43 above right, 47, 52, 53, 57, 62, 65, 73, 76–77, 81 above, 86, 89, 92, 100–101, 120, 129, back jacket center right; Burns/FPG International: 147 center; Caesar's Palace, Courtesy of: 225 above; Campbell, Tom/FPG International: 12–13; CBS: 111, 147 above center, center left, center right, below center; Christopher Collection: 128; Columbia University Rare Book and Manuscript Library, Joseph Urban Collection: 80; Culver Pictures: 16, 21, 22, 23, 25 above, 40, 43 above left, below left, below right, 51, 61 above, 82, 85 below, 95, 114, 119 above left, below left, below right, 121; Dean, Loomis/Life Magazine: 163 left; de'Espinasse, Hank/Image Bank: 225 below left; Dixon, Dean/Photo Fair: 211 above center; Edwardo Jaffe Collection: 125 above right; Elvis Presley Enterprises, Inc., Courtesy of: 243 below; Fishback, Glen/FPG International: 155 above left; FPG International: 56, 60, 64, 75, 91, 98, 102, 103 above, 113, 125 above left, 139, 145, 147 above right, 148, 193 center right, 194, 201 below, 223 above, 225 below right, back jacket center left; Frank Driggs Collection: 44, 55, 63, 71, 136 below, 185, 187, 189 above, 190–191, 192, 193 center left, below left, below right, 207 above, 214, 221, 232, 233, 256, back jacket above center; Freeburg, Andy/Retna Ltd.: 153; Gehr, Herbert/Life Magazine © Time Inc.: 135; Gershoff, Gary/Retna Ltd.: 211 below left; Granger Collection: 107; Gubb, L./Gamma-Liaison: 212–13; Hanley, Dick/FPG International: 193 above left; Hooper, Robert Scott: 130 below right, 147 below left, 149 below, 155 above right, below left,

205 above left, 223 below, 235, 236; Howard, Leslie: endpapers, 157, 158; Jacobs, Lou/FPG International: 205 below right; Kalinsky, George: 2–3, 9, 14, 154 above, 160, 174, 181 below, 196 below, 208 below, 216, 251 below; Karger, George/Life Magazine © 1942 Time Inc.: 134; Kobal Collection: 97, 161, 171, 182, 209; Las Vegas News Bureau: 1, 6, 193 above right, 220, 228, 229 below, 230, 231 above, below, 243 above; Lerario, Marty/Martin Photography: 132, 133, 141, 147 below right, 151, 152, 154 below, 205 below left, 239, 251 above, 254; Library of Congress: 94, 189 below, back jacket center; Michael Ochs Archives: 46, 125 below left, 197 left, 201 above, 204 above, 209 above; Museum of the City of New York Theatre Collection: 26 below, 31, 35, 38 above, below, 39, 42, 70 left, 81 below, 85 above, 87, 109, 110 above, 140, 173, 218; National Broadcasting Corporation, Courtesy of: 204; National Broadcasting Corporation Radio: 106; Neal Peters Collection: 197 right, 229 above, 240; New York Public Library at Lincoln Center, Billy Rose Theater Collection: 37 (Otto Nelson), 61 below, 70 right, 78 (Otto Nelson), 103, 115, 119, 126 (Otto Nelson), back jacket above right; Putland, Michael/Retna Ltd.: 219; Redfern, David: 199, 207 below, 208 above, 211 above right, center, below center, below right; Rex Features: 163 right, 165, 178, 179, 183; Sandler, Roger/Gamma-Liaison: 198; Schapiro, Steve/Gamma-Liaison: 10; Steingart/Concord Hotel: 142, 147 above left; Stock, Dennis /Magnum: 150; Strock, George/Life Magazine © Time Inc.: 136 above; Swope, Martha: 127, 130 above, below left, 181 above; University of Florida Libraries, The Belknap Collection for the Performing Arts: 25 below left, 117, 123; Watkins, E. S./FPG International: 201 center; Wisconsin Center for Film and Theater Research: 45, 54, 58, 67, 68–69, 79, 83, 93, 96, 99, 106, 108, 110, 116, 128 above, 247, back jacket above left, below all; Yale University Library, Crawford Theater Collection: 25 below right, 28, 32, 48.

SONG CREDITS

Excerpts from the following songs are used by permission. All rights are reserved and international copyrights secured.

"All Shook Up" by Elvis Presley and Otis Blackwell (p. 244), Copyright © 1957 by Shalimar Music Corp. All rights for the U.S.A. assigned to Elvis Presley Music (Unichappell Music, Admin.) and Unart Music Corp. "Anatole of Paris" by Sylvia Fine Kaye (p. 168), courtesy of Sylvia Fine Kaye. "Don't Sit Under the Apple Tree (with Anyone Else but Me)" by Lew Brown, Charlie Tobias, and Sam Stept (p. 188), Copyright © 1942, 1954 Robbins Music Corporation, Copyright © renewed 1970, 1982 Robbins Music Corporation and Ched Music Corporation. Rights assigned to CBS Catalogue Partnership. All rights administered by CBS Robbins Catalog Inc. and Ched Music Corporation. "Everybody Step" by Irving Berlin (p. 185), Copyright © 1921 Irving Berlin. Copyright © renewed 1948 Irving Berlin. Reprinted by permission of Irving Berlin Music Corporation. "Heartbreak Hotel" by Mae Boren Axton, Tommy Durden, and Elvis Presley (p. 241), Copyright © 1956 Tree Publishing Co., Inc. Copyright © renewed. "How 'Ya Gonna Keep 'Em Down on the Farm? (After They've Seen Paree)" by Walter Donaldson, Joe Young, and Sam M. Lewis (p. 92), Copyright © 1919 Mills Music, Inc. Copyright © renewed 1947 Mills Music, Inc., Warock Corp., and Donaldson Publishing Co. "I Couldn't Sleep a Wink Last Night" by Harold Adamson and Jimmy McHugh (p. 250), Copyright © 1943 T. B. Harms Company. Copyright © renewed (c/o The Welk Music Group, Santa Monica, CA 90401). "I Know That You Know" by Vincent Youmans and Ann Caldwell (p. 186), Copyright © 1926 (Renewed) Warner Bros. Inc. "If Love Were All" by Noel Coward (p. 175), Copyright © 1929 (Renewed) Chappell & Co., Ltd. Warner Bros., Inc., Publisher and Owner of all rights for United States and Canada. "If You Knew Susie" by B. G. DeSylva and Joseph Myers (p. 90), Copyright © 1925 Renewed Shapiro, Bernstein & Co., Inc. "Louise" by Leo Robin and Richard A. Whiting (p. 162), Copyright © 1929 by Famous Music Corporation. Copyright © renewed 1956 by Famous Music Corporation. "Lovie Joe" by Joe Jordan and Will Marion Cook (p. 88), printed by the permission of the copyright owner Jerry Vogel Music Co., Inc., 501 Fifth Avenue, NY 10017. "My Mammy" by Walter Donaldson, Sam M. Lewis, and Joe Young (p. 50), Copyright © 1920 Irving Berlin, Inc. Copyright © renewed 1948 Bourne Co., Warock Corp., and Donaldson Publishing Co. "My Man (Mon Homme)" Words by Albert Willemetz and Jacques Charles, Music by Maurice Yvain, English Lyric by Channing Pollock (pp. 88, 90), Copyright © 1920, 1921. Copyright © renewed 1948, 1949 Francis Salabert, Paris, France. Rights assigned to CBS Catalogue Partnership. All rights for North America administered by CBS Feist Catalog Inc. "One for My Baby (and One More for the Road)" by Harold Arlen and Johnny Mercer (p. 253), Copyright © 1943 Harwin Music Co. Copyright © renewed 1971 Harwin Music Co. "San Fernando Valley (I'm Packin' My Grip)" by Gordon Jenkins (p. 217), Copyright © 1943 Edwin H. Morris & Company, A Division of MPL Communications, Inc. Copyright © renewed 1971 Edwin H. Morris & Company, A Division of MPL Communications, Inc. "Thanks for the Memory" by Leo Robin and Ralph Rainger (p. 112), Copyright © 1937 by Paramount Music Corporation. Copyright © renewed 1964 by Paramount Music Corporation. "White Christmas" by Irving Berlin (p. 218), Copyright © 1940, 1942 Irving Berlin. Copyright © renewed 1968, 1969 Irving Berlin. Reprinted by permission of Irving Berlin Music Corporation.

BIBLIOGRAPHY

Adams, Joey. *Here's to the Friars*. New York: Crown Publishers, Inc., 1976.

Adamson, Joe. *Groucho, Harpo, Chico and Sometimes Zeppo: A Celebration of the Marx Brothers*. New York: Simon and Schuster, Inc., 1983.

Barnes, Ken. *Sinatra and the Great Song Stylists*. London: Ian Allen, Ltd., 1972.

Berger, Phil. *The Last Laugh: The World of the Stand-up Comics*. New York: William Morrow and Co., Inc., 1975.

Burke, Peter. *Popular Culture in Early Modern Europe*. New York: New York University Press, 1978.

Cantor, Eddie. *My Life Is in Your Hands*. New York: Harper and Brothers, 1928.

Collins, Pete. *No People Like Show People*. London: Frederick Muller, Ltd., 1957.

Corio, Ann, and DiMona, Joseph. *This Was Burlesque*. New York: Grosset and Dunlap, Inc., 1968.

Csida, Joseph. *American Entertainment*. New York: Watson-Guptill Publications, Inc., c. 1978.

DiMeglio, John E. *Vaudeville, U.S.A*. Bowling Green, Ohio: Bowling Green State University, Popular Press, 1973.

Douglas-Home, Robin. *Sinatra*. New York: Grosset and Dunlap, Inc., c. 1962.

Farren, Mick, ed., *Elvis Presley in His Own Words*. New York: Quick Fox, Putnam Publishing Group, 1981.

Fisher, John. *Call Them Irreplaceable*. London: Elm Tree Books, 1976.

Freedland, Michael. *Maurice Chevalier*. New York: William Morrow and Co., Inc., 1981.

Frost, Thomas. *The Old Showmen and the Old London Fairs*. London: Chatto and Windus, Ltd., 1874.

Gaver, Jack, and Stanley, Dave. *There's Laughter in the Air*. Sykesville, MD: Greenberg Publishing Co., 1945.

Gilbert, Douglas. *American Vaudeville, Its Life and Times*. New York: McGraw-Hill, Inc., 1940.

Goldman, Albert. *Elvis*. New York: Avon Books, 1982.

Gorham, Maurice. *Showmen and Suckers: An Excursion on the Crazy Fringe of the Entertainment World*. London: P. Marshall, Ltd., 1951.

Haney, Lynn. *Naked at the Feast*. New York: Dodd, Mead and Co., c. 1981.

Harbinson, William Allen. *Elvis Presley: An Illustrated Biography*. London: Michael Joseph, Ltd., 1975.

Irving, Gordon. *Great Scot: The Life Story of Sir Harry Lauder, Legendary Laird of the Music Hall*. London: L. Frewin, Ltd., 1968.

Katkov, Norman. *The Fabulous Fanny: The Story of Fanny Brice*. New York: Alfred A. Knopf, Inc., 1953.

Laurie, Joe, Jr. *Vaudeville: From the Honkey-tonks to the Palace*. New York: Henry Holt, 1953.

————, and Green, Abel. *Show Biz, from Vaude to Video*. New York: Henry Holt, 1951.

Liberace. *Liberace*. New York: Putnam Publishing Group, 1973.

Lichter, Paul. *Elvis in Hollywood*. New York: Simon and Schuster, Inc., c. 1975.

McKechnie, Samuel. *Popular Entertainments through the Ages*. New York: Stokes Publishing Co., 1931.

Marks, E. B., and Liebling, A. J. *They All Sang: From Tony Pastor to Rudy Vallee*. New York: The Viking Press, 1935.

Morley, Sheridan. *Marlene Dietrich*. London: Elm Tree Books, 1976.

Oberfirst, Robert. *Al Jolson: You Ain't Heard Nothin' Yet*. New York: A. S. Barnes, 1982.

Pearl, Ralph. *Las Vegas Is My Beat*. Secaucus, NJ: Lyle Stuart, Inc., 1973.

Richards, Dick. *The Life Story of Danny Kaye*. London: Convoy Publications, 1949.

Samuels, Charles, and Samuels, Louise. *Once Upon a Stage: The Merry World of Vaudeville*. New York: Dodd, Mead and Co., 1974.

Seldes, Gilbert. *The Seven Lively Arts*. New York: A. S. Barnes, 1962.

Shaw, Arnold. *Sinatra: Twentieth-Century Romantic*. New York: Holt, Rinehart and Winston, 1968.

Simon, George T. *The Big Bands*. New York: Macmillan Publishing Co., Inc., 1975.

Singer, Kurt. *The Danny Kaye Saga*. London: Robert Hale, Ltd., 1957.

Smith, Bill. *The Vaudevillians*. New York: Macmillan Publishing Co., Inc., c. 1976.

Smith, Lorna. *Judy with Love: The Story of Miss Show Business*. London: Robert Hale, Ltd., 1975.

Sobel, Bernard. *Pictorial History of Burlesque*. New York: Bonanza Books, 1956.

————. *Pictorial History of Vaudeville*. Secaucus, NJ: Citadel Press, 1961.

Welsford, Enid. *The Fool: His Social and Literary History*. New York: Farrar and Rinehart, 1935.

Wilson, Earl. *Sinatra: An Unauthorized Biography*. New York: Macmillan Publishing Co., Inc., c. 1976.

PAGE ONE:

Phyllis Diller's raucous high spirits and absurdist material helped to distinguish her from the ordinary brash comedienne. "I had a classmate so fat," she'd say, "they used to pull her through the Lincoln Tunnel just to clean it." Being funny—which Diller tremendously was—counted for a lot in her act, but opening doors to fancy and escape counted for more.

PAGES TWO AND THREE:

When Diana Ross left the Supremes, their act had transcended the race music from which it sprang. No longer one among many stereotyped, choreographed black singing groups, the Supremes were playing the top white showrooms in Las Vegas and Miami Beach, slicked up, decked out, and made chic. Ross achieved still greater success as a solo, becoming a dominant force on the concert and arena circuits.

PAGES FOUR AND FIVE:

Michael Jackson started out as a youngster in his brothers' act, the Jackson Five. Like Stevie Wonder, he was a show-business veteran at twenty, knowing no other life but performing. Although he has had stupendous success in records and music videos, he remains a live entertainer in spirit. In fact, what Jackson really is, is a good old-fashioned song-and-dance man.

PAGE SIX:

One of the rare performers who bestride the legitimate theater and solo performance, Liza Minnelli has remained a singer of traditional songs—a "belter"—in a world of synthesized rock music. If the so-called standards of American popular song are to be performed in the future, if the Richard Rodgers–Cole Porter style of music is to endure in any way, there will have to be singers to sing them. No one as yet outclasses Minnelli.

PAGE SEVEN:

Peter Allen's exuberance as a performer tended to overshadow his immense gifts as a composer and lyricist. His songs are often rueful and melancholy toasts to lost innocence. Even in the rollicking "I Go to Rio" there is a suggestion of bruise and regret.

PAGE EIGHT:

Although "mime" was coined to describe the broad entertainment that lightened matters between the acts of Greek tragedies, in later times the term came to refer to a special kind of silent, often serious clowning. Marcel Marceau mastered this dancelike form and made it so perfect a thing that he became an international artist. All others are compared to Marceau, the ultimate mime.

PAGE NINE: PAGE TEN:

Bob Hope   *Barbra Streisand*

PAGE ELEVEN:

Challenging the medium's dehumanizing force, Lily Tomlin brought warmth, sensitivity, and humanity to her televised monologues and monodramas. Hers was an artistry and sophistication rare in those tough and impatient times. Like the great monologist Ruth Draper, Tomlin created story lines and multiple characters with breathtaking ease—and she could do it with the same success alone and alive on a stage.

PAGES TWELVE AND THIRTEEN:

The floor show at the MGM Grand Hotel in Las Vegas

PROJECT DIRECTOR: *Robert Morton*
EDITOR: *Ellyn Childs Allison*
DESIGNER: *Judith Michael*
PHOTO EDITOR: *John K. Crowley*

LIBRARY OF CONGRESS CATALOGING IN PUBLICATION DATA
Gottfried, Martin.
In person.

Bibliography: p. 258
Includes index.
1. Performing arts—United States—History.
2. Performing arts—History. I. Title.
PN2221.G67   1985   790.2′09   85–6031
ISBN 0-8109-1613-4